CYBORG WORLDS

the military information society

What is the connection between working on the Star Wars programme, operating an 'intelligent automation' system, learning 'higher-order' cognitive skills through computer-aided instruction, and losing oneself in a home computer 'microworld'? Common to such activities is a search for total control through simulation. This book explores the hidden military origins of that project for transforming the social and psychic order.

In these 'post-modern' times we often behave as if we were cybernetic organisms – confusing the mechanical and the organic, the inner and outer realms, simulation and reality, even omnipotence and impotence. This book demonstrates that such cyborg worlds are structured by military paridigms of power, widely disseminated through information technology. The contributors cite pervasive military models and fantasies in order to demonstrate the role played by infotech in redefining public institutions and human identity.

Illuminating a blind spot in most social science research, our overall approach is to treat the military paradigm as a prism through which to analyse the wider role of infotech. The book's central heresy is that all of infotech bears the stamp of its military origins – not just as hardware or software, but as 'liveware'. The contributors show how infotech's uses for social control derive from the conceptual framework that guided its original military development. And they show how today's applications involve a new internalized discipline for high-tech researchers, educators, soldiers, political strategists and social engineers.

At all those levels, the military is playing a central role in current restructuring, which is often glibly heralded as a 'post-Fordist' reskilling, even liberation. Yet in reality this means extending control to the parts that Fordism didn't fully reach. Through the 'man/machine interface', people are more effectively reduced to 'human components' of a system whose purposes are pre-programmed. Such a systems model, increasingly writ large as a military information society, can blur any meaningful distinction between military and civilian versions of infotech.

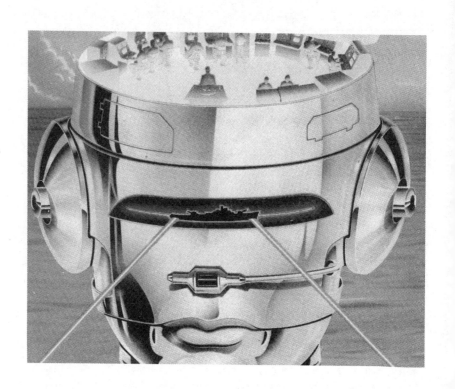

CYBORG WORLDS
the military information society

Edited by Les Levidow and Kevin Robins

'... an association in which the free development of each
is the condition of the free development of all'

Free Association Books / London / 1989

First published in Great Britain 1989 by
Free Association Books,
26 Freegrove Road,
London N7 9RQ

British Library Cataloguing in Publication Data
Cyborg worlds : the military information society.
   1. Military operations. Applications of computer systems
   I. Levidow, Les II. Robins, Kevin
355.4′028′5

ISBN 1-85343-093-5

Typeset by Photosetting, Yeovil

Printed and bound in Great Britain by
Billing and Sons Ltd, Worcester

Contents

Introduction

LES LEVIDOW and KEVIN ROBINS

In these 'post-modern' times we often behave as if we were cybernetic organisms – confusing the mechanical and the organic, the inner and outer realms, simulation and reality, even omnipotence and impotence. This book demonstrates that such cyborg worlds are structured by military paradigms of power, in particular through the military constitution of information technology (infotech). The contributors cite pervasive military models and fantasies in order to illuminate the role played by infotech in redefining both the social order and human identity.

How is the military connection evaded in popular consciousness? Where the promise of a bountiful information utopia coexists alongside the barbarism of high-tech warfare, it is easy to reassure ourselves with simple distinctions. We mentally separate the ominous from the apparently benign: Star Wars versus computer-aided learning, Aegis air defence system versus Apple PC, 'smart weapons' versus 'intelligent automation', 'command and control' versus 'user-friendly'.

However, those examples have more in common than we would like to think. As this book argues, an evolving paradigm of military discipline has shaped infotech in its very essence. Whenever we extend the 'guns versus butter' analogy to the realm of infotech, we blind ourselves to the continuities between its military and civilian versions.

Of course, it is well known that the military gave birth to infotech and still provide its single greatest application. Yet the military's role is widely seen as an exception to the otherwise benign promise of technological progress. People find ways of mentally dissociating themselves from the military aspects – either by disavowing the connection, or by splitting off the supposedly beneficial applications from the harmful ones.

However, military values have always guided the course of infotech research, development and application – in areas ranging from advanced weaponry to industrial design to educational methods. Such influence extends far beyond particular techniques, to entire models of social organization and aspirations for the kind of society we consider possible, necessary or desirable. It defines each person's place within the technological order, imposing profound changes in psychic organization, social identity, human nature.

As contributors to this book demonstrate, infotech systems promote new models of rationality, cognition and intelligence, all derived from military world-views. Such models are founded on the pursuit of a logic of total control, both internal and external. Far more profound than externally imposed commands, the 'military information society' involves internalizing a self-discipline, technologies of the self, in ways that come to be seen as normal, rational, reasonable.

The post-World War II paradigm has been 'cybernetics', the science of automatic, self-regulated control. Although first devised with the intention of human liberation, this science was soon appropriated by industry and the State, particularly the military, which extended the potential for cybernetic control to the depths of human behaviour. Its military-based developments have helped to bring us not only 1970s 'deskilling' but also a 1980s 'reskilling' and 'flexible specialization', terms with which futurologists euphemistically welcome a new 'post-Fordist' era now irrevocably upon us.

Underlying that rhetoric, though barely in public view, are military paradigms, particularly the latest cybernetic control model, which we call the 'cyborg' (cybernetic organism). It has been conceived as a way to shape people into perfectly flexible 'human components' of a control system. When high-tech firms use quasi-military language to market 'intelligent automation systems', in which 'robotics and vigilant operators form an efficient team', this holds a significance far greater than a civilian spin-off from military R&D. For, in such ways, the military acts as vanguard of capital's long-standing dream: an orderly, consensual, profitably productive society.

In practice, while that project has become the ruling paradigm, its rule has often failed to operate as planned. The fantasy has encountered inherent limitations in reducing people's behaviour to that of machines, 'intelligent' machines or cyborgs. Like any scientific model, cybernetics must create an ideal, imaginary, world in order to impose its order on the real world. Yet it is impossible to design a system that perfectly simulates and anticipates the real-world events that it is assigned to control. Moreover, despite heroic attempts to adapt humans perfectly to such elaborate systems, people often resist such adaptation.

If we are to recognize how best to use those limitations to promote an alternative future, a different project for human nature, then we will need a better understanding of what we are up against. Indeed, our cyborg worlds extend from the military itself, to video games, to advertising, to home appliances, to the work-place, to 'defence' debates. In all those realms, the military information society not only defines the ruling order but also sets the terms for what counts as an effective opposition.

The remainder of the Introduction briefly sketches the areas explored by the contributors to this collection. Contrary to those who would neatly distinguish civilian and military realms, our overall approach is to treat the military paradigm as a prism through which to analyse the wider role of infotech in adapting human identity to the technological order. The book's central heresy is that all of infotech bears the stamp of its military origins – not just as hardware or software, but as 'liveware', as 'man/machine interfaces', as social relations. The contributors show how infotech's uses for social control derive from the conceptual framework that guided its original military development. And they show how today's applications involve a new internalized discipline for high-tech researchers, educators, soldiers, political strategists and social engineers.

Computer-based instruction, with its underlying cognitive psychology, has been widely celebrated as a means for fulfilling the potential of individual learners. As Douglas Noble shows, however, this project has meant militarizing education by reducing the learner to 'mental materiel'. Human performance is redefined according to cognitive models derived from weapons systems, where the priority is to optimize the system's potential. Human thinking, memory, problem-solving and learning are modelled after their anthropomorphic counterparts in machine intelligence systems. Beneath its benign veneer, such education serves at once as laboratory, production site and legitimation for this military-based agenda, which in turn is increasingly writ large as a military information society.

That tendency in education finds a striking parallel in the training of the new model soldier – who holds responsibility for expensive, sophisticated weapons – which the military has adopted to overcome human unreliability. Military strategists have been posing the question, 'Now that we have these machines, what kind of machine shall we put in charge of them?' One answer has been the cyborg, the cybernetic organism – or, somewhat less fantastically, a human trained to behave like one. As Chris Gray shows, the military is devising psychological and pharmacological methods for inculcating the necessary self-discipline in their brave new recruits. At the same time, these high-tech systems encounter other 'post-modern warriors', both armed and unarmed, who subvert the rules of the game.

The professional workers who design the military technology are, in effect, soldiers of a different kind. As Dennis Hayes reveals, through interviews and anecdotes, they operate under military secrecy, enforced not only by an extreme division of labour but also by self-censorship, by implicit vows of ignorance. As if cloistered in a monastery, they avoid discussing or even recognizing the military applications of their work, shrouded in abundant technical euphemisms for deadly weapons. All those separations become further institutionalized through the 'structured techniques' that firms feel compelled to adopt if they are to stay in the running for military contracts.

The distinction between military and civilian infotech has become further eroded by the USA's massive expenditure on the Strategic Defense Initiative (SDI). While critics have amply refuted government claims that it can ever work 'as seen on TV', Vincent Mosco shows how SDI has already been working very well to achieve other, unofficial goals. As part of a wide-ranging strategic offensive, SDI has been militarizing the entire society. Not only do its technical achievements facilitate military attack in Earth wars, but its economic clout has pressured industry into adopting R&D pro-grammes more suited to military purposes. It has also exploited our nuclear nightmares so as to make us psychologically dependent on an imagined 'nuclear umbrella', personified in a father-protector President; at the level of mass culture, SDI has served to infantilize us.

The fantasy of technological omnipotence, epitomized by SDI, has for long been pursued by the military in its drive to make all performance predictable. Even though many weapons systems have notoriously failed to meet the mark, the military have continued to win funds for ever more elaborate versions, and thus to lead industry to bid for producing them. Tom Athanasiou analyses the wishful thinking involved in the military's holy grail of 'artificial intelligence', with the artificially tidy world that AI simulates. In order to explain the persistent fantasy of omnipotent control, he roots it in the practical and ideological imperatives of the USA's military Keynesianism.

Long before current AI programmes, there have been computer models that acknowledged only those parts of the world considered amenable to reliable control. Surveying developments since World War II, Paul N. Edwards traces the confluence of systems engineering and military thinking, towards a 'closed-world discourse'. He shows how it gained impetus, paradoxically, in order to accommodate anti-militarist objections against maintaining a large peacetime army, as well as to sustain the pretence of the USA's role of global protector in the face of instabilities that have not really fitted the systems model. Thus military aspirations and computer myth-ology have been symbiotically sustained, permeating the entire political culture with a systems discourse of omnipotence. At the same time, this approach has found itself repeatedly disoriented by rebellions unanticipated by the model.

In the final essay, the editors develop the concept of a 'military information society'. They juxtapose the writings of social critics, cybernetic rhetorical fantasies and management practices that attempt to turn such dreams (or nightmares?) into reality. Involved here are contending models of the human mind, discipline and skill; these bear on industry and education as well as the military itself. The editors also discuss an emerging redefinition of human identity – the 'cyborg self' – in which the most primitive emotions become inseparable from apparent rationality.

Having read this Introduction, readers may ask: if the military information society is truly totalitarian – that is, if militarism runs so deeply, so subtly, throughout our daily lives – then where lies the basis for any alternative future? As we suggested earlier, the 'man/machine interface' never functions exactly as intended: the fantasy of total control can never perfectly contain reality. The more the system attempts to specify every detail, the more it may fall short of its ever more ambitious aims, as neither human nor machine behaves precisely as intended. The control mission cannot avoid that internal contradiction. For that reason, every day we face the choice of either helping to perfect it or resisting its definition of perfection, its programmed purposes and the role that it assigns us. That is, we either help to construct or subvert the military information society.

How might that subversion lead to a different society? What different kinds of technology might emerge? Might cybernetic tools themselves be used to break open 'closed' systems? How can infotech be used to construct different kinds of knowledge? While this book doesn't presume to answer such questions, it does intend to shift attention to them, in theory and in practice. Such are the questions needed to defend ourselves against being programmed into a military information society.

Innovation

Art Edmondson on advances in real-time software technology.

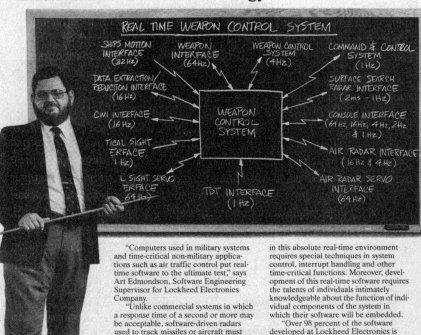

"Computers used in military systems and time-critical non-military applications such as air traffic control put real-time software to the ultimate test," says Art Edmondson, Software Engineering Supervisor for Lockheed Electronics Company.

"Unlike commercial systems in which a response time of a second or more may be acceptable, software-driven radars used to track missiles or aircraft must respond in milliseconds.

"Modern digital gun and missile fire control systems require software which can simultaneously communicate with command and control and weapon control subsystems; interface with track-while-scan surface and air-search radars; filter and predict at various rates for the two radars; perform ballistic computations for individual components of the weapons suite; compute and output gun orders complete with position and rate commands; and interface with weapon control consoles and operator displays.

"To develop software for application in this absolute real-time environment requires special techniques in system control, interrupt handling and other time-critical functions. Moreover, development of this real-time software requires the talents of individuals intimately knowledgeable about the function of individual components of the system in which their software will be embedded.

"Over 98 percent of the software developed at Lockheed Electronics is intended for time-critical applications. Each software package poses a unique challenge since no two real-time systems are alike.

"We're utilizing cross-assemblers, cross-compilers, debuggers and emulators to accommodate computer and language mix. We also are pursuing introduction of Ada to our real-time systems.

"Our diverse systems in weapons control, air traffic control, EW, communications, C³I, radar signal processing and automatic testing require efficient, reliable real-time software to meet their specific performance requirements."

Lockheed Electronics
Giving shape to imagination.

Lockheed Electronics, Plainfield, New Jersey 07061

1   MENTAL MATERIEL
The militarization of learning and intelligence in US education

DOUGLAS D. NOBLE

Materiel: '... weapons, equipment, supplies, etc., of armed forces: distinguished from "personnel".'

Our final hope is to develop the brain as a natural resource... Human intelligence will be the weapon of the future.
– Luis Alberto Machado[1]

'Problem-solving', 'critical thinking', 'reasoning', 'learning skills': such 'higher-order' mental capacities have recently surfaced as new goals for US education. Curriculum planners throughout the country, at all levels of education, are designing courses in critical thinking and problem-solving. 'Teaching for thinking', we are told, 'is ... the great educational discovery of the '80s' (Costa, 1984, p. 62). Teachers of every subject routinely talk about 'learning strategies' as their instructional focus. Articles and books promote the 'new three R's: Reading, 'Riting and Reasoning', while standardized tests are revised to reflect increased intellectual expectations. Instruction is being recodified in terms of 'comprehension strategies', 'cognitive objectives' and 'metacognitive skills'.

There are several reasons given by educators for this sudden new emphasis on higher-order abilities in public education. Of course, a small cadre of progressive teachers have been promoting critical thinking, logic instruction, and independent learning for years. Many others have suddenly become alarmed by the deficiencies of their students, who do not know how to learn, do not know how to think, do not know how to question what they read, do not know how to solve problems in mathematics and science. Still others have been motivated by the presence of computers, with their alleged potential to foster just such higher-level intellectual activity. Many are encouraged by a recent flurry of new research on learning and intelligence that, they are told, promises techniques to train complex cognitive functioning. Meanwhile, education leaders are heeding the call of business-men who urge that international competition, rapid technological change, and the complexities of the information age all demand a work-force of 'problem-solvers': people who can interpret information, who can learn new tasks, who can 'think for a living' (Carnegie Forum, 1986).

From all accounts, a growing number of educators sincerely believe that the time is ripe for such higher intellectual expectations within public education, signalling a vigorous transition from an ineffective, deadening traditional pedagogy to an era of universal intellectual empowerment and educational excellence.

However, things are not as they seem. In fact, this sanguine new celebration of cerebration, of intellect and learning, is for the most part a confused blend of scientific hyperbole, wishful thinking and irrepressible ideology.

For one thing, 40 percent of urban high-school students drop out before graduation, while 25 percent of US adults nation-wide cannot read. Such statistics belie any simplistic faith that a new intellectual focus on thinking and learning skills, coupled with new technologies, will turn the nation's students – however ill-prepared, however impoverished, however dis-affected – into motivated learners, let alone intelligent, reflective thinkers. Second, the sudden new appreciation for intellectual competence on the job and in school is baffling, juxtaposed beside the general derogation of intellectual competence in our society – a devaluation reflected in the in-crease of mind-numbing service-sector jobs and in the vacuous content of typical television fare.

Third, the belief in the possibility of an intellectual reformulation of education is based largely on recent cognitive research on learning and intelligence; yet there is little evidence that this research has anything to offer the classroom at this time.[2] Last, but not least, the new research on learning and intelligence underlying educators' elevated expectations has been sponsored not by the Department of Education, as one might expect, but rather by the Department of Defense, curiously enough, which leads one to wonder what is really going on.

Clearly, the sudden celebration of intellect and learning within an educational and intellectual wasteland, a celebration largely underwritten by the military, requires a deeper explanation. Could it be that educators have unwittingly adopted the framework of a larger military/scientific enterprise that only appears to be an agenda for public education because the language – intelligence, learning, thinking, and problem-solving – is the same?

This essay provides just such an alternative analysis of the sudden interest in the cultivation of human intellect within education. Its thesis is that this new educational impulse is in fact a derivative venture. It is both a 'spin-off' from and a corollary of a much deeper and more pervasive enterprise, fuelled by military research and mirrored in corporate practice. This is the enterprise to harness intelligence, both human and machine, for use within complex military and corporate technological systems. Here the promise of 'expert systems' and 'artificial intelligence' (AI) captures the collective imagination of generals and chief executives, for whom the interest in 'understanding [and improving] how people reason . . . [is] clearly motivated by the pressing needs to make effective use of technology' (Sheil, 1982, p. 104). The new goal for education unwittingly reflects the need to fulfil this technological promise, rather than reflecting any new-found appreciation for the developed potential of enlightened, empowered human beings.

In fact, the new appreciation of intellect represents the desiccation of human intellectual potential at the very moment it appears to be celebrating it. This is because cognitive processes of learning and thinking, needed as components in the complex information systems of the military and industry, are cultivated only with such needs in mind. The new 'higher order' education consists in the training of cognitive procedures derived not from a deep appreciation of human ingenuity but instead from computer models of machine learning and artificial intelligence. In the 'age of the smart machine', according to Shoshana Zuboff (1988, p. 309), 'successful utilization of intelligent systems requires maximizing the cognitive capacity and learning ability of the work force'. This in turn requires the schools to serve as both laboratory and production site, bending human minds into technologies themselves – imbued, no less than machines, with a reliable, controllable, flexible 'artificial' intelligence. Human beings, already reduced to the status of 'human resources', or 'personnel', defined in terms of their function within institutional systems, are thus further reduced to hardly animate, 'mental materiel' – cognitive processing units within the interstices of large technological systems.

Structure of this essay
This essay is in three parts:

Part I briefly outlines the two historical paths leading to the current scenario.

1. First, in order to show that US education has been following military prerogatives for decades, I sketch the importance of military research and development in the emergence of technologies, systems and methods used in public education since the 1950s.

2. Next, I trace the development, also since the mid-1950s, of a militarized science of mind, based on human cognition viewed as an information-processing system. I show how an interest in cognitive 'human factors' arose within the military context of engineering complex weapon systems, giving

rise to the fields of artificial intelligence and cognitive science, as well as to a preoccupation with human problem-solving.

Part II discusses the latest phase of military funding in cognitive science and educational technology, begun in the mid-1970s, which involves the wedding of these two military ventures. This part describes the motives of researchers and their military sponsors in this new unified enterprise.

Part III describes the new field of 'cognitive engineering', born of the unification of cognitive science and educational technology. Two examples of cognitive engineering will be discussed: the amplification of intelligence through man–computer interaction, and the direct training of cognitive processes, including thinking skills and learning strategies. The critical analysis is completed with the question, 'Who is ultimately in control of these skills and strategies?'

The Conclusion returns to the role of public education in this scenario. In it, I suggest that public education, in its heightened emphasis on applications of new research in thinking and learning, serves unwittingly as an instrument of educational engineering. It is at once a locus of legitimation, a laboratory for developing and testing cognitive theories, and, ultimately, a site for the production of 'mental materiel' for technological systems.

I. HISTORICAL BACKGROUND

Militarized pedagogy

Although it might appear strange to suggest that impulses within public education are part of military agendas, the fact is that the US military since at least World War I has had a substantial impact on school practice. Because of its enormous budget, protected in the name of national security, the military serves as a vanguard innovator in technological research and development. By seeding new research and by shielding the products of this research from market and democratic forces (Smith, 1985), the military permits many esoteric technological enterprises to mature. Some of these – the transistor, the chip – manage to survive later commercialization and legislative politics; others – teaching machines, nuclear power – collapse from their own insufficiencies when they emerge from the protected military umbrella. The military nurture and protection of educational innovations, and, as the next section will show, of artificial intelligence and cognitive psychology as well, have followed just this pattern.

In education, it is widely acknowledged that standardized testing in the USA is a legacy of Army Alpha and Beta tests originally used for selection and classification purposes in World War I. Less well known are the wartime training origins of the influential 'educational engineering' movement in the 1920s, which resurfaced as 'educational technology' after World War II

(Neumann, 1979). Since World War II, in fact, military research and development (R&D) has served as the dominant incubator of educational technology, and it is the source of most of the technologies, instructional systems and learning models that have entered the schools in the last three decades.

During World War II, educators and experimental psychologists mounted a massive effort in training R&D, characterized by intensified use of behavioural objectives and task analysis, and by the use of audio-visual technologies, including instructional films, training devices, and simulations. After the war this research effort, rather than being disbanded, was intensified within a panoply of new military laboratories. These included the Air Force Personnel and Training Research Center (AFPTRC), the Air Force's Rand Corporation and System Development Corporation (SDC), the Army's Human Resources Research Office (HumRRo), and the Navy Personnel Research and Development Center (NPRDC). In addition, an 'enormous body of psychological literature on learning and training was generated' (Neumann, 1979, p. 86) under contract with such military funding agencies as the Office of Naval Research (ONR), the Air Force Office of Scientific Research (AFOSR), the Army Research Institute (ARI), and the Defense Advanced Research Projects Agency (DARPA, formerly ARPA).

Educational technologies that have emerged from this military research effort include overhead projectors, language laboratories, instructional films, instructional television, teaching machines, computer-assisted and computer-managed instruction, and video-disc applications. Educational models and methods derived from this research include programmed instruction, instructional design, criterion-referenced testing, individualized instructional packages, the 'systems' approach to educational administration, simulation software, skill taxonomies, behavioural objectives, the mastery learning model, and intelligent tutoring systems.[3] Anyone familiar with US education will recognize in this list a rather exhaustive compendium of educational innovations that have entered the schools, and that have fuelled much of the direction of educational research since the 1960s.

These military-sponsored educational innovations reflect the distinctive needs of military training. These needs include: efficiency, particularly the shortest possible training time; task-specific performance, avoiding both 'undertraining' and 'overtraining'; the use of technologies and simulations, to supplant the use of instructors and actual weapons systems in training; and instructional systems design, to ensure the compatibility of training to ongoing changes in mission and in weapons systems technology. All of these characteristics reflect the military need for complete control of the training process, which is viewed as a 'personnel subsystem' ancillary to the design, development and implementation of complex weapons systems.

The considerable influence of military research on public schools is not a result of some Pentagon conspiracy. Rather, military educational innovations have been incorporated into public school practice and research through a convergence of efforts and motives. These include researchers seeking wider funding and laboratory opportunities, education leaders seeking ways to improve the schools and to modernize their profession, and commercial interests seeking to exploit new education markets. They also involve political leaders capitalizing on public outrage over educational failure, and a population encouraged to believe in the prestige of science and space-age technology, offering educational solutions to technological and economic threats to US hegemony.

In any event, educational agendas have been influenced enormously by the massive military research and development enterprise, although this influence is rarely discussed. So, too, have the recent cognitive thrust in modern psychology and the celebrated impulse to build intelligent machines.

Militarized mind

During World War II, psychologists and engineers, responding to the problems facing pilots and operators in increasingly complex weaponry, worked together to design weapons that better matched the capacities and limitations of men. Out of this human factors engineering, or 'psychotechnolgy', came 'a new view of man': 'The human operator served as information transmitter and processing device interposed between his machine's displays and ... controls' (Lachman, 1979, p. 7). The result was a single operating unit, a new hybrid of man and machine, the 'man/machine system'. This new conception stimulated substantial research into the processes of human intellectual, perceptual and motor functioning: '[W]e have the human operator surrounded on both sides by very precisely known mechanisms and the question comes up, "What kind of machine have we placed in the middle?"' (Edwards, 1985, p. 42) After the war, psychologists, biologists and engineers began a concerted effort to provide answers to this question by applying models and metaphors from wartime developments in computers and cybernetic theory to human functioning.

The result, according to Paul Edwards (1985, pp. 1, 13), was the 'militarization' of the mind and the body: 'Wartime cybernetic psychology militarized the mind in theorizing ... the antiaircraft gunner, the communications man, the airplane and submarine crewman, and the naval artilleryman ... inserted into mechanical and electromechanical systems.' With such mechanistic models and metaphors in the air, and with a growing body of empirical research on human performance, it remained for another military event to provide the context for the first concrete demonstrations of the machinery of human intellectual performance.

In 1949, in response to the first Soviet atomic bomb detonation, the US military began development of the SAGE system, a massive air defence system which eventually consisted of twenty-three 'direction centres' across North America. Among the many research facilities involved in this effort was the Systems Research Laboratory (SRL) of the Rand Corporation, later to become the System Development Corporation. The SRL was the site of a large-scale simulation of a SAGE direction centre for team training research involving radar operators.[4]

According to the account by McCorduck (1979), training director Allen Newell successfully simulated aircraft radar blips for training purposes at SRL, the first use of the computer for symbol manipulation rather than number crunching. Within the simulated training environment, Newell came to view the human operators, too, as 'information processing systems' (IPS) which processed symbols just as his program 'processed' the symbols of simulated radar blips (p. 127).

In the early 1950s Newell began to collaborate with Rand consultant Herbert A. Simon, whose work involved analyses of administrative decision-making in industrial organizations. Simon saw the mind as a logic machine, 'which took some premises and ground them up and processed them into conclusions' (p. 127). Signal detection by radar operators was understood as a form of complex decision-making: 'Did I see it or not?' Accordingly, Simon mapped Newell's militarized language of 'information processing systems' on to a theory of management decision-making. Newell had written programs that simulated the symbols of radar information. Since they viewed human decision-making as another form of symbol-manipulation, or 'information processing', Newell and Simon began to write programs that would *simulate* human decision-making. Their personal interests led them to start by programming simulations for playing chess and for proving theorems in mathematical logic; they then moved on to arithmetic and logic puzzles (p. 132; see also Newell and Simon, 1972).

Newell and Simon's work was part of the military endeavour to understand the 'human factor' within a complex man/machine weapon system. In an early report on their work (Newell, Shaw and Simon, 1958, p. 151), they explained, 'If one considers the organism to consist of effectors, receptors, and a control system for joining these, then [ours was] a theory of the control system.' They asserted that if one could simulate such complex intelligent behaviour, actually reproduce it on a computer, then one could claim to understand the processes behind that behaviour. This was the motivation behind their work, which they called 'cognitive simulation' and which was later dubbed 'artificial intelligence' (AI). Although others were exploring this new research terrain at the time, Newell and Simon were the first to produce concrete examples of programs simulating intelligent behaviour.

These origins of AI were also the origins of 'information processing' cognitive psychology. In 1960 the psychologist George Miller and two colleagues first translated the Simon and Newell IPS into 'plans and the structure of behaviour' in their highly influential book of that name (Miller, Galanter and Pribram, 1960). Their efforts and others' soon replaced the opacity of the 'black box' of behaviourism with the transparent 'processes' of what Ulric Neisser eventually labelled 'cognitive psychology' (Neisser, 1967). By now IPS cognitive psychology has swallowed up so much of contemporary psychology that the terms 'cognitive psychology' and 'psychology' have for many become synonymous (Knapp, 1986, p. 30).

Theories in this new psychology 'represent a specific layer of explanation [that is, computer models] lying between behaviour, on one side, and neurology, on the other' (Newell and Simon, 1972, p. 876). '"Cognition" [is] thus objectified through a new standard of psychological explanation: formal modeling [via computer programs]... [a] newly constructed psychological object' (Edwards, 1985, p. 22). In 1980, together with artificial intelligence and neurobiology, cognitive psychology became a part of a new science of the mind based on IPS models, christened 'cognitive science' (Norman, 1981).

These origins of artificial intelligence and cognitive psychology also marked the beginning of an intense preoccupation with human problem-solving that has recently captured the imagination of educators. At SRL, Simon adopted the term 'problem-solving' for what he earlier had called 'decision-making'; he also used the term 'problem-solving' synonymously with Newell's 'information processing' (McCorduck, 1979, p. 132; Newell and Simon, 1972, p. 880). The heightened emphasis within education on complex problem-solving is a direct result of this early military human factors work in man/machine systems.

According to Simon and Newell (1972, p. 870), 'the basic point inhabiting our work has been that the programmed computer and the human problem-solver are both species belonging to the genus "information processing system"'. The recent interest of educators in AI, cognitive psychology and problem-solving relies, wittingly or unwittingly, on this view of mind as computer, which in turn stems from the view of mind as a 'human factor', an 'arsenal' (Simon, 1980, p. 93) of cognitive components within complex weapons systems or advanced industrial systems. According to Edwards (1985, p. 12), 'cybernetic psychology began as an effort to theorize humans as component parts of weapons systems and continue[s]... to draw crucial models and metaphors from that problematic. Cognitive science may be read both metaphorically and literally as a theory of technological worker-soldiers.'

II. EDUCATIONAL TECHNOLOGY MEETS COGNITIVE SCIENCE

The development of educational technologies and cognitive science within military man/machine research is not simply a matter of historical interest. Military sponsorship of these enterprises continues to the present day, and has in fact intensified in recent years.

In education, much recent research in computer-based education and computer-managed instruction (CMI) has been sponsored by the military services (Ellis, 1986); these institutions, particularly the Army, have been very active in video-disc research for training applications (OTA, 1982, p. 251). Practically all research on 'intelligent tutoring systems', or 'intelligent computer-assisted instruction' (ICAI), has been a military-sponsored enterprise (Ellis, 1986). In cognitive science, almost all research on artificial intelligence has been sponsored since the 1950s by DARPA, the Defense Advanced Research Projects Agency (Bellin and Chapman, 1987; Davis, 1985); and the Office of Naval Research continues to be a prime sponsor of research in cognitive psychology.[5]

By far the most important military-sponsored efforts in educational technology and cognitive science since the 1970s have involved the wedding of the two areas into a single enterprise. As we shall see, one legacy of this union is the present emphasis in education on thinking, intelligence, problem-solving and learning strategies. All of these rely upon research supported almost entirely by military funds.

Researchers in educational technology and cognitive science realized by the mid-1970s that each of their fields was at a standstill. Educational technologists recognized the limitations of behaviourist principles of learning (Gropper, 1980; Resnick, 1983), which served as the theoretical basis for programmed instruction and teaching machines in the 1960s. Early researchers in computer-assisted instruction such as Patrick Suppes began to realize that advances in this educational technology required 'an explicit theory of learning and instruction' (Dreyfus and Dreyfus, 1986, p. 143), which required further reliance on the unfolding revelations of cognitive psychology.

Cognitive psychologists and artificial intelligence researchers, meanwhile, also realized that they had gone as far as they could in the development of intelligent machines and in the modelling of human cognition, especially because of their inadequate understanding of human intellectual functioning in real-life situations. They recognized that 'the major progress in automated . . . systems will come from a better understanding and representation of the human machine' (Towne, 1987, p. 59). AI researchers attempting to stimulate such real-life human cognitive activity turned their attention from expert performance to learning processes in search of a short cut. Simon (1983, p. 36), for one, realized that 'for big, knowledge-based systems, learning [is] more efficient than programming', which quickly requires an unmanageable number of instruction steps when one attempts to simulate real-life complex behaviour.

A unification of cognitive science and educational research, focused on learning and intellectual development, thus came to serve as the solution to the problems of both fields. According to Roy Pea (1985b, p. 179), researchers recognized that 'important advances in instructional technology and in basic cognitive science will occur as an integrated activity'. Future achievements in these fields would depend on a more complete understanding of the processes of learning and of intellectual development.

Why military sponsorship?

As mentioned, the military has been a prime sponsor of this unified enterprise up to the present time; however, its interest in learning and in the development of intelligence is not simply scientific or technological, but practical, dictated by its mission.[7]

Three explanations have been offered by the military for this sponsorship: (1) the development of fully automated 'intelligent systems' and 'autonomous weapons'; (2) the acceleration of learning and instruction in training; and (3) the 'amplification' of human intelligence within man/machine systems.

(1) Total automation, in training systems and in weapons systems, has been a central theme in military research and development since World War II (Bellin and Chapman, 1987; Shaker and Wise, 1988); and the military is the force behind industry's drive for the 'automated factory'. The failure of this endeavour to create autonomous intelligent machines has forced the military (and corporations) to retain the 'man in the loop' within complex technological systems. But one underlying focus of the new research on learning and intelligence remains this endeavour to codify human intellectual functioning sufficiently to produce automated machines. In this sense, the military (and corporate) preoccupation with improving human learning and intelligence is merely an interim measure.

(2) The complexity of its increasingly esoteric weapons systems has staggered military efforts to train maintenance, trouble-shooting and operations personnel. According to Evans (1986, p. 11), learning to repair the tracks on the M-1 tank is considered equivalent in difficulty to a first-year college course, AEGIS cruiser fire controlmen spend twenty-seven months in school, and the maintenance publications for the Navy's F-14 interceptor total 300,000 pages. These training problems are compounded

by the educational deficiencies of many new recruits (p. 12).

Not surprisingly, then, the military has turned to exotic new training approaches, in conjunction with its use of sophisticated instructional technologies. McCoy (1986, p. 61) of the Air Force Human Research Laboratory, for example, contends that 'the unobservable mental acts required for skillful information processing constitute important elements of technical competence across many Air Force specialties'. For this reason, Wittrock (1979, p. 309) explains, 'the armed services are in the forefront of applications of ... cognitive psychology to instruction.' (See also Halff *et al.*, 1986.) Their goal is to permit direct intervention, manipulation and reorganization of these 'unobservable mental acts' in order to accelerate and strengthen learning capacities.

(3) The military also needs to 'amplify' and 'accelerate' the cognitive processes of pilots and other operators of complex high-speed weapons systems in order to bring them 'up to speed' with the systems themselves. This in turn ensures the optimal utilization of these technologies. A high-performance, computer-based weapon system such as the F-14 jet fighter requires a pilot capable of split-second performance in response to the continuous flow of information generated by on-board computers. To meet such high-performance specification in the 'human factor', in order to make the human more 'machine-friendly', the military needs to 'redesign ... the operator' (WGBH, 1988), through an understanding of human abilities and their amplification.

In other words, the military wants to 'engineer' the 'human factor' just as it designs and engineers the hardware and software. According to cognitive psychologist Donald Norman (1980), 'any situation in which the human mind is a relevant part of the system could use a systematic engineering application of the lessons from cognitive psychology'. This engineering approach involves reorganizing human functioning based on computer models, which in turn requires a fuller understanding of the principles of learning and instruction.

The urgency for this engineering project was clearly recognized early on in the development of intelligent machines. In 1964 at a symposium entitled 'Computer Augmentation of Human Reasoning', Ruth Davis (1965, p. 171), representing the military sponsor of the symposium, warned that 'it is much easier to improve computers than it is to improve people ... It takes twenty years to develop a person to the extent that we are now developing the computer. And we are getting out of phase very rapidly.'

III. COGNITIVE ENGINEERING: REDESIGNING MIND

We are going to retool our industry, and ... we must, at the same time, retool ourselves.

– J. C. R. Licklider (1982)

For all the reasons above, a new field has emerged in the last decade called 'cognitive engineering'[8] – an amalgam of the 'knowledge engineering' of the cognitive scientists and the 'educational engineering' of the educational technologists. This new field is sometimes referred to as 'AI in reverse' (Pea, 1985a, p. 77) because it ultimately involves the engineering of human learning and human intellectual functioning modelled after AI procedures. AI researchers, Brown, Collins and Harris (1978, p. 108) explain: 'AI has developed a variety of formalisms that in turn provide a new basis for analyzing [human] cognitive processes.' Thus, although AI itself depends upon an analysis of human learning and functioning to arrive at sophisticated computer models, one central purpose of AI is to turn things around and to apply these models to improve human learning and performance.

As John L. Kennedy (1962, p. 18), an early systems researcher, noted years ago, 'The most important point to be made is this: the design problem [in man/machine systems] is not how to design a machine – it is how to design an organism.' Cognitive-science researchers, adopting this view, have often remarked on the 'prescriptive' nature of their work. Simon (1981, p. 23) notes that 'artificial intelligence . . . addresses itself to normative goals, and ought to. It is interested, in its applied aspects, not only in understanding intelligence but in improving it . . . We need to recognize this explicitly by speaking of cognitive engineering as well as cognitive science.' Posner (1973, p. 167), another cognitive scientist, asserts that 'cognitive psychology must face the problem of design, discussing not only what is but also what ought to be'. Still another (Reif, 1980, p. 44) asks, 'Can one design or invent modes of human information processing that can specifically enhance human cognitive performance?' Answering his own question, he concludes that one goal of cognitive science is 'prescriptive': ' . . . to design . . . the information processor of interest, either a computer or a human being' (p. 43).

In 1980, the birth year of cognitive science, Simon (1981) announced that cognitive science is a 'science of the artificial'. By this he means that the human mind is most appropriately viewed, for scientific purposes, as a contingent, artificial 'system', something that is malleable and adaptable, that could be other than what it is. He argues that cognitive science should think of human functioning 'as if' it were designed. In this way one can consider 'redesigning' it to suit the outer environment – which, in the case of cognitive scientists, consists of huge, complex computer systems. The redesign of human functioning, therefore, takes its cues from this environment by viewing mind as an information processing system, modelled after the computer.

We turn now to two examples of this 'redesign', two central thrusts in 'cognitive engineering', each substantially supported by the military: (1) the indirect 'augmentation' of intelligence through the 'symbiotic' fusion of mind and computer; and (2) the direct training of cognitive processes involved in thinking and learning, modelled on computer procedures and strategies.

Cockpit cognition

Early on in the development of computers, the military was concerned with the availability of 'real-time' interactivity between computers and military decision-makers, whose combat decisions could not wait for results. This led to 'time-sharing', which permitted this instantaneous interactivity. Time-sharing was the first instance of 'man/computer symbiosis', where the human and the computer worked as a partnership. Time-sharing was also considered to be the first computer-based 'augmentation of human intellect' via the computer (Fano, 1965). This meant that the computer and human working in tandem served as an amplification of human intellectual decision-making and memory.

During this DARPA-funded project, a number of leaders in the new computer field began to write and to fantasize about the further possibilities of intellectual amplification through this 'symbiosis'.[9] For example, Harold Sackman (1967, p. 564) a participant in the SAGE project discussed earlier, predicted that 'a fundamental consequence of . . . [the idealized] maximum linkage of . . . man-to-computer communication . . . is the vast potential for the . . . realization of a far more intelligent type of human being, on the average and at most levels, than we have today'.

This idea of intellectual augmentation through symbiosis remains a potent form of cognitive engineering within the military, and among cognitive scientists and educational technologists, in the 1980s. A recent NOVA television show on pilot training (WGBH, 1988) spoke of the 'magic cockpit' of the near future, in which the aircraft serves as a 'pilot's associate' talking to the pilot (in a female voice) about ongoing conditions and responding to the pilot's spoken orders. Air Force spokesmen talked about the near possibility of arranging for the intelligent cockpit computers to respond to the pilot's eyesight or even his/her brain waves – 'controlling by thinking is no more than thirty years away'. Through this symbiosis of the pilot and the aircraft, it is claimed, the pilot's memory and decision-making capacities are tremendously increased.

Such military aspirations have found their way into the thinking of researchers working at the juncture of cognitive science and educational technology. Some are captivated by similar fantasies of symbiosis. John W. Loughary (1970), an early promotor of 'man–machine systems in education', predicted that laser-beam technology and advances in endocrinology and biochemical control of genetics would provide the capacity to make direct changes in human learning ability. More recently, a leading Soviet proponent of educational computing recommended linking the nerve cells of teachers and students with circuitry in the computer, thereby multiplying the intelligence of both learners and teachers (Zender, 1975, p. 139). He and others also speak of implanting computer chips in the brain to augment intelligence (Pea, 1985a, p. 92). Finally, robotics scientist Hans Moravec (1988) suggests the possibility of 'downloading' the entire contents of persons' brains into a computer, transforming education into the merging of computer files.

But some promoters of symbiosis in education arrive at this position via an apparently more respectable pedagogical path. For example Roy Pea (1985a), an ardent spokesman for computers in education, has fashioned theories of his mentor, cognitive psychologist and educator Jerome Bruner, and of the Russian psychologist Lev Vygotsky, into a similar man/computer symbiosis scenario. Bruner and Vygotsky argue that human intelligence evolves as a function of its surrounding culture and the tools at its disposal. Thus, written language, musical notation and mathematical symbols have all amplified human intelligence. Pea argues that the computer can do the same: amplify, restructure and reshape human intelligence.

Computers thus can be considered new 'organs of intelligence', 'cognitive props', or 'extracortical organizers of thought', according to Pea (1985a, pp. 88–93), which provide additional 'cognitive workspace' as 'adjuncts to processing capacity'. But, more important, they serve as 'a mirror of the learner's thought processes by providing an external representation of internal cognitive processes' (Kozma, 1987, p. 24). Some cognitive engineers (Klein, 1985) speak of 'process highlighters' and 'cognitive traces' provided by the computer to the user, permitting the user to externalize his or her steps in the solution to a problem, retaining the 'traces' of intermediate 'processes' not otherwise available. For example, if one is graphing an equation, the computer would provide graphic representations of all early attempts, so that the student can learn from his or her mistakes and corrections in the course of solving the problem. Such transparency of one's thought processes, made possible through human/computer symbiosis, serves to augment intellectual capabilities, according to some cognitive engineers.

Perhaps the most well-known instance of this form of cognitive engineering applied to education involves the use of 'microworld learning environments' derived from AI research, to generate powerful ideas in young children. An early leader in AI research, Seymour Papert (1980), speaks of 'mindstorms' made possible in young children through their interaction with a computer microworld utilizing the LOGO programming language. LOGO is perhaps more responsible than any other single circumstance for the introduction of computers in US classrooms. Unfortunately, early predictions that children would arrive at 'powerful mathematical ideas' through its use, or even that they would learn sophisticated forms of problem-solving and planning through their interaction with the LOGO microworld, have been disappointing (Dudley-Marling and Owston, 1988; Leron, 1985). As a result, many cognitive engineers are turning to a more direct approach (Klahr and Carver, 1988); rather than wait for the symbiosis to work its magic, they have opted instead to focus on directly training the reorganization and amelioration of human intellectual processes.

Cognitive process instruction

1. *Thinking skills*. Symbiosis is indirect; cognitive engineers have therefore focused the better part of their attention on training higher-order intellectual activity directly, utilizing the view of mind as an 'information processing system'. This is variously referred to as 'cognitive process instruction' (Lockhead and Clement, 1979) and 'training thinking skills'. A leading promotor of teaching thinking skills in schools, Robert Sternberg, derived a 'componential' model of intelligence, under ONR and ARI contracts, that has served as a basis for identifying the 'components' of thinking that can be modified and reorganized through direct intervention (Keating, 1984; Sternberg, 1977). Another military researcher, Raymond S. Nickerson (1985) has also championed a public education focus on training thinking skills.

This approach to education 'assumes that if we can specify in enough detail the tacit processes that underlie various thinking skills, then we can find methods to teach students to master those skills' (Sternberg and Detterman, 1982, p. 173). The search for general thinking and problem-solving skills has, in the last few years, run into a problem that has also plagued AI research: namely, problem-solving and thinking is domain-dependent to a degree not previously expected (Resnick, 1987). The skills used to solve a problem in algebra, for example, may have little in common with those involved in figuring out the causes of the Civil War – or even a proof in geometry.

This conclusion, still very controversial, has led to an emphasis on domain-dependent 'expert systems' in AI research. Such systems, though starting to be commercially successful, none the less represent a failure in the AI project to design flexible, adaptable intelligent machines. In cognitive engineering, then, the principal focus has been on cognitive processes that are perhaps not so domain-dependent – namely, the processes of learning.

2. *Learning strategies*. Learning is the central preoccupation of cognitive

science at this time (Langley and Simon, 1981; Simon, 1983). As mentioned earlier, the renewed interest in learning research is a product of scientific and military interests, rather than a focus initiated by educators. Researchers in AI arrived at this new emphasis on learning in their search for efficient techniques of building flexible intelligent systems (that is, for techniques in 'machine learning'), and in their scientific quest for general 'first principles' or invariants, in intellectual functioning. For reasons discussed earlier as well, the military has sponsored this research since the early 1970s; in fact, 'the most ambitious recent program of research on learning strategies was funded by the Defense Advanced Projects Agency' (Rigney and Munro, 1981, p. 133), which has been responsible for the publication of many of the seminal books in the field.[10]

The study of learning processes offers more promise of arriving at domain-independent 'invariants' than thinking skills; that is, learning involves more general processes than thinking does. This means that training learning skills promises to be more efficient than training thinking skills. But learning is itself rather inefficient, so the goal of the cognitive engineer is not merely to train learning skills, but, more important, to improve on these skills.

The military and its researchers share an interest in improving the efficiency of learning, which is typically defined by them in terms of temporal efficiency. According to Langley and Simon (1981, p. 367), 'learning is taking place if solution times decrease as a person solves a sequence of [similar problems]'. Simon (1983), still a key player in the cognitive fields he kindled, espouses a distaste for normal human learning, shared as well by many of his colleagues and sponsors: 'Human learning is horribly slow. It takes decades for human beings to learn anything' (p. 26). Thus his goal is to search for 'tricks that manage to escape the tediousness of human learning' (p. 26). He is also concerned that there is no 'copy process' in human 'learning programs', in contrast to computer programs, which can be copied at will: 'When one computer has learned it, they've all learned it – in principle . . . Only one computer would have to learn; not every one would have to go to school' (p. 35). Simon's frustration, and his motivation, is clear: 'I find it terribly frustrating trying to transfer my knowledge and skill to another human head. I'd like to open the lid and stuff the program in' (p. 27).

The closest the new research on learning has come to such aspirations has been to focus, not on learning, but rather on 'learning mechanisms' within the human 'information processing system' (IPS). Here learning is viewed as the 'modification of any component in the IPS' (Langley and Simon, 1981, p. 368). That is, the human being, in the language of machine learning, is an 'adaptive production system'. 'Production systems' are discrete sets of condition–action pairs of the form 'If A and B, then do C' that are the heart of AI programs; 'adaptive production systems' are such systems that can add, delete or rearrange the order of these productions automatically or through instruction (Simon, 1980, p. 87). That is to say, they can learn. Human learning, then, is taken to be identical to machine learning: 'If we are really simulating people with computers, then the only way to improve people is to understand the procedures that the computer goes through and attempt to teach . . . people like we . . . teach computers' (Davis *et al.*, 1965, p. 171).

The processes directly involved in learning are thought of as 'strategies', originally a military term. They are 'human information-processing activities that facilitate acquisition, retention and retrieval of representational and procedural knowledge' (Rigney and Munro, 1981, p. 128). Examples include mnemonic devices, elaboration schemes like underlining key words in a text, looking for central ideas, and linking an idea to an analogous idea. Although these sound simply like study skills, the focus of cognitive engineering is to isolate, represent externally, and then train efficiently the internal processes and subprocesses involved in these activities. This will, in theory, equip the learner with an 'armoury' (Simon, 1981, p. 20) of strategies applicable to a variety of domains.

Does all of this reduce entirely to study skills when one eliminates the jargon? That is a controversial issue. The key difference seems to be that learning strategies are grounded in a computer model of the learner. According to Pressley (1985, p. 36), 'in the best of all possible worlds, learners would have a well-develooed repertoire of strategies, they would . . . know when to deploy each one, and they would know how to modify the strategies . . . Learners would keep track of their cognitive activities, with such monitoring directing strategy shifts.'

The learner, then, is viewed as a processing system equipped with strategies applicable to cognitive purposes such as memorizing and comprehending texts. All of these strategies are accessible to conscious control by the learner, by the instructor, or by the instructional system. Learning strategies, then, are control processes (Snow *et al.*, 1980, p. 307). Thus Tessmer and Jonassen (1988) suggest that, while 'low-ability learners . . . may require "embedded" learning strategies, where cues and prompts for a student to use a specific learning strategy are actually built into the instructional materials' (p. 41), for most other learners, 'the appropriate learning strategies . . . [and] the proper learning interventions are not so much provided for the learner as generated by him' (p. 34).

The question of control of learning strategies has led cognitive engineers to still another level of generality in cognitive process instruction: the 'meta-level' of 'metacognition', to which we now turn.

3. *Metacognition.* Developmental psychologist John Flavell (1977)

originated the discussion of 'metacognitive strategies' in the mid-1970s in describing children's knowledge of what they remember. This approach to 'metamemory' soon set off a frenzy of interest in metacognitive strategies of all kinds. A decade later, Flavell (1987, p. 28) asserts that no one knows 'what metacognition is, how it operates, [or] how it develops'. Ann Brown (1987, p. 105), a leader in the study of metacognition, refers to the concept as 'a monster of uncertain origin'. This realization has not, however, stopped cognitive engineers from applying the concept liberally throughout education.

One thing is clear. Metacognitive theory presupposes that the human mind is an IPS, and that metacognition is itself the 'executive routine', as in a computer program (Spitz, 1986, p. 209; Yussen, 1985, p. 262). Metacognitive strategies occur at a level 'higher' than both learning strategies and thinking skills. According to Brown (1987, p. 66), they consist of 'one's knowledge and control of one's own cognitive system'. For this reason, it is considered to be more efficient to train metacognitive skills than to train the particular skills for which they are responsible.

4. *Who's in control?* A key question arising from the cognitive engineering of thinking skills, learning strategies and metacognition is whether the learner or the instructional system is in control. The purpose of all three cognitive engineering approaches is to intervene in the learner's cognitive processes in order to improve them – which is to say, in order to get them to function more efficiently or otherwise appropriately. A central contradiction in the work of cognitive engineers, then, is their claim that their goal is to place the learner in control of his or her own cognitive system. Some researchers speak of transforming learners into 'managers of their own cognitive resources', 'information managers', even 'entrepreneurs' controlling their cognitive investments (Pea, 1985a, 1985b). Others, preferring the language of the technologist to that of the capitalist, speak of 'giv[ing] students the power to reprogram their own biocomputers' (Dansereau, 1978, p. 3).

However, remembering the military origins of the field of cognitive engineering, we must bear in mind that 'the idea of automated control of information processes ... has shaped more than any technology the contemporary American armed forces' (Bellin and Chapman, 1987, p. 60). Control is the name of the game: the goal of engineering, cognitive or otherwise, is to establish control. Thus, while the emphasis of these ventures in cognitive engineering is 'self-programming' and 'self-monitoring', the underlying theme is self-discipline as a convenient substitute for imposed discipline. Just as 'autonomous weapons' in the military 'internalize' their mission and their orders, relieving some of the minute-to-minute responsibilities of the chain of command, so metacognition and learning strategies involve the internalization of external control of appropriate modes of thinking and learning. Students are set free, with their self-monitoring skills, to 'match their processing resources to learning task-requirements' (Rigney, 1978, p. 200). Such is the extent of their control over their own learning and thinking.

Furthermore, the higher the level of self-control, from thinking skills to learning strategies to metacognition, the more accessible as well is the learner to external control. This is because the more general the cognitive process, the more efficient the external control. More general skills are more generic skills. The learner with most control over his or her cognitive system is most easily adaptable to a wide range of jobs. In the military, 'from the point of view of the higher-order planning system, individual men are considered to be rather independent components who might, at one time or another, be required to operate in *any* man–machine system' (Kennedy, 1962, p. 18, his emphasis). The metacognitive manager, in other words, constitutes an extreme form of abstract labour.

Finally, the very accessibility to one's own cognitive apparatus, defined in generic terms, leaves one that much more open to external control: 'The more transparent is the [black] box, the more efficient can be the control of its processes' (Landa, 1976, p. 51). And the potential is real. In the military, of course, with its 'instructional systems design', the entire training enterprise is one of control. But as military technologies and methods of cognitive engineering enter the schools, systematic control of learning and thinking activities become the order of the day. In the prescient words, once again, of a SAGE pioneer Harold Sackman (1967, p. 568): 'As we advance toward computer-service cultures, the educational process in society is likely to take on attributes of realtime control systems.'

CONCLUSION: THE ROLE OF EDUCATION REVISITED

> The final difficulty that . . . must be faced in the attempt to integrate the science of learning and the technology of education is that of gaining access to children of school age for . . . experimental investigations.
> – Arthur W. Melton[11]

Cognitive engineering is, then, a cognitive technology which combines a science of mind with a technology of learning and intelligence. While cognitive engineering depends upon the study of human learning and intelligence to develop its models, it also uses these models to redesign those human capacities. In the words of Roy Pea (1985b, p. 169), it 'reshapes human nature' to fit the new technological landscape.

Where does public education fit into this enterprise? For their own reasons, educators have adopted the techniques of cognitive engineering. By now, 'thinking skills', 'learning strategies' and 'metacognition' are all accepted entries in the educational lexicon; they serve as objectives of new instructional practices. So, too, are computer microworlds and intelligent tutoring systems, designed to improve problem-solving and thinking skills through 'symbiosis', steadily becoming fixtures within the public education arena.

In order to improve instruction and in order to legitimate their profession, through the incorporation of new technologies and the latest applications of 'scientific' research, the schools have unwittingly welcomed the Trojan horse of military prerogatives within their gates. These prerogatives include a view of human minds – of students and teachers alike – as information-processing systems, layered with the procedures, strategies and heuristics of an 'artificial' intelligence. They also include the idea of persons reduced to their generic cognitive components, disembodied, decontextualized and depersonalized, infinitely adaptable to any and all technological man/machine systems. They include as well the reduction of education to task-specific training, with its emphasis on performance outcomes and 'time-on-task' efficiency. And they include, finally, a desiccated redefinition of key educational concepts – intelligence, learning, thinking – into information-processing procedures which are highly 'mindful' yet unreflective and pre-determined.

Of course, such models and their related methods and technologies take on new shapes once they enter the public education arena. More often than not they are diluted as they are fitted to the bureaucratic and pedagogical prerogatives of the schools. Metacognitive strategies, as mentioned earlier, are taught as 'study skills', for example. Researchers in programmed instruction, computer-based problem-solving, individualized learning programs and other educational innovations certainly complain about such dilution (Popkewitz et al., 1982). Yet neither do these innovations work exactly as planned even in the military contexts within which and for which they were originally designed.[12]

Are such models and practices inappropriate to begin with? Or do they lose their potency only once they enter the schools? In either case they ultimately contribute little or nothing to education or to educational change. They serve instead as massive 'scientific' distractions, redirecting attention and funding away from genuine avenues of reform, approaches that might take into account the larger social, political, economic and cultural considerations that are at the real root of school problems.

To the extent, on the other hand, that such models and innovations take hold within the schools, retaining their original character and intent, they represent a militarized debasement of education. This is because, ultimately, the design and production of human components appropriate for optimal performance of technological systems – rather than the fulfilment of human potential for its own sake – is the criterion of success of such 'education'. In fact, as mentioned earlier, the underlying goal of military attempts to understand human capacities is the eventual replacement of human beings, by autonomous weapons and automated battlefields. This is because human limitations in cognitive processing are viewed within military technological development as the source of 'human errors' in weapon systems. Thus, if education is a celebration of the potential of human beings, military cognitive R&D constitutes, at bottom, a celebration of their dispensability.

Military prerogatives, and those of cognitive researchers themselves, invade the school alongside the introduction of cognitive models, methods and technologies. According to Reif (1980, p. 45), education ought to be considered a component of cognitive engineering, with schools serving as laboratories for empirical research by cognitive engineers. The best way to understand human learning and cognition is to observe it in action – to do detailed 'microanalyses' of instruction and learning processes. And the schools serve this agenda as the perfect laboratories in which to test hypotheses and to formulate new theories about learning, instruction and intelligent technologies. 'Instruction on how or what to think', say Belmont and Butterfield (1977, p. 439), 'can be a potent and subtle *tool* for cognitive research.' No wonder, then, cognitive engineer Reif (1980, p. 49) announces that 'the time is ripe for ... achiev[ing] a symbiotic interaction of cognitive scientists and persons interested in practical education'.

In addition to their role as laboratories, schools also serve as a locus of legitimation for cognitive engineers, who are caught between several fields, with little to show as yet for their years of research. In the words of researcher David Klahr (1976, p. 331), 'neither instructors nor learners could benefit from the thinking about the design of learning models. The payoff, at present, appears to be for the people who fall into the intersection of the categories of instructional designer and cognitive psychologist: "learning engineers"'.

Vanguard of corporate capital

Educators have gone further than acquiesce in the prerogatives of military research and of military researchers. They have also, more and more, aligned their goals with the goals of a 'high-technology' corporate economy that is itself, as it always has been, the inheritor of military technological imperatives. From the very beginning of industrialization, military enterprise, 'owing to its enduring character, its scale, and its demand for materiel of the highest quality ... has exerted a powerful influence in determining the institutional and technical dimensions of the modern industrial era' (Smith,

1985, p. 1). Consequences of this early influence included scientific management, mechanized production, standardization and hierarchical organizational structures.

Since World War II this influence has escalated manifoldly. Daniel Bell (1967, p. 166), first ideologue of post-industrialism, recognized early on that 'military technology [will be] the major determinant of social strucure'. The entire economic landscape of 'post-industrial society', later dubbed by Bell (1981) the 'information society', has been shaped by military technological enterprise, from information theory, systems analysis, nuclear energy and transistors to automation, robotization, bio-engineering, and semiconductors.[13]

This is part of the reason why a number of noted scholars refer to the postwar US economy as a 'permanent war economy'.[14] The 'militarization of high technology' (Tirman, 1984) represents the latest phase in a century-long history of 'pervasiveness of military enterprise in the American [corporate] economy' (Smith, p. 5). Because it is at the cutting edge of information technologies, and is in fact used as the protected technological R&D arm of corporate capital, military enterprise is the advance guard of the information society.

To the extent, then, that public education aligns itself with the supposed new 'intellectual' requirements of the information economy, it is to that extent further saturating itself with the militarized redefinition of mind, intellect, thinking and learning that has been the subject of this essay. Public education thus becomes not only laboratory and locus of legitimation; it also becomes the site for the actual production of 'mental materiel' – for the design and manufacture of 'intellectual capital' (Greeno, 1985, p. 21) needed by corporate enterprise. The production of cognitive components for complex weapon systems – mind as materiel – is also the production of cognitive components for the global systems of information technology that are transforming the character of corporate capital. Only the battlegrounds are different.

Twenty-five years ago, Herbert Simon (1964, p. 82), management theorist turned cognitive pioneer, noted that 'the bulk of the productive wealth consists of programs... stored in human minds', and that 'the principal under-utilized resources [are] ... learning programs of the employed population'. Around the same time, Jerome Bruner, cognitive pioneer turned educator, became instrumental in Federal education reform, as Headstart initiator, leader of the new social-science curriculum movement and theorist of learning and instruction. Looking back on those early years, Bruner (1983, p. 62) recently remarked, 'It seems plain to me now that the "cognitive revolution" ...was a response to the technological demands of the "post-industrial revolution". You cannot properly conceive of managing a complex world of information without a workable concept of mind.' He recognized that if you 'develop a sufficiently complex technology ... [then] there is no alternative but to create cognitive principles in order to understand how people can manage it.'

Elsewhere, Bruner (1985, p. 599) recently added that 'it is almost the essence of the post-industrial revolution to place a high premium on the skills of the generalist, the troubleshooter, the problem-solver ... Once "mindful performance" becomes a practical necessity for the conduct of technology, the issue of mind and its status ceases to be governed by philosophical ... debates.' Thus, Bruner (1983, p. 274) insists, 'the cognitive revolution ... lies at the center of the post-industrial society ... The new capital is know-how, forecast, intelligence [and] the result has been not simply a renewal of interest in how the "mind" works, but rather a new search for ... how mindfulness is cultivated.'

This cultivation of cognitive resources for advanced technological systems is the new cognitivist agenda for the schools, and it lies at the heart of new corporate demands for employees who can 'think' and 'problem-solve', 'reason' and 'learn'. In her recent book, *In the Age of the Smart Machine*, Harvard Business School professor Shoshana Zuboff (1988) calls the skills involved in this new 'mind work' of corporate employees 'intellective skills'. Zuboff's book has been highly acclaimed as the clearest expression of how new corporate information technologies, rather than deskilling or displacing masses of workers, can instead create entirely new opportunities, available to more workers than ever before, for intellectual participation in the workplace.

Motivated by such new pressing needs for their wares, public education leaders are tripping over themselves to transform the schools, unwittingly, into a staging ground for playing out militarized scenarios. These scenarios are shaped by the requirements of advanced military-weapon systems, by cognitive researchers' need for laboratories and legitimation, and by new 'intellective' requirements of corporate capital in a militarized information economy. Now, just as educators are being told that their long-standing desire to teach students how to think now happily coincides with the new intellectual needs of corporate employers, the ongoing, militarized degradation of education and human intelligence is important to bear in mind ... while we still have one.

NOTES

1 Machado (1981), former Minister for the Development of Intelligence in Venezuela, sponsored Project Intelligence, which, from 1979 to 1984, was conducted by the Massachusetts

consulting firm Bolt, Beranek & Newman. Among the participants were Allan Collins, Jack Lochhead, Raymond Nickerson, and other individuals who play a significant role in the USA in thinking skills research funded by the military. For further information on Project Intelligence, see Walsh (1981) and Nickerson (1986).

2   Critical reviews of the state of the art include Dudley-Marling and Owston (1988); Resnick 1987, p. 47, 1988/9, p. 12); and Rosenberg (1987).

3   For evidence of the seminal military contribution to the research and development of these educational technologies, see Blaschke (1967); Hitchens (1971); Lumsdaine and Glaser (1960); Office of Technology Assessment (1982); Olsen and Bass (1982); and Saettler (1968).

4   For more information on the SAGE system and the Systems Research Laboratory, which later became the System Development Corporation, see Baum (1982); Chapman and Kennedy (1956); Rowell and Streich (1964); and Sackman (1967).

5   Cognitive psychologists and scientists whose work has been sponsored recently by ONR, NPRDC, DARPA, AFHRL or ARI include: John R. Anderson, Richard C. Anderson, John Seely Brown, Allan Collins, D. F. Dansereau, Robert Glaser, James Greeno, David Klahr, Raymond Nickerson, Donald A. Norman, David Rumelhart, Roger Schank, Richard Snow, Robert Sternberg and M. C. Wittrock.

6   It must be made clear that military sponsorship of research in the 1980s is far more mission-oriented than such sponsorship in the 1950s. Military funding of 'basic research' is a thing of the past; now all military funding, even for what it may call 'basic research', is focused on specific military applications (Dickson, 1984, p. 140; Piller and Yamamoto, 1988, p. 211).

For example, the mission of AI research by DARPA has for the first time been identified explicitly as the development of pilot associates, 'intelligent surface vehicles', and battle management systems for the Air Force, Army and Navy, respectively (*Datamation*, 1984; Davis, 1985).

The point here is this: if research in educational technology and cognitive science is substantially funded by the military, and subsequently adopted by the schools, the military purpose or mission of this sponsorship must be examined, and the compatibility of this mission with educational goals must be addressed. Claims that military support is unrelated to the goals of this 'educational' research are no longer valid, since such research has 'strong practical military implications' (Snow *et al.*, 1980, p. xiii).

7   I am speaking as though the military were a monolith, with a singular motive and mission. It is not. There are many conflicting views on these projects within the military, in particular those of the opposing technocratic and 'military reform' contingents. However, there is no question that the dominant dynamic in the military is the one represented here.

8   According to Donald Norman (1987), he coined the term 'cognitive engineering'. Others who have used this term include DiVesta and Rieber (1987), Robert Glaser, Harold F. O'Neil, Roy D. Pea, Frederick Reif and Herbert A. Simon.

9   The term 'symbiosis', applied to man/machine interaction, was first used by J. C. R. Licklider (1960), former director of DARPA's Information Processing Techniques Office, key leader in time-sharing technology, and later a prime supporter of 'computer literacy' instruction (1982). John Kemeny (1972), inventor of the BASIC programming language, was another early user of the term. It is now in widespread usage, by Pea (1985 a and b) and others.

10   Among the publications generated by the DARPA program are: Brown, Collins and Harris, 'Artifical Intelligence and Learning Strategies'; Dansereau, 'The Development of a Systematic Training Program for Enhancing Learning Strategies and Skills'; Logan, *An ISD Approach for Learning Strategies*; O'Neil, *Learning Strategies*; O'Neil and Spielberger, *Cognitive*

and Affective Learning Strategies; Rigney, 'Learning Strategies: A Theoretical Perspective'; Singer and Gerson, *Learning Strategies for Motor Skills*; and Sticht, *Literacy Training*. See Rigney and Munro (1981), pp. 133–4.

11 Psychologist Arthur W. Melton (1959, p. 103) was director of the Air Force Personnel and Training Research Center in the 1950s and has been instrumental in applying military training concepts to civilian education. Recently he has been the editor of the Experimental Psychology Series for Erlbaum publishers, a series which includes the first work by Robert Sternberg on his componential theory of intelligence (1977).

12 See Anderson (1986), Binkin (1986), Ellis (1986), Hoos (1972).

13 See Hounshell (1984), Piller and Yamamoto (1988), Smith (1985), Tirman (1984).

14 See Lens (1987), Melman (1985), Mills (1959), Mumford (1963).

REFERENCES

Anderson, C. L. (1986) 'Where did we go wrong? An analysis of the way ISD was mustered out of the Army', paper presented at AERA annual convention, San Francisco. (ED 270 632.)

Baum, C. (1982) *The System Builders: The Story of SDC*. Santa Monica, Ca.: System Development Corp.

Bell, D. (1967) 'The post-industrial society; a speculative view', in E. Hutchings *Scientific Progress and Human Values*. New York: American Elsevier, pp. 154–70.

———— (1981) 'The social framework of the information society', in T. Forester, ed. *The Microelectronics Revolution* Cambridge, MA: MIT Press.

Bellin, D. and Chapman, G. eds (1987) *Computers in Battle: Will They Work?* New York: Harcourt Brace-Jovanovich.

Belmont, J. M. and Butterfield, E. C. (1977) 'The instructional approach to developmental cognitive research', in R. V. Kail and J. W. Hagen *Perspectives on the Development of Memory and Cognition*. Hillsdale, NJ: Erlbaum, pp. 430–50.

Binkin, M. (1986) *Military Technology and Defense Manpower*. Washington, DC: Brookings Institution.

Blaschke, C. L. (1967) 'The DOD: catalyst in educational technology', *Phi Delta Kappan* 48:204–14.

Brown, A. (1987) 'Metacognition, executive control, self-regulation, and other more mysterious mechanisms', in F. E. Weinert and R. H. Kluwe eds *Metacognition, Motivation, and Understanding*. Hillsdale, NJ: Erlbaum, pp. 65–140.

Brown, A. and Campione, J. (1977) 'Memory and metamemory development in educable retarded children', in R. V. Kail and J. W. Hagen *Perspectives on the Development of Memory and Cognition*. Hillsdale, NJ: Erlbaum, pp. 367–407.

Brown, J. S. Collins, A., and Harris, G. (1978) 'Artifical intelligence and learning strategies', in H. F. O'Neil, Jr ed. *Learning Strategies*, New York: Academic Press, pp. 107–39.

Bruner, J. S. (1983) *In Search of Mind*. New York: Harper & Row.

———— (1985) 'On teaching thinking', in S. F. Chipman, J. W. Segal and R. Glaser, eds *Thinking and Learning Skills*, vol. 2. Pittsburgh, PD: University of Pittsburgh Press, pp. 590–9.

Carnegie Forum on Education and the Economy (1986) *A Nation Prepared: Teachers for the 21st Century*. Washington, DC: Carnegie Forum.

Chapman, R. L. and Kennedy, J. L. (1956) 'The background and implications of the systems research laboratory studies', in G. Finch and F. Cameron, eds *Air Force Human Engineering,*

Personnel and Training Research. National Academy of Sciences/National Research Council, pp. 65–73.

Costa, A. L. (1984) 'Mediating the metacognitive', *Educational Leadership* 42:56–61.

Dansereau, D. (1978) 'The development of a learning strategies curriculum', in H. F. O'Neil, Jr *Learning Strategies*. New York: Academic Press, pp. 1–29.

Datamation (1984) 'DARPA's big push in AI' 30:50.

Davis, D. B. (1985) 'Assessing the strategic computing initiative', *High Technology* 5:41–9.

Davis, R. *et al.* (1965) 'Potential implementation', in M. A. Sass and W. D. Wilkinson, eds *Computer Augmentation of Human Reasoning*. Washington, DC: Spartan, pp. 151–87.

Dickson, D. (1984) *The New Politics of Science*. New York: Pantheon.

DiVesta, F. J. and Rieber, L. P. (1987) 'Characteristics of cognitive engineering: the next generation of instructional systems', *ECTJ* 35:213–30.

Dreyfus, H. L. and Dreyfus, S. E. (1986) *Mind over Machine*. New York: Free Press.

Dudley-Marling, C. and Owston, R. D. (1988) 'Using microcomputers to teach problem solving: a critical review', *Educational Technology* 28:27–33.

Edwards, P. N. (1985) *Technologies of the Mind*. Santa Cruz, Ca: University of California. (Silicon Valley Research Group Working Paper no. 2.)

Ellis, J. A., ed. (1986) *Military Contributions to Instructional Technology*. New York: Praeger.

Evans, D. (1986) 'Losing battle: the army and the underclass', *New Republic* 194:10–13.

Fano, R. M. (1965) 'The MAC system: a progress report', in M. A. Sass and W. D. Wilkinson, eds *Computer Augmentation of Human Reasoning*. Washington DC: Spartan, pp. 131–49.

Flavell, J. H. (1977) *Cognitive Development*. Englewood Cliffs, NJ: Prentice-Hall.

———— (1987) 'Speculations about the nature and development of metacognition', in F. E. Weinart and R. H. Kluwe *Metacognition, Motivation, and Understanding*. Hillsdale, NJ: Erlbaum, pp. 21–9.

Greeno, J. (1985) 'Looking across the river: views from the two banks of research and development in problem solving', in S. F.Chipman, J. W. Segal and R. Glaser, eds *Thinking and Learning Skills*, vol. 2, pp. 209–14.

Gropper, G. L. (1980) 'Is instructional technology dead?' *Educational Technology* 20:39.

Halff, H. M. Hollan, J. D., and Hutchins, E. L., (1986) 'Cognitive science and military training', *American Psychologist* 41:1131–8.

Hitchens, H. B. (1971) 'Instructional technology in the armed forces', in S. G. Tickton *To Improve Learning: An Evaluation of Instructional Technology*, vol. II. New York: R. R. Bowker, pp. 701–21.

Hoos, I. R. (1972) *Systems Analysis in Public Policy: A Critique*. Berkeley, CA: University of California Press.

Hounshell, D. A. (1984) *From the American System to Mass Production, 1800–1932*. Baltimore, Md: Johns Hopkins University Press.

Keating, D. P. (1984) 'The emperor's new clothes: the "new look" in intelligence research', in R. J. Sternberg *Advances in the Psychology of Human Intelligence*, vol. 2. Hillsdale, NJ: Erlbaum, pp. 1–45.

Kemeny, J. G. (1972) *Man and the Computer*. New York: Charles Scribner's Sons.

Kennedy, J. L. (1962) 'Psychology and systems development', in R. M. Gagne, ed. *Psychological Principles in System Development*. New York: Holt, Rinehart & Winston, pp. 13–22.

Klahr, D. (1976) 'Designing a learner: some questions', in D. Klahr, *Cognition and Instruction: Tenth Annual Carnegie Symposium on Cognition*. Arlington, VA: Office of Naval Research, pp. 325–32.

Klahr, D. and Carver, S. M. (1988) 'Cognitive objectives in a LOGO debugging curriculum: instruction, learning, and transfer', *Cognitive Psychology* 20:362–404.

Klein, E. I. ed. (1985), *Children and Computers*. San Francisco, CA: Jossey-Bass.

Knapp, T. J. (1986) 'The emergence of cognitive psychology in the latter half of the twentieth century', in T. J. Knapp and L. C. Robertson, eds *Approaches to Cognition: Contrasts and Controversies*. Hillsdale, NJ: Erlbaum, pp. 13–35.

Kozma, R. B. (1987) 'The implications of cognitive psychology for computer-based learning tools', *Educational Technology* 27:20–5.

Lachman, R. *et al.* (1979) *Cognitive Psychology and Information Processing: An Introduction*. Hillsdale, NJ: Erlbaum.

Landa, L. N. (1976) *Instructional Regulation and Control*, ed. F. Kopstein, Englewood Cliffs, NJ: Educational Technology.

Langley, P. and Simon, H. A. (1981) 'The central role of learning in cognition', in J. R. Anderson, ed. *Cognitive Skills and Their Acquisition*. Hillsdale, NJ: Erlbaum, pp. 361–80.

Lens, S. (1987) *Permanent War: The Militarization of America*. New York: Schocken Books.

Leron, U. (1985) 'Logo today: vision and reality', *The Computing Teacher* February: 26–32.

Licklider, J. C. R. (1960) 'Man–computer symbiosis', *IRE Transactions on Human Factors in Electronics*, HFE-1 (March): 4–11.

———— (1982) 'National goals for computer literacy', in R. J. Seidel *et al.*, eds *Computer Literacy: Issues and Directions for 1985*. New York: Academic.

Lochhead, J. and Clement, J. (1979) *Cognitive Process Instruction*. Philadelphia, PA: Franklin Institute.

Loughary, J. W. (1970) 'Teaching technology', in A. C. Eurich, ed. *High School 1980*. New York: Pitman, pp. 240–51.

Lumsdaine, A. A. and Glaser, R. (1960) *Teaching Machines and Programmed Learning*, vol. 1. Washington, DC: NEA.

McCorduck, P. (1979) *Machines Who Think*. San Francisco, CA: W. H. Freeman.

McCoy, T. W. (1986) 'New ways to train', *Air Force Magazine* 69:55–61.

Machado, L. A. (1981) 'Élite babies: the weapon of the future', *Times*, 30 August: no page. Cited in J. Crouse and D. Trusheim (1988) *The Case against the SAT*. Chicago, IL: University of Chicago Press, p. 1.

Melman, S. (1985) *The Permanent War Economy*. New York: Simon & Schuster.

Melton, A. W. (1959) 'The science of learning and the technology of educational methods', *Harvard Education Review* 29:97–105.

Miller, G. A., Galanter, E. and Pribram, K. H. (1960) *Plans and the Structure of Behavior*. New York: Holt, Rinehart & Winston.

Mills, C. W. (1959) *The Power Élite*. New York: Oxford University Press.

Moravec, H. (1988) *Mind Children*. Cambridge, MA: Harvard University Press.

Mumford, L. (1963) *Technics and Civilization*. New York: Harbinger Books.

Neisser, U. (1967) *Cognitive Psychology*. New York: Appleton-Century-Crofts.

Neumann, W. (1979) 'Educational responses to the concern for proficiency', in G. Grant, ed. *On Competence: A Critical Analysis of Competency-Based Reforms in Higher Education*. San Francisco, CA: Jossey-Bass, pp. 67–95.

Newell, A. and Simon, H. A. (1972) *Human Problem Solving*. Englewood Cliffs, NJ: Prentice-Hall.

Newell, A. Shaw, J. C. and Simon, H. A. (1958) 'Elements of a theory of human problem solving', *Psychological Review*, 65:151–66.

Nickerson, R. S. (1986) 'Project Intelligence: an account and some reflections', *Special Services in the Schools* 83–102.

———— Perkins, D. N. and Smith, E. (1985) *The Teaching of Thinking*. Hillsdale, NJ: Erlbaum.

Norman, D. A. (1980) 'Cognitive engineering and education', in D. T. Tuma and F. Reif, eds *Problem Solving and Education*. Hillsdale, NJ: Erlbaum, pp. 81–95.

_____ (1987) 'Cognitive science – cognitive engineering', in J. M. Carroll, ed. *Interfacing Thought*. Cambridge, MA: MIT Press, pp. 325–36.

_____ ed. (1981) *Perspectives on Cognitive Science*. Hillsdale, NJ: Ablex/Erlbaum.

Office of Technology Assessment (OTA) (1982) *Informational Technology and Its Impact on American Education*. Washington, DC: US Government Printing Office.

Olsen, J. R. and Bass, V. B. (1982) 'The application of performance technology in the military: 1960–1980', *NSPI Journal* 21:32–6.

Papert, S. (1980) *Mindstorms: Children, Computers, and Powerful Ideas*. New York: Basic.

Pea, R. D. (1985a) 'Integrating human and computer intelligence', in E. I. Klein, ed. *Children and Computers*. San Francisco, CA: Jossey-Bass, pp. 75–96. (New Directions for Child Development 28.)

_____ (1985b) 'Beyond amplification: using the computer to reorganize mental functioning', *Educational Psychologist* 20:167–82.

Piller, C. and Yamamoto, K. R. (1988) *Gene Wars: Military Control Over the New Genetic Technologies*. New York: William Morrow.

Popkewitz, R. S. *et al.* (1982) *The Myth of Education Reform*. Madison, WI: University of Wisconsin Press.

Posner, M. I. (1973) 'Cognition: natural and artificial', in R. L. Solso, ed. *The Loyola Symposium: Contemporary Issues in Cognitive Psychology*. Washington, DC: V. H. Winston & Sons, pp. 167–75.

Pressley, M. *et al.* (1985) 'Children's use of cognitive strategies', in M. Pressley and C. J. Brainerd, *Cognitive Learning and Memory in Children*. New York: Springer-Verlag, pp. 1–48.

Reif, F. (1980) 'Theoretical and educational concerns with problem solving: bridging the gaps with human cognitive engineering', in D. T. Tuma and F. Reif, eds *Problem Solving and Education*. Hillsdale, NJ: Erlbaum, pp. 39–50.

Resnick, L. (1983) 'Toward a cognitive theory of instruction', in S. G. Paris, ed. *Learning and Motivation in the Classroom*. Hillsdale, NJ: Erlbaum.

_____ (1987) *Education and Learning to Think*. Washington, DC: National Academy Press.

_____ (1988/9) 'On learning research', *Educational Leadership* 46:12–16.

Rigney, J. W. (1978) 'Learning strategies: a theoretical perspective', in H. F. O'Neil, Jr, ed. *Learning Strategies*. New York: Academic Press, pp. 165–205.

Rigney, J. W. and Monro, A. (1981) 'Learning strategies', in H. F. O'Neil, Jr *Computer-Based Instruction: A State-of-the-Art Assessment*. New York: Academic, pp. 127–59.

Rosenberg, R. (1987) 'A critical analysis of research on intelligent tutoring systems', *Educational Technology* November: 27: 7–13.

Rowell, J. T. and Streich, E. R. (1964) 'The Sage system training program for the Air Defense Command', *Human Factors* October: 4: 537–48.

Sackman, H. (1967) *Computers, System Science, and Evolving Society: The Challenge of Man-Machine Digital Systems*. New York: Wiley.

Saettler, P. (1968) *A History of Instructional Technology*. Washington, DC: NEA.

Shaker, S. M. and Wise, A. R. (1988) *War without Men: Robots on the Future Battlefield*. Washington, DC: Pergamon-Brassey's.

Sheil, B. A. (1982) 'Coping with complexity', in R. A. Kasschau, R. Lachman and K. R. Laughery, eds *Information Technology and Psychology*. New York: Praeger, pp. 77–105.

Simon, H. A. (1964) 'Decision-making as an economic resource', in L. H. Seltzer, ed. *New Horizons of Economic Progress*. Detroit, MI: Wayne State University Press, pp. 81–3.

_____ (1980) 'Problem solving and education', in D. T. Tuma and F. Reif, eds *Problem Solving and Education*. Hillsdale, NJ: Erlbaum, pp. 81–96.

_____ (1981) 'Cognitive science: the newest science of the artificial', in D. A. Norman, ed. *Perspectives on Cognitive Science*. Hillsdale, NJ: Ablex/Erlbaum, pp. 13–25.

_____ (1983) 'Why should machines learn?' in R. S. Michalski *et al.*, eds *Machine Learning: An Artificial Intelligence Approach*. Palo Alto, CA: Tioga, pp. 25–37.

Smith, M. R. ed. (1985) *Military Enterprise and Technological Change*. Cambridge, MA: MIT Press.

Snow, R. E. *et al.*, eds (1980) *Aptitude, Learning and Instruction*, vol. 2. Hillsdale, NJ: Erlbaum.

Spitz, H. H. (1986) *The Raising of Intelligence*. Hillsdale, NJ: Erlbaum.

Sternberg, R. J. (1977) *Intelligence, Information Processing and Analogical Reasoning: The Componential Analysis of Human Abilities*. Hillsdale, NJ: Erlbaum.

Sternberg, R. J. and Detterman, D. K. (1982) *How and How Much Can Intelligence be Increased?* Norwood, NJ: Ablex.

Tessmer, M. and Jonassen, D. (1988) 'Learning strategies: a new instructional technology', in D. Harris, ed. *Education For the New Technologies: World Yearbook of Education*. London: Kogan Page, pp. 20–45.

Tirman, J. (1984) *The Militarization of High Technology*. Cambridge, MA: Ballinger.

Towne, D. M. (1987) 'The generalized maintenance trainer', in W. B. Rouse, ed. *Advances in Man–Machine Systems Research*, vol. 3. Greenwich, CT: JAI.

Walsh, J. (1981) 'A plenipotentiary for human intelligence', *Science* 214:640–1.

WGBH (1988) 'Top gun and beyond', NOVA television programme (20 January).

Wittrock, M. C. (1979) 'Applications of cognitive psychology to education and training', in H. F. O'Neil, Jr and C. D. Spielberger, eds *Cognitive and Affective Learning Strategies*. New York: Academic, pp. 309–17.

Yussen, S. R. (1985) 'The role of metacognition in contemporary theories of cognitive development', in D. L. Forrest-Pressley, G. E. MacKinnon and T. G. Waller *Metacognition, Cognition, and Human Performance*. New York: Academic, pp. 252–83.

Zender, B. (1975) *Computers and Education in the Soviet Union*. Englewood Cliffs, NJ: Educational Technology.

Zuboff, Shoshana (1988) *In the Age of the Smart Machine*. New York: Basic.

2   THE CYBORG SOLDIER
The US military and the
post-modern warrior

CHRIS HABLES GRAY

> Recall that it is not only that men make wars, but that wars
> make men.
> – Barbara Ehrenreich (1987)

Wars do make men. And not just real wars. Possible wars, imagined wars, even unthinkable wars are shaping men, and women, today. Just as modern war required modern soldiers; post-modern war[1] needs soldiers with new military virtues who can meet the incredible requirements of high-technology war. These new soldiers are moulded, in part, by personnel science and marketing analysis in uneasy alliance with traditional military discipline and community. But in another sense it is the weapons themselves that are constructing the US soldier of today and tomorrow.

Weapons have always played an important role in war, from before the Greek hoplite to the tankers of the world wars. Today, however, it is not just that the soldier is influenced by the weapons used; now he or she is (re)constructed and (re)programmed to fit integrally into weapon *systems*. The basic currency of war, the human body, is the site of these modifications – whether it is of the 'wetware' (the mind and hormones), the 'software' (habits, skills, disciplines) or the 'hardware' (the physical body). To overcome the limitations of yesterday's soldier, as well as the limitations of automation as such, the military is moving towards a more subtle man/machine integration: a cybernetic organism ('cyborg') model of the soldier, that combines machine-like endurance with a redefined human intellect subordinated to the overall weapons system.

Current US Department of Defense policy is creating a post-modern army of war machines, war managers and robotized warriors. The post-modern enlisted soldier either is an actual machine or will be made to act like one through the psychotechnologies of drugs, discipline and management. The post-modern officer is a skilled professional who manages weapons systems and sometimes applies them in combat. In all cases soldiers are to be intimately connected with computers through hard wiring, lasers and more traditional soldier–machine interfaces.

Despite governmental restrictions on information, conscious official disinformation, and a secret military 'black' budget of over $35 billion for 1988 – that is 11 percent of the Pentagon's planned $312 billion budget (Weiner, 1987) – a great deal can be discovered about these developments from obscure journals, public documents, and concerned participant-observers. It is just too big to hide, dominating much of science, a huge hunk of the economy, and most of military discourse. A little investigation reveals, in some detail, the outlines of the arcane policies and classified R&D that is making this science-fiction scenario a reality.

Relentless and massive changes in the basic technologies of war are the key reason behind this transformation of the modern soldier into the fragmented and interpenetrating identities of fighters, supporters, administrators, and machines, humans, cyborgs. It's not just nuclear weapons that are causing these changes, although they are both physically and symbolically central to our post-modern situation – a situation in which the superpowers are restrained from total war while they seem structurally incapable of real peace.

Yet, the great accomplishments in nuclear-war technology (the world's leading industry by many measures) are only part of the general advance of technoscience that has meant the extraordinary changes in the speed, scope and destructiveness of war. If any technoscience is crucial to post-modern war, it is not nuclear but computer. Computers not only make nuclear technoscience possible, they form the underlying basis and rationale for most post-modern war doctrines, policies and weapons, both materially and metaphorically (Gray, 1988b).

All kinds of war are being fought now on our planet. Religious and racial conflicts, neo-colonial struggles, border clashes, insurgency, counter-insurgency and pro-insurgency still rage; usually they involve weapons not much different in form from those of World War II, though much more powerful functionally (rate of fire, accuracy, explosive force). But these killings take place in a world-wide context where there cannot be total war. That would be unthinkable – though Herman Kahn in his 'thinking about the unthinkable' called it, revealingly, 'wargasm'. Total war is now 'imaginary war', in Mary Kaldor's phrase. It is getting ready for the war that must never be fought. Israel, South Africa, Pakistan, Libya, India, Taiwan and others will soon join the nuclear club – in some cases admitting to already having those awesome weapons they dare not use. France, China, the UK and the superpowers continue to expand their own arsenals. Meanwhile Iraqi poison gas chokes down Kurdish holy warriors as Israeli robot drones and the satellites of the great powers look on. So comes Sylvere Lotringer's chilling insight: 'War is perhaps impossible: it continues nonetheless everywhere you look' (Baudrillard and Lotringer, 1987, p. 111).

POPULAR IMAGES OF US SOLDIERS

This is why in North America the cosy images from modern war of US soldiers (Kilroys, dog faces, GI Joes) and Commonwealth soldiers (wisecracking Tommys, soft-spoken Canadians, loud Anzacs, and silent Gurkas) from World War II (*Combat, 12 O'Clock High*) have been shattered. In film portrayals of the first post-modern war, Vietnam, multi-ethnic teams of clean-cut-born-in-America guys (*Green Berets*) coexist with men trapped in an insoluble moral dilemma (*Deerhunter, Platoon*) or even inside of *Apocalypse Now*. Vietnam War means Vietnam Protests (*Coming Home, Fields of Stone*) as even the charmed circle of all-American guys (*Tours of Duty*) now must recognize. The first TV show about Vietnam, *M*A*S*H*, was set in Korea during that conflict but it was always, psychologically and ideologically, about Vietnam. One of the most successful TV shows in the USA, it still plays out its ironic anti-war message every day in syndication. Although its dark humour is copied by some (*Good Morning, Vietnam!*) and its feminine healing focus by others (*China Beach*), *M*A*S*H* remains unique, marking in the mass media the critique of modern war first elaborated by the poet veterans of World War I and then by the novelist veterans of World War II.[2]

Consider the billions of dollars spent, the complex weapons built, the 50,000 nuclear warheads in the world, the constant skirmishing of the Cold War (aka: Pure War, High Technology War, Permanent War, Technowar, War without End, the Dance of the Superpowers, Exterminism), the smart bombs, and the high-tech low-intensity wars (but sometimes locally total, as in Vietnam, East Timor, Cambodia, Afghanistan). These forces now generate a wild range of bizarre characters. Bad guys and good guys are harder to keep separate when one compares:

- Stateless terrorists (IRA, PLO, Contras) and state terrorists (Col. North and his friends, British and Israeli Commandos);
- Communist military officers (Poland, Ethiopia) and Fascist military officers (Chile, El Salvador) holding State Power;
- 'Right stuff' astronauts ('one giant step for mankind') and 'Top Gun' pilots (killing Muammar Gaddafi's four-year-old daughter with a 'smart bomb');

- Jedhi Knights (modelled on the Vietcong according to Lucas) and Rambo (a Nam vet whose first movie is all about killing policemen);
- Fat Pentagon officers smoking cigars with briefcases full of money (as shown in countless political cartoons) and naïve soldier-engineers (Jimmy Carter);
- Defeated superpower soldiers riding their tanks and helicopters out of Afghanistan and Vietnam, and the winners;
- Good cyborgs ('Robocop', hundreds of cartoon and sci-fi characters) and bad cyborgs ('The Exterminator' and more hundreds of cartoon and sci-fi characters);
- Elite US soldiers invading countries (Grenada), training death squads (Latin America), killing civilians with high-tech weapons (Persian Gulf, Libya) and as victims of terrorism (Marines in Beirut, woman soldier in West Germany, black sailor on hijacked plane);
- Boring, nerdy, war researchers (David Broad's book *Star Warriors*) and Dr Strangelove scientists.

GI Joe is now a TV character who fights more battles with transformers (robots that can turn into cars and planes) and dinosaurs than any normal human enemies. All the violent children's cartoons involve cyborgs and other strange mixes of the human, the beastly, the alien, and the technological. The newest shows allow the kids at home to join in the fight as well by using expensive interactive toys. In just the last four years the main war cartoons have included the interactive *Captain Power and the Soldiers of the Future* (Mattel Toys), interactive *Photon* (MCA-Universal), interactive *TechForce* (Axlon Toys), *Inhumanoids* (Hasbro Toys), *Centurians: Power Xtreme* (Kenner Toys), *GI Joe* (Hasbro), *Challenge of the Gobots* (Tonka Toys), *Transformers* (Hasbro), *Dungeons & Dragons* (TSR, CBS), *Rambo: Force of Freedom* (Coleco Toys), *Star Wars: Droids* (Kenner, ABC), *She-Ra, Princess of Power* (Mattel), *Thundercats* (MCA-Universal), *Jaycee and the Wheeled Warriors* (Mattel), *Superpowers* (Marvel Comics, ABC), *Voltron* (Matchbox), *Lazer Tag* (Worlds of Wonder, NBC), *Star Wars: Ewoks* (Kenner, ABC), *Silverhawks* (Kenner), *HeMan & Masters of the Universe* (Mattel), *Robotech* (Matchbox), *Dinosaucers* and *Dinoriders* (Leggoes).[3]

War today is equally disjointed even if it lacks dinosaurs. We now witness the extrapolation of modern war motifs and weapons into their *reductio ad absurdum* and their unabsurd opposite images. So the atomic bomb and the computer, the two great military brain children of World War II, become nuclear overkill facing hijackers armed with hand-guns, and the electronic battlefield is overrun (and undermined) by the agrarian Vietnamese. And, as alluded to above, the common-man foot soldier has assumed any number of other identities, from a female soldier-tech repairing a faceless machine to an élite bloody-minded covert-action warrior using a satellite to call in a killer droid.

Autonomous weapons, such as the Aegis anti-aircraft system, have already been deployed in combat. The Aegis on the cruiser USS *Yorktown* was armed and put on automatic in the Gulf of Sidra during confrontations with Libya in spring 1986, when it fired on its own at an unidentified target with results still undetermined to this day (Grier, 1986). More recently its unreliability has been cited to explain both the attack on the USS *Stark* in April 1988 and the shooting down of an Iranian commercial airliner by the USS *Vincennes* in the Persian Gulf a few months later.[4]

Various artificially intelligent expert systems are being used to maintain high-tech weapons, play war games and bring together logistical and crisis information. At the same time most soldiers are now involved in support work for the war machines and the few élite warriors who fight them; all under the direction of a growing stratum of technobureaucratic war managers. Post-modern war is still in its infancy. One possible future, the official one, is formalized in Pentagon future studies. A look at two such reports, one from the Army and one from the Air Force, will show what the United States war managers expect of po-mo soldiers after the year 1999.

AIRLAND BATTLE 2000:
THE TWENTY-FIRST-CENTURY ARMY

The twenty-first century is less than one procurement cycle away, as Capt. Ralph Peters (1987), US Army, recently wrote in an article on 'The army of the future'. Many of today's junior officers will serve more of their careers in that century than this one, notes a retired general in a piece on stress in future combat (Sarkesian, 1980). Ever since World War I, with the crucial role given to new technologies (machine-guns, planes, poison gas, trucks, tanks, radios, fire control, submarines, and operations research), the US military have understood the importance of new scientific and technological developments. Since World War II the Pentagon has institutionalized and magnified this understanding into a 'Strategy of High Technology' that posits technological innovation as the decisive factor in shaping strategy and winning actual wars.

Starting in 1944 with *Toward New Horizons*, the US military has initiated a number of studies aimed at systematically understanding future war. They have brought together futurists, scientists, science-fiction writers, military and civilian technobureaucrats in a series of conferences. The US Air Force's *Project Forecast* of 1964 was followed by *Forecast II* in 1985. The approaching millennium has encouraged a number of looks at the soldier of the next century, including *AirLand Battle 2000*, *Army 21*, *Air Force 2000*, and *Focus 21* (a joint Army and Air Force product).

Produced in 1982, *AirLand Battle 2000* was a 'jointly developed concept agreed to by the United States Army and the German Army'. It has since been distilled into the official US Army plans for war in Europe and also been recycled as *Army 21*.

AirLand Battle (ALB) gets its name from the assumption that the post-modern battle will be three dimensional, requiring intimate co-ordination between land and air-space forces. ALB doctrine is based on manoeuvre and aggression in the context of a hyper-lethal chaotic battle 'field' of hundreds of cubic miles. Nato plans are for deep counter-attacks in the rear of the attacking Warsaw armies immediately after (or perhaps immediately before) a presumed invasion of Europe. Pre-emptive strikes are an integral part of ALB plans. Despite the unlikelihood of a Soviet assault on Nato, the ALB has a concrete function in that it supplies a pretext for a whole set of new strategies (of multi-arm co-ordination) and weapons (especially remote-controlled and autonomous drones, vehicles, and sensors) that have almost certainly already been used in Grenada, Nicaragua, and other 'little wars' and low-intensity conflicts (Miller, 1988).

AirLand Battle 2000, addressing post-modern war in general, puts forward a number of technological solutions to the problems expected to result from the mind-rending impact of high-technology weapons in continuous combat lasting days at a time. Many units will be obliterated, others merely broken. All evidence suggests that most soldiers, as we now know them, will not be able to fight with any effectiveness under these conditions (Hunt and Blair, 1985).

To deal with the post-modern battlespace, *AirLand Battle 2000* advocates improved support services – medical, logistical, and even such marginal aids as video chaplins, talking expert systems to give legal advice, and computer war games for 'recreation and stress reduction'. It also proposes stronger measures to integrate the individual soldiers into parts of a complex fighting unit. See-through eye armour and other 'personal bionic attachments to improve human capabilities' are planned to go along with artificial bones, artificial blood, and spray-on skin for the wounded. For those with major wounds, WHIMPER (Wound Healing Injection Mandating Partial Early Recovery) shots would allow their evacuation or even their quick return to combat. Universal anti-viral, anti-bacterial and anti-VD vaccines are to be developed along with mycotoxin antidotes. A universal insoluble insect repellent is supposed to save on time and aggravation – as will chemicals to stunt hair growth, retard body functions, and keep teeth clean without brushing for six months.

Miniature sensors will warn soldiers of chemical, biological or radiological threats. Miniature data discs will hold his or her records. Other 'automated devices' will judge the soldier's 'physical and psychological fitness' and

decide who must keep fighting.

The Strategic Computing Program is working on an expert system battle-manager to advise AirLand Battle commanders on the corps level. It is to predict enemy activity, track and filter the extraordinary amount of information that post-modern battle generates, advise the humans and even issue their orders. It is expected that satellites in near space will direct individual artillery rounds, send messages between commands, and pinpoint every single friendly soldier and machine. While the outside command and control of the individual combatant is being computerized, various interventions are planned for his or her insides as well. Combat rations will be spiked with 'additives to assist in preventing disease or effects from CBR (Chemical, Biological, or Radioactive) contamination', and they will be 'fortified with... anti-stress components'.

AirLand Battle 2000 warns starkly that 'Battle intensity requires: stress reduction...' New anti-fatigue and anti-stress medicines that work 'without degradation to performance' are a high priority. The noted military psychiatrist Dr Richard Gabriel claims that this research for 'a nondepleting neurotrop' ('... a chemical compound that will prevent or reduce anxiety while allowing the soldier to retain his normal levels of acute mental awareness') is nearing success with grave implications:

> Both the US miliary and the Soviets have initiated programs in the last five years to develop such a drug; the details of the American program remain classified... The US military has already developed at least three prototypes that show great 'promise'. One of these drugs may be a variant of busbirone. If the search is successful, and it almost inevitably will be, the relationship between soldiers and the battle environment will be transformed forever... if they succeed... they will have banished the fear of death and with it will go man's humanity and his soul. (Gabriel, 1987, pp. 143–4)

While unique in terms of their potential effectiveness, these current projects to develop such drugs are part of a US research programme going back to the 1950s and military traditions thousands of years old. Until they are successful in developing a drug that encourages aggressiveness and obedience, blocks fear and confusion, and allows for clear thinking (at least in terms of the specific tasks of the soldier), the US military is stressing improved weapon systems and stronger training.

Training for ALB involves a central paradox, however. Potential external stimuli (death and destruction) are much greater than in previous wars but the duties of the soldiers are more technical and complicated. How can psychological limits be overcome and yet human judgement preserved? This was one of the central problems addressed at a symposium held by the Army Institute for the Behavioral and Social Sciences at Texas Tech University in Lubbock, Texas, in 1983.

In order to avoid 'cognitive freezing' in battle, the many academic and military experts at this symposium proposed various approaches to training, including 'overtraining', so that under stress the desired behaviour occurs, creating quantitative instead of qualitative tasks (spraying automatic weapons fire instead of aiming single shots at people), forming strong peer groups, and using hypnotism and drugs (Hunt and Blair, 1985). Officers, technical specialists, and even the ordinary soldiers, to some extent, will have to be helped to be innovative and show initiative, two qualities required by high-technology weapons in general and ALB in particular. Many analysts see such conflicting advice as indicative of the unrealistic assumptions of ALB, which is probably true. But it also shows that post-modern war calls for more than one type of soldier. At a minimum there must be those who can perform almost mindlessly under extreme conditions that most humans cannot bear, and at the same time there is a need for experts in management, technical repairs and weapon-system application.

The US Air Force, in a way, has already solved part of this problem. Machines are for the mindless fighting, and humans are still needed for some of the management, maintenance and manipulation of the weapon systems. For the future the Air Force plans to take this approach even further, as can be seen in its own blueprint for the next century.

FORECAST II:
THE TWENTY-FIRST-CENTURY AIR FORCE

Project Forecast II comes from a large collection of experts: 175 civilian and military experts divided into eighteen technology, mission and analysis panels (US Government, 1986). A related three-day conference at Wright Patterson Air Force Base called *Futurist II* brought together thirty Air Force officers, eight science-fiction writers and ten futurists (Cooper and Shaker, 1988, p. 39). A little think-tank, Anticipatory Sciences Inc., got $44,105 to organize it. Seventy specific suggestions from *Forecast II* and *Futurist II* are being pursued by the Air Force.

Indeed, Gen. Lawrence A. Skantze, Commander, Air Force Systems Command, makes a convincing case in his briefing at 'Aerospace '87' that *Project Forecast II* has shaped Air Force R&D to a great extent. He claims that in 1987 the project's suggestions absorbed over 10 percent of the $1.6 billion Air Force Laboratories budget (his command) with a similar level being planned to 1993. The Air Force as a whole kicked in another $150 million for 1988. In 1987, twenty-four key aerospace companies put up $866 million of their own for the *Forecast II* proposals: 44 percent of their $2 billion of internal R&D (Skantze, 1987). This 'private' research on military proposals doesn't officially count as military work, although it is along military lines, with military specifications, aimed at winning military contracts, and only possible because of the profits from earlier military work.

So, easily over $1 billion in fiscal year 1987 was spent on R&D on the proposals from this conference, with another $1.2 billion or more slated for 1988. Clearly 'The United States Air Force is committed to implementing the results of *Project Forecast II*', as the Executive summary proclaims on page 1. What are they?

There are too many to list here. New materials are proposed. The use of photons in place of electrons in computers is advocated to speed them up and make them harder to disrupt electromagnetically in combat. There is the dream of 'optical kill mechanisms' and more deadly lasers to blind and kill sensors and people on the battleground. Many of the proposals are to help fulfil the Air Force's desire for 'rapid, reliable, and affordable access to space'. Others are members of 'a family of weapons which autonomously acquire, track, and guide to a broad spectrum of air and surface targets in all environments'. Specific examples include low-cost drones for surveillance, homing in on radar sites, or carrying their own 'smart' anti-armour weapons with a 'fire & forget terminal maneouvering' capability. 'Smart skins' combining sensors, new materials, and computers in a system capable, they hope, of a 'total situational awareness' will be used to cover both independent brilliant weapons and piloted aircraft.

One of the most significant projects for understanding the role of the future soldier is that to introduce artificial intelligence into the cockpits of Air Force planes and Army helicopters. Through the Army Air Force programme to build the AI Virtual Cockpit and DARPA's 'phantom flight crew' of five expert systems in the Strategic Computing Program's Pilot's Associate demonstration project, the pilot will be intimately connected to his or her flying-fighting machine.

The goal is to improve 'man–machine interaction', including 'control through line of sight, voice, and psychomotor responses'. Computerized 'decision aids' are proposed along with a vague call for techniques to 'effectively and efficiently couple operators to advanced systems'. General Skantze is a little clearer in his speech. He refers to 'pilot state monitoring' in the Virtual AI Cockpit, slated to be done by 1996. This interface is being built by 'human factors engineers' from 'our Human Systems Division'.

As Kenneth Stein (1985) reports, with the Pilot's Associate 'all on-board systems' will be monitored and diagnosed for their 'health and current/ projected operational status'. This includes the human pilot. Stein goes on to note that the 'tactical planning manager ... may wait for pilot confirmation or may initiate responses' itself. 'Where there is time for the pilot to make a judgement', it will graciously suggest possible actions and recommend one. The 'pilot state monitoring' is intended to include systems that read the pilot's brain waves, follow eye movements and test the conductivity of sweaty palms. By gauging the pilot's mood, the computer will know how to communicate with the pilot or even when to take over the plane if deemed necessary (Faludi 1986; Wilford, 1986).

Work is also proceeding on a number of subroutines that will plan the possible future duties of the Pilot's Associate by predicting the pilot's requests and actions ahead of time. As a team from the Artificial Intelligence Laboratory at the Air Force's Institute of Technology coyly notes: 'Because the pilot and computer have trained together, the pilot expects the computer to begin problem solving when the situation dictates it'. The team goes on to propose a 'goal detector' to 'deduce' the goals of the pilot 'by observing his actions' (Cross *et al.*, 1986, pp. 152, 163). According to some of the other Virtual AI Cockpit researchers, this 'mindware' is supposed to create a 'fully interactive "virtual computer space" wherein the human and the computer live together' (Wilford, 1986).

For the more distant future the military is clearly aiming for direct brain–computer connections. It could be through computer monitors 'reading' the pilot's specific thoughts. A Stanford Research Institute (now called SRI) research project in the early 1970s, funded by the Department of Defense, aimed not only at reading minds but also at having a computer insert ideas and messages into people's brains. Although project director Dr Lawrence Pinneo reported that his computers were 30 to 40 percent accurate in 'guessing' what a person was thinking, it doesn't seem that the work was that successful (*Counterspy*, 1974, p. 5). Recent research at Johns Hopkins University has managed to sort out enough brain waves to predict when a monkey will move its arms by reading its electrical mental patterns before it acts.

Then again, perhaps the connections will be hard-wired: neuron to silicon. The Air Force has paid for much of this biocybernetic research since the 1970s (Davies, 1987, p. 78), including work in its own labs that puts computer chips into dog brains in experiments aimed at giving pilots 'an extra sensing organ'. But it is the Army that has paid for the work at West Texas State (and possibly the similar work at Stanford) that has succeeded in growing rat and monkey neurons to silicon chips (Goben, 1987; *Scientific American*, 1987 p. 62). The goal is to develop biochips that can be activated by hormones and neural electrical stimulation and which can, in turn, initiate hormonal and mental behaviour in humans. It is hoped that such human–machine integration will result in quicker reaction times, better communication, improved control and greater reliability overall.

Important as this cyborg research is, just as central to current plans are totally mechanical systems that will allow for the complete replacement of the soldier by the machine – in other words, autonomous weapons.

WAR MACHINES

The US military has on hand, or under development, hundreds of robots, artificial intelligences, dedicated computers and autonomous weapons. They include various industrial robots, automated production lines, three-, four- and six-legged mechanical walkers, at least two different artificial hands, security robots, fire-fighting robots, runway repair robots, robotic refuellers, robotic cargo handlers, automatic decontaminators of clothing and equipment, automated repair systems for the B-1 bomber, and expert systems for finances, logistics, and systems analysis. They also have numerous programs to analyse photo data, to sort captured electronic information and to enhance radar images.

There are projects to create autonomous land vehicles, minelayers, minesweepers, obstacle breachers, construction equipment, surveillance platforms, and anti-radar, anti-armour and anti-everything drones. They are working on smart artillery shells, smart torpedoes, smart depth charges, smart rocks (scavenged meteors collected and then 'thrown' in space), smart bombs, smart nuclear missiles and brilliant cruise missiles. Computer battle-managers are being developed for AirLand battle, tactical fighter wings, naval carrier groups, and space-based ballistic-missile defence. Complex AI computer programs are already at the heart of the Pentagon's vast computer-gaming system, where people can now duel with AI 'agents' instead of human opponents. They also control the new crisis management centre and many command, control and communication systems from the tactical in range to interplanetary in scope (Earth and Moon). By 1995 the Army even hopes to have a robot to 'decontaminate human remains, inter remains, and refill and mark the graves' (Commandant, undated).

These systems range from tele-operated (controlled by a human at some distance through wires or broadcasts) to the fully autonomous. In many cases the plan is for tele-operated systems to become autonomous over the next few decades as expert systems and automatic controls are developed. Many current weapons, such as the Aegis, have both automatic and operator modes, although certain analytical functions may remain computerized and outside human control. In a battle situation, where microseconds are seen as critical, tele-operated systems involve inevitable delays along with their other problems (protecting the operators, staying connected with the operators). Thus the more autonomous weapons are being highly favoured, even though the only role human judgement often has with them is whether or not they should be released. If a fighter had been sent to intercept flight 655 over the Persian Gulf, the pilot would have seen it was an airliner. Manned planes almost always close to visual range before firing because of the extreme danger of fratricide (shooting down their own planes), which is always possible because they lack any absolutely effective system to distinguish friend from foe. Instead, the Captain of the USS *Vincennes* had his Aegis system send a missile which did as it was told and blew the Iranian airliner out of the sky.

Why this mania for tele-operated and automatic weapons? One reason, often ignored, is that in a discourse system dominated by technophilia, profit-making and fear, as is the military discourse system, every shiny machine, or even plan for a machine, becomes an argument in itself for more mechanization (Dickson, D., 1974). This argument by artifact explains much about the computerization of war today. We should also consider the extreme political pressures against risking civilians (or even US military personnel) in dangerous war situations (the 'Vietnam War syndrome'), along with the supposed (but seldom, realized) reliability of automatic systems and their potential for close control by the higher command (often over-exercised, as it was during President Ford's Mayaquez affair, Carter's botched Iranian raid, and Reagan's clumsy Grenada invasion). Thus it becomes somewhat understandable that the US military has staked so much on these unproven technologies.

Finally, the nature of the post-modern battlefield has also become a key rationale for 'warbots'. Chemical, biological and nuclear (CBN) weapons make the killing zones of late twentieth-century battle as lifeless as the surface of the moon. Command and fighting vehicles will be CBN-proof and the soldiers inside will also wear protective suits that allow 'the wearer to drink and eat special food developed at the [US Army's] Natick R&D Center and to eliminate body waste while wearing the suit . . . using technology from the space programme . . .' (United States Government, 1984, p. 15).

Robots are also supposed to be able to work twenty-four hours a day without fatigue, absorb the vast amounts of information necessary, react well under stress, survive greater amounts of destructive fire, and keep up with the accelerating speed of battle, now keyed by machines instead of human bodies. Building and maintaining all these robots is a massive managerial job. Bureaucrats see robots as a way of making war a science and an industry – or at least something that can be managed. Inevitably, there is great pressure to turn the human soldiers that remain into manageable units as well.

WAR MANAGERS

In the long history linking hierarchical organizations and war, successful armies could never become pure bureaucracies because very unbureaucratic virtues – physical courage, loyalty and leadership for example – were needed to win real battles. 'Wars ruin more good armies', military officers used to joke, referring not to defeat on the battlefield but to managers and office-holders losing control of the military system to warriors and officers with battlefield promotions.

In many ways, trying to make soldiers into machines has preceded making machines into soldiers. Lewis Mumford (1967) claimed that the very first machine was the first army and the soldiers were its parts. Uniforms, hierarchies, discipline, training and rules of war have all been used for some time to try to control soldiers, to make them interchangeable and mould them into a single unit of fighting force. Since the turn of the century, modern labour management (capitalist and State socialist) has co-evolved with military personnel management. Both aim at fitting the individual worker-soldiers into the military-industrial system. The 'American system' of manufacturing, Taylorism, scientific management, psychological testing, counselling, operations research, systems analysis and similar social technologies have all been developed within a military context.

Lawrence Radine, in his book *The Taming of the Troops: Social Control in the United States Army*, traces how current military managers have added to their traditional forms of 'coercive' and 'professional paternalist control' a new form he calls 'co-optive rational control through behavioral science and management' to manage their troops. In his view personal leadership is being replaced by 'testing, attitude surveys, various utilitarian and life-style incentives, and weapons systems...' (Radine, 1977, p. 91). He points out that:

> One application of this social engineering approach is the way the military matches men to machines (as well as matching some aspects of machines to men). The man is the extension of such machines as artillery pieces or weapons systems generally; he is an adjunct for some limitation the machine has due to its incomplete development. (p. 89)

An important part of this is the very detailed study of the humans in their system context. '[The soldier's] performance is measured and predicted to a degree of precision unmatched in previous human experience.' Measurement of behaviour leads to more effective social control and might even 'provide a nearly unlimited potential for the bureaucratic or administrative domination of man'. He cites C. Wright Mills for first describing this style of domination and coining the term 'cheerful robots' for the type of subjects it produces. Radine concludes that 'the ultimate result of co-optive rational controls is cheerful states of mind, with no values or beliefs other than one's own comforts, and automatic, mechanical performance' (p. 90).

The rationalization of social control in the US military has many applications. In training it involves using B. F. Skinner's principles of reinforcement and punishment for operant conditioning. Survey research is used to identify effective reinforcers and they are administered carefully to maximize their impact (Radine, p. 130).

Just as important is the systems approach. Noting that 'social control is more effective when it is embedded in the totality of a situation', Radine reflects upon the importance technology can have in maximizing the control of individual soldiers.

Two developments have emerged somewhat simultaneously that have elements of this type of situational or nonpersonalized social control. One is a result of technological development in weaponry. As weaponry gets more complex and is based more on hardware than on manpower, the interaction of various components becomes emphasized and is termed a system or a weapons system. The weapons system becomes, perhaps in an unanticipated way, a new and effective technique of domination. It elicits obedience and makes resistance appear senseless. The other development associated with the modernization of weaponry and hardware is the principle of training men who operate weapons systems through simulating the environment with a computer. (p. 134)

As part of a system, the individual soldier has less of a chance to deviate from expected behaviour. Realistic simulations also serve as 'a means of indoctrination' – both because they serve to validate the system itself and because, for a technosoldier launching a missile, simulated conditions and real war conditions are almost identical. Through systems analysis, social psychology, behavioural sociology, personnel management and computer-mediated systems the individual soldier becomes part of a formal weapons system, bureaucratic and technical, that is very difficult to resist. It produces 'a kind of isolation' from the violence of war that allows for its unrestrained prosecution because the bomber pilots and other distant killers are removed from the bloody results of their decisions. And 'the structuring of a situation through the use of technologically developed equipment and realistic team training' produces a 'degree of conformity and effectiveness' that is much more effective than traditional leadership because it 'is very difficult for the individual to sense the degree to which this form of domination can control his behavior' (Radine, p. 142).

Similar formal systems, with their roots in the computer paradigm, are used by the bureaucracy to try to manage war itself. Many of the strange and stupid decisions of the US military in the areas of strategy, tactics and the development of weapons systems can be traced to the limited and self-referential logics of game theory, economic bargaining theory (which assumes the enemy fits your definition of a 'rational' actor), systems analysis, crisis management, mathematical modelling and computer simulations.

Complex calculations have been used to justify everything from thousands of strategic nuclear weapons (Kaplan, 1983) to the way the USA fought the Vietnam War (Gibson, 1986). This process, only rational in the crudest sense, depends more on the psychodynamics that turn fear of war into love of weapons and the angst of nuclear destruction into the creation of more powerful instruments for just that end, than any sensible idea of national security. The drive to manage war seems to be rooted in the repression of uncontrollable human and emotional forces to the greatest extent possible, both among the actual soldiers and the war managers (Gray, 1988b).

CYBORG WORLDS

These hidden emotions return in the form of hubris and hatred. Under President Reagan they took over US foreign policy, as a tight circle of military officers and spies with control of the National Security Council and the ear of the president tried to 'manage' the rollback of the 'Communist menace' around the world (Kennedy, 1988; Zakaria, 1987). Ollie North, the zealous killer who *on his own time* returned to Vietnam and went on dangerous combat missions, is the exception (Ehrenreich, 1987). Most officers who rise to power are cooler technocrats in better control of their impulses, such as the 'intelligence' admirals, Inman, Turner and Poindexter.

Their illusions are the same as North's, by and large: great faith in technology, unreflective belief in the rightness of the American Empire, incredible hubris combined with the fear and anger of those whose profession is poised on the brink of exterminating the human race. But they don't get excited. They send a memo, make a proposal, procure that new weapon or management system that will really get the problem under control. And they don't forget their career.

Thus, most of today's officers are technocrats, not combat leaders. In the Air Force almost 60 percent of the officers have graduate degrees and even the Army boasts that a quarter of its officers have a Master's or a PhD (Satchell, 1988). Roughly half the Navy's officers are line officers who might see combat; the other half are in non-combat specialities. There is no combat speciality while three systems of technomanagerial specialization coexist, each with powerful bureaucratic sponsors. While 200 Navy officers were in senior-service colleges learning 'warrior craft' in 1985, 1,200 were in full-time pursuit of advanced degrees in science, engineering and management. While the Navy has over 200 public affairs officers, fewer than thirty officers teach co-ordinated battle group tactics. Instead of 'the management of violence', there is 'management for its own sake' (Byron, 1985).

Psychological and other studies in World War II showed that less than 25 percent of the men in combat were really shooting at the enemy. Some men didn't want to kill; others were too afraid to try (Keegan, 1976). These studies and later ones also showed that almost every human has a limit. Only 2 percent of all examined soldiers were capable of continued heavy combat of more than a few months. The vast majority of this 2 percent tested out on standard psychological profiles as pure psychopaths with no conscience or emotional involvement in the killing and dying around them. They can act coldly, with calculation and aggression but not blood-lust. Producing more such soldiers seems to be the aim of many current training schemes and significant military drug research (Gabriel, 1987).

To the bureaucrats, one of the biggest management problems is finding, or making, more men like this. To manage war there needs to be a way to facilitate the average soldier performing well under the extraordinary stress

58

of war today. The World War II studies showed that traditional training does not suffice. So, years ago, the Pentagon began its search for ways to improve the integration of human soldiers into the inhuman battlefield, at least until there are more effective killer robots. They will try almost anything.

PSYCHOTECHNOLOGIES: BE ALL THAT YOU CAN BE MADE INTO

Since the Spanish–American War more US soldiers have been lost to psychiatric collapse than are killed in action. Recent wars have seen the rate climb to twice the number killed and almost a third of all casualties. In a conventional war in Europe it is estimated that 50 percent of the casualties will be psychiatric. On a nuclear (or chemical/biological) battlefield they will certainly be even higher (Gabriel, 1987).

To solve this problem, the US Army set up the Human Resources Research Office (HUMRRO), among other think-tanks. HUMRRO coined the term 'psychotechnology'. It has sought to apply its vision of 'human engineering', 'human quality control' and the 'man/weapon system' to US military problems since its founding in 1951. Paul Dickson notes just how important this view has been:

> HUMRRO's influence has been deep and fundamental. It has been the major catalyst in changing traditional training and task assignment procedures from those in effect during World War II to new ones dictated by 'the systems-orientation', or training geared to the system that a man is to be part of, whether it be a 'rifle system', a helicopter or a missile battery. The HUMRRO approach – and subsequently the Army's – is to look at men as integral parts of a weapons system with specific missions. (Dickson, P., 1971, p. 149)

But this systems view is just the beginning. The human must be modified if it is not to be the weakest link in an integrated weapons system. The incredible demands of post-modern war have precipitated a bureaucratic scramble for technological solutions.

Jeffrey Moore, a scientist in the élite advanced weapons group at the Los Alamos National Laboratory, wants to use the biocybernetic brain–computer connection work of the Pilot's Associate and related programmes to allow the foot soldier to control a 200-lb suit of armour called Pitman. It would be capable of stopping a 50-calibre bullet and offer CBN protection. A series of small electric motors would move the massive limbs, and a mind-reading computer would control them. Los Alamos even calls it 'a mind-reading protective suit' (Davies, 1987, p. 78).

Even more extreme is the research by the Delta Force, who coined the

Army's motto, 'Be All You Can Be'. Delta Force got its name from the belief that technology was the difference, or delta, between the USA and USSR. (It is unrelated to the anti-terrorist strike teams of the same name.) A Delta Force spin-off proposed the First Earth Battalion plan in 1981 for the 'warrior-monk' who had mastered extra-sensory perception (ESP), 'leaving his body at will, levitation, psychic healing and walking through walls'.

Lt-Col. Jim Channon, US Army, the originator of the First Earth Battalion, explains that we lost in Vietnam because 'We relied on smart bombs instead of smart soldiers' and 'Stronger than firepower is the force of will, stronger still is spirit, and love is the strongest force of all.' But actually Channon's ideal is more in the line of the cyborg. Believing the future of war belongs to psychoelectronic weapons, he explains why the 'free world' will have an advantage in developing them.

> If you look for clear examples of where the free world has an advantage over the world of nonbelievers, you will discover two resources that clearly stand out in our favor. They are God and microelectronics. The beauty in that is you can use the microelectronics to project the spirit ... brains work like that. Hence the field of psychoelectronic weaponry. (McRae, 1984, p. 124)

A number of Channon's ideas on training are being investigated by the Pentagon, and the First Earth Battalion has over 800 officers and bureaucrats on its mailing list, including eight generals and an Undersecretary for Defense. Not a major research effort, it gets less than $10 million a year (McRae, 1984, p. 6). More important, it symbolizes how desperately the US military is searching for solutions to the paradoxes of post-modern war, and how even the most 'spiritual' formulations can suddenly be twisted around to become part of the general hyper-computerization of the US military.

This technoscience turn is a common one when the military describes its attempts to find strategic advantage in occult practices. Studying Soviet ESP becomes research in 'novel biological information transfer' (the CIA); psychically tracking submarines becomes investigating 'the ability of certain individuals to perceive remote faint electromagnetic stimuli at a noncognitive level of awareness' (US Navy). The Army has even let a number of contracts to buy psychic shields for missile silos to prevent psychics from detonating the warheads before they can be launched. Other studies have explored performing and preventing psychic computer programming. As Ron McRae notes in his book on military psychic research, *Mind Wars*, the military point of view is that 'Psychic control of computers would indeed be analogous to a nuclear monopoly, and this fact has not escaped the attention of the Pentagon' (pp. 5, 54).

Related projects include SRI's numerous studies by researcher W. F. Hegge for 'controlling automatic responses to stress and injury' for the 'non-drug management of wound-related pain' (Mazione, 1986), and the US Army's use, in 1981, of remote-viewing psychics to look for one of its officers, Brigadier General Dozier, kidnapped in Italy by the Red Brigades. Three years later the US military launched Project Jedi (yes, named after the *Star Wars* movie knights) to see if neurolinguistic programming could improve soldier performance (Squires, 1988). All of these programmes involve reconceptualizing New Age and occult knowledges with metaphors of information transfer, networking and programming from computer science. They also share a very low success rate.

In light of the failure of these esoteric methods, and their social context, it is unsurprising that the US military would put more energy into developing more direct and traditional (at least in the United States) ways of controlling stress: drugs.

JUST SAY YES TO DRUGS

There is a long history of using drugs to improve performance in war. Dr Gabriel notes that the Koyak and Wiros tribes of Eurasia used a drug, made from the mushroom *Amanita muscaria*, that was probably quite effective. He also discusses the *hashshashin* ('assassins') who used hashish, the Inca warriors chewing their coca leaf, and the traditional double jigger of rum for British soldiers about to face battle. In the USSR during World War II, 250 officers were shot for cowardice and thousands of lower rank were executed; the Soviets combine strict discipline with issues of vodka and valerian to calm Soviet soldiers and caffeine to wake them (Gabriel, 1987, pp. 136–40).

Official US interest in drugs other than alcohol can be traced to the 1950s. As early as 1954 the Air Force was testing the performance effects of dextroamphetamine, caffeine and depressants on men at Randolph Air Force Base, Texas (Payne and Hauty, 1954). Three years later the amphetamine was tested again (Hauty, *et al.*, 1957).

When it was revealed that the CIA had secretly dosed unsuspecting subjects with LSD and sought ways to psychoprogramme killers – with drugs as well as 'psychology, psychiatry, sociology, and anthropology' – a giant scandal ensued (US Government, 1975, p. 610). An important side-effect of the resulting investigation was the public unveiling of most military human-subjects research up to the mid-seventies. Bearing in mind that each human-subjects study was probably based on many more animal studies, it becomes clear that millions of dollars were spent between 1950 and 1975 on the search for drugs that would lower stress and fear while raising or maintaining performance levels.

For example, between 1956 and 1969 the US Air Force sponsored over $1 million in research by doctors at Duke, Baylor and the University of Minnesota on the effects of stress. This included Dr Burch's work on 'psychophysiological correlates of human information processing' that he claimed had 'direct potential applications to problems of interrogation... and may be employed in programming an on-line automatic analysis of data'. In other words he hoped his work would help develop a machine to interrogate prisoners. The guiding principles of this work were clearly stated by the Duke doctors: '... to develop specific means to alter or modify responses [of humans to stress] in any desired fashion' (US Government, 1975, pp. 1135-8). In 1971 two researchers at the US Army's Aberdeen Research & Development Center and Proving Ground published an annotated bibliography on behaviour modification through drugs for the Human Engineering laboratories, showing the ongoing military interest (Hudgens & Holloway, 1971).

The Congressional investigation of 1975, chaired by Senator Edward Kennedy, revealed that at that time there were at least twenty human-subject studies on controlling stress being conducted by the military. At Walter Reed, an Army hospital, there were experiments on the effects of stress on 'higher-order... human performance', 'psychophysiological changes... of problem solving', and 'military performance'. At the US Army Research Institute of Environmental Medicine they examined 'the effect of emotional stress' and assessed 'visual response times' under stress. 'Metabolic, physiological, and psychological effects of altitude' were measured at the Letterman Army Institute of Research. The US Army Medical R&D Command sponsored in-house research on recovery from fatigue. The Navy in Oakland, California, took a much mellower line and looked into hypnosis for pain relief and relaxation through meditation. Meanwhile their fellows at the Navy Research lab did large studies on 'effects of combined stresses on naval aircrew performance' and the 'psychological effects of tolerance to heat stresses', along with a dozen studies on the effects of cold, water pressure, acceleration, and biorhythms on military performance (US Government, 1975, pp. 620-7, 640).

The biggest programme reported was run by the Edgwood arsenal and involved an attempt to make a self-administered antidote for soldiers exposed to chemical weapons, specifically oximes. The antidote tested was a combination of atropine, the mysterious TMB4 and the anti-phobic drug benactyzine (US Government, 1975, pp. 765-91).

Considering all this reseach it is no surprise that the US military issued illegal drugs during Vietnam to élite units and probably still does. As Elton Mazione, a former LURP (a member of a Long Range Reconnaissance Platoon) reports: 'We had the best amphetamines available and they were supplied by the US government.' He also quotes a Navy commando:

> When I was a SEAL team member in Vietnam, the drugs were routinely consumed. They gave you a sense of bravado as well as keeping you awake. Every sight and sound was heightened. You were wired into it all and at times you felt really invulnerable. (Mazione, 1977, p. 36)

Dr Gabriel argues that major advances in the esoteric disciplines of molecular biology, biocybernetics, neurobiochemistry, psychopharmacology and related fields mean that much more effective drugs can be developed. As noted above, he fears that both the USA and USSR are about to develop such a drug with the effect of not only keeping soldiers from feeling fear but almost anything else as well, making them functional psychopaths (Gabriel, 1987).

The post-modern battlefield also requires humans to fight twenty-four hours a day. So there has been research like Project Endure by HUMRRO and various programmes to develop night goggles and scopes or even to modify the human eye for night vision by using atropine (a belladonna derivative) and benactyzine for dilating pupils. The 1978 experiments by Optical Sciences Group of San Rafael, California (chief investigator A. Jampolsky), brought in $700,000 for one of the experiments (Mazione, 1977).

This programming of soldiers with drugs is analogous to the programming of computers. Imagine your immune system programmed against VD, viruses, bacteria and various toxins; your body with attached bionic parts and eye inserts; your brain hard-wired to a mechanical associate; your mind drugged or psychoprogrammed against stress, fear, altitude, depths, heat, cold and fatigue; yourself continuously connected and monitored by the computer systems that you watch and use, riding in some secure CBN micro-environment protected by autonomous and slaved weapon systems, and controlling vast resources in destructive power and information manipulation. You are a cyborg soldier.

POST-MODERN WARRIORS
Col. Frederick Timmerman Jr, US Army, director of the Center for Army Leadership, and former editor-in-chief of *Military Review*, embraces this creature with pleasure, naming it the future warrior.

> In a physiological sense, when needed, soldiers may actually appear to be three miles tall and twenty miles wide. Of course in a true physical sense nothing will have changed. Rather, by transforming the way technology is applied, by looking at the problem from a biological perspective – focusing on transforming and extending the soldier's physiological capabilities ... (the superman solution)? Robots? Remote television control? Controllable sensor fields? Imbedded computer chips? Bionics?

> Flying suits? In the ideal, we might hope to create future warriors that we could send forward surrounded by protecting robots or remote control aircraft. These would be responsive to the soldier's every biological command. These transformed warriors would not have to be retrofitted or resupplied for months. (Timmerman, 1987, p. 51)

Consider the range of Col. Timmerman's speculations. And they are not just his, but military policy devised by breathing people with healthy budgets. They are embodied in real weapons and real soldiers.

So far his proposals don't seem very coherent. They are a search, a recognition that if war is to remain central to human culture, as it is now, and technological development continues, the soldier will have to change. They will have to 'transform' their bodies and also their role. Col. Timmerman again:

> It sounds radical, but the time when soldiers are merely soldiers may be ending. Because of an enhanced social role, soldiers of the future may have to be social engineers, appreciate the political implications of their every move and be able to transform themselves to perform missions other than those currently classified as purely military...
>
> The key will be to recognize the importance of education... Language skills so long neglected may become a primary means by which the soldier is made militarily effective... detailed training on enemy social weaknesses and strengths may be as common as qualifying with a rifle... Finally, we may actually be able to use enhanced social capabilities to degrade an opponent's social cohesion. (Timmerman, 1987, p. 53)

The good Colonel has slipped through an elision in time. This is what covert soldiers do. They may be called spies, spooks, mercs, operatives, special forces, commandos, Delta Force, Spetsnik. They operate from Central America to Central Africa to Central Asia. Today. And hasn't Nato's arms race ('enhanced social capabilities') had some effects on the Warsaw Pact's 'social cohesion'? 'Language skills' are to be a primary weapon.

In many strange ways, then, certain themes – information, high technology, computerization and speed – remain consistent. When they collide with traditional military culture – as institutionalized in the armies, navies, and air forces of the most powerful human empire ever – they produce the many cyborg images and realities of the US military today. But they represent just some of the potential developments of the post-modern soldier. Even as they come to pass, they are inevitably confounded and contrasted with other facets of the warrior icon. This is because the same conditions (especially the advances of technoscience) that have forced the US military to reconceptualize itself have led others, soldier and civilian, to appropriate the warrior mythos within an argument that war itself must end.

For some military writers and soldiers, this very refusal might be the next step in the evolution of warriors (Gray, 1959; Keegan, 1976). It is not a new idea. Through the ages some soldiers have become non-violent; and some non-violent activists, such as Gandhi, have called for pacifist warriors. But the idea has certainly been gaining strength in the last few decades. It started in the USA with Vietnam. Widespread draft resistance, desertion and mutinies in the field (and even at air bases in Guam) shook the US military. Only American English has a special word, 'fragging' (from fragmentation grenades), for soldiers killing their own officers. Once back in 'the World', veterans formed a number of anti-war groups, most notably Vietnam Veterans Against the War. Today such activism continues within the mainstream veterans' organizations and in special veterans' groups such as the Veteran Action Teams that have gone to Central America and the Veteran's Peace Convoy that recently managed to take humanitarian aid to Nicaragua despite US government obstructions.

Even groups of Nato and Warsaw Pact generals have met and drafted statements saying that soldiers now must prevent war and that the first principle of military virtue is 'to serve peace'. They claim high technology has made war impossible (Generals, 1984, p. 23). Admiral Rickover, the 'father' of the US nuclear Navy, served until he was over eighty years old; soon after retirement he denounced his own career. As with the vast majority of the military repentants, he waited until his career was finished to renounce war and its preparations.

Such dissent is only a part of post-modern military culture. The dominant discourse remains controlled by the generals and admirals still in uniform and by colonels such as North and Timmerman. They will find wars or make them. They will also rearticulate the military's role so as to recoup the fear of total war into more military power. The slogan of the Strategic Air Command (Minuteman and MX missiles, B-52 and B-1 bombers) is 'Peace is Our Profession'. The justification of Star Wars is framed in the same way. The success, and ambiguity, of such conceptions can be seen in the recent awarding of the Nobel Peace Prize to the United Nations military forces.

Just as interesting are the inversions of the warrior ethos and its seizure by non-violent activists. As mentioned above, some soldiers and many veterans have made this turn, which can lead to bitter irony. Brian Wilson, who served as an Air Force intelligence officer in 'the Nam', recently lost his legs trying to block a weapons shipment at the Concord Naval Air Station in California. Being a peace activist in 'peacetime' has proved much more dangerous to Brian Wilson than serving as a soldier in a war.

This points to a seldom-noticed paradox. Many 'peace' activists around the world, even in the Western countries, have had friends murdered by the

State, seen people killed, been chased by cars, trucks, police; they've been captured, beaten and tortured, locked up. These activists have seen more violence than most military people. Their emotional experience can be quite similar to that of men and women who have been in combat. Only their refusal of killing makes them not warriors.

So, unsurprisingly, in the peace movement proper there are also strong currents by those trying to remake the warrior metaphor and claim it for themselves. Native Americans and their supporters have often called themselves rainbow warriors – a title also taken up by Greenpeace eco-activists. Within grass-roots anti-war and peace groups, there have been proposals for activists to make a commitment of several years to a peace army (from the First Strike Project)[5] or to work for peace (Beyond War). Established pacifists have an international peace-brigade programme that inserts peace 'soldiers' into war zones as varied as Guatemala and Sri Lanka, as the religious Witness for Peace and the Veterans Action Teams are doing in Nicaragua.

While most peaceniks still manifest an open aversion to militarism and military metaphors, the influence of the warrior image is quite powerful, infecting draft resisters, veterans, feminists, Christians and non-Christian alike. Even some neo-pagan peace activists are putting forward 'The Path of the Pagan Warrior as Revolutionary Activism today ... [in] ... Defence of Mother Earth & the Web of Life'. The pagan revival highlights an intriguing aspect: these peaceful warriors are quite often women. Of course, in the official US military 10 percent of the soldiers are women, although strict divisions are made between 'warrior specialties' and 'technical' ones; the officer/managers are mostly male.

War is still gendered, if slightly more subtly. The symbiotic relationship between war and patriarchy is now a triangle, with technoscience as the anchoring side. The manager and the scientist occupy all three sides now. Post-modern warriors future and present exist in relationship to this structure, supporting it or subverting it.

At the intersections between warrior images and iron triangles come variations of the military identities, especially cyborgs. For some, cyborgs aren't a horror to recoil from, but an opportunity to break old relationships of domination. The feminist philosopher Donna Haraway has said it best. For her the cyborg means

... embracing the skillful task of reconstructing the boundaries of daily life, in partial connection with others, in communication with all of our parts. It is not just that science and technology are possible means of great human satisfaction, as well as a matrix of complex dominations. Cyborg imagery can suggest a way out of the maze of dualisms in which we have explained our bodies and our tools to ourselves. This is a dream not of a common language, but of a powerful infidel heteroglossia. (Haraway, 1985, p. 100)

Dream and nightmare, warriors and cyborgs and warrior-cyborgs are with us and of us. What do they have in common? Opportunity. If postmodernism means anything in relation to war, it is the necessity of change. Modern war was certainly never stable as an institution, but before it became suicidal it at least made limited sense. Now, perhaps, it can be ended or changed enough so that we can survive. Is appropriation the best strategy for dealing with warriors or cyborgization or both? Perhaps, though, it is certainly not a total answer. But it seems to me an acceptable part of any possible change.

In Europe and North America we are cyborgs in many ways already: medical implants in our bodies, mechanical connections close at hand, products from around the world in every corner of our lives. Look at the people on the street, anyone. Take that one with his walkman in his ear, gold in his teeth, anti-polio programming in his immune system, chains on his shoulders, and his Spanish black boots on a skateboard. Such intimacy with technology is relatively recent.

Not so the warrior ethos. It is so old that I don't see how it can just be purged from public discourse or the cultural unconsciousness. If sacrifice can be separated from savagery and some of its energy can be turned to peace-making, then I can live with the idea of non-violent warriors. But it is not how I choose to portray myself. There is a little too much courting of conflict and domination in the idea of the warrior for my comfort.

Appropriation of either of these ideas will only work, anyway, in concert with the social mobilization of various subjugated knowledges that include a rejection of violence and dehumanization. And this must take place in a social situation where total critiques of militarism, mechanism and warriorism are made forcefully by many people. There is a need for many different voices, of that I am sure.

My role here is just to sketch out some of what is happening now. What it means to the future-present is in part already determined, fixed in artefacts and inscribed on our bodies. But there is that other part that has yet to be formed. Empires fall. Icons are shattered and reformed. Definitions change. New metaphors are forged. The rules of the dominant discourse are always shifting and sometimes they are even up for grabs. The French philosopher Michel Foucault pointed out how important this can be.

The successes of history belong to those who are capable of seizing these rules, to replace those who had used them, to disguise themselves so as to pervert them, invert their meanings, and redirect them against those who had initially imposed them; controlling this complex mechanism, they will make it function so as to overcome the rulers through their own rules. (1971, p. 86)

Foucault claims we can always have a say, even if it is disguised, perverted or inverted at times. And to such deceptions go 'the successes of history'. But some things are better not said at all. Still, I see no danger in rejecting the role of victim (of science, of the warrior ethos) to embrace instead whatever moral possibilities there are to be active shapers of these cultural constructions. Most of these, I believe, involve confronting the discourses that bind us directly where they contradict themselves and reveal their true values, not twisting them. But subversion is needed with conversion and revision and every other possible lever of redefinition.

The crisis of post-modern war – it is impossible yet it continues all the same – appears so deep to me that only the most extreme changes will prevent human self-destruction. The war system will eventually create the final war if it is not dismantled, even if it is only a computer error, after all. It will not surrender but it may well self-destruct. Not alone. In light of possible apocalypse inverting the warrior ethos to aid in wars, deconstruction seems quite acceptable. This is not the case with real military options. Maybe we don't have to do away totally with warriors – and how can we resist being cyborgs? Yet cyborg-soldiers, autonomous weapons, war managers and technobureaucrats will have to go if we are to survive. And war itself.

These are times of great change so there are possibilities. They just aren't all that good. They are just not simple.

NOTES

1 Fredric Jameson originally coined the term, calling Vietnam 'the first postmodern war' (Jameson, 1984, p. 84). Most military writers have recognized that modern war, as exemplified by World Wars I and II, is no more. For now I advocate calling its successor post-modern war (or even pomo war). It is open to definition because 'post-modern' doesn't mean much specifically yet; it comes after something labelled the 'modern', with vague intimations of fragmentation, bricolage (elements of the modern distilled, rearranged and juxtaposed with their opposites), and crisis thrown in. Science is a central question but there is no easy (no single?) answer. My understanding of post-modernism has been most influenced by David Dickson (1984), Lyotard (1985) and Harding (1986).

2 *Combat* and *12 O'Clock High* were TV shows in the 1960s about WW II. *The Green Berets* was a best-selling Robin Moore novel, a hit record and a John Wayne movie. *Deerhunter*, *Platoon*, *Apocalypse Now*, *Coming Home* and *Fields of Stone* are movies about Vietnam. *Tour of Duty* is a 1989 TV series about a platoon in Vietnam during 1986–9. *M*A*S*H* was a successful book, movie, and TV comedy about a Mobile Army Service Hospital (MASH) during the

Korean War. *Good Morning, Vietnam!* is a recent movie about a wild disc jockey in Vietnam. *China Beach* is a current dramatic series centred around a nurse at a hospital in Vietnam, also 1968-9. On World War I poets see Fussell's remarkable work *The Great War and Modern Memory* (1977). The definitive World War II novel is perhaps Joseph Heller's *Catch-22* but Norman Mailer's *The Naked and the Dead* and Kurt Vonnegut's *Slaughterhouse Five* are equally extraordinary in their own ways.

3 Information from the National Coalition on Television Violence and watching TV with my three-year-old son.

4 Rear Admiral Wayne E. Meyer, USN ret., Aegis project manager from 1970 to 1983, even goes so far as to claim that the USS *Vincennes* was given the right to open fire when it did only because it had an Aegis expert system (Meyer, 1988, p. 102). Not that this makes the Iranian and other civilians of flight 655 any less dead.

5 The peace army has since been endorsed by the national Mobilization for Survival and numerous other activists in the USA. A nation-wide meeting is being planned for 1989 (*Test Banner*, 1988, p. 7).

REFERENCES

Baudrillard, Jean, and Lotringer, Sylvere (1987), *Forget Foucault & Forget Baudrillard.* New York:. Semiotext(e).

Byron, Commander John (1985) 'Warriors', *U.S. Naval Proceedings* June: 63-8.

Commandant, US Army Quartermaster School (n.d.) 'Robotics/artificial intelligence fact sheet' (mimeo hand-out).

Cooper, Earl, and Shaker, Steven (1988) 'The military forecasters', *The Futurist* May-June: 37-43.

Counterspy Staff (1974) 'Thought control, *Counterspy* 1, fall:5.

Cross, Stephen *et al.* (1986) 'Knowledge-based pilot aids: a case study in mission planning', in Thomas and Wyner, eds *Artificial Intelligence and Man-Machine Systems.* Springer-Verlag: 141-74.

Dasey, Charles (1984) 'Biotechnology and its applications to military medical R&D', *Army Research, Development & Acquisition Magazine* July-August: 12-13.

Davies, Owen (1987) 'Robotic warriors clash in cyberwars', *Omni* January: 76-88.

Dickson, David (1974) 'Technology and the construction of social reality', *Radical Science Journal* 1:29-50; reprinted in L. Levidow, ed. *Radical Science Essays.* London: Free Association, 1986, pp. 15-37.

———— (1984) 'Radical science and the modernist dilemma', in Radical Science Collective, eds *Issues in Radical Science.* London: Free Association.

Dickson, Paul (1971) *Think Tanks.* New York: Atheneum.

Ehrenreich, Barbara (1987) 'Iranscam: the real meaning of Oliver North – can a member of the warrior caste survive in the horror of peace?', *Ms* May.

Faludi, Susan (1986) 'Billion dollar toy box', *San Jose Mercury News, West Magazine*, 23 November: 14-25.

Foucault, Michel (1971) 'Nietzsche, genealogy, history', in *Hommage à Jean Hyppolite.* Paris: Presses Universitaires de France.

Fussell, Paul (1977) *The Great War and Modern Memory.* Oxford: Oxford University Press.

Gabriel, Richard (1987) *No More Heroes: Madness and Psychiatry in War.* New York: Hill & Wang.

Generals (1984) *Generals for Peace and Disarmament*. New York: Universe.

Gibson, J. (1986) *The Perfect War - The Technowar in Vietnam*. New York: Atlantic Monthly Press.

Goben, Ron (1987) 'Human nerve repair may be possible'. *Stanford Observer* spring.

Gray, Chris Hables (1988a) 'The Strategic Computing Program at four years', *AI and Society* 2: 141-9.

_____ (1988b) 'Artificial intelligence and real war: the shaping of postmodern conflict in the United States military today', unpublished qualifying essay, History of Consciousness Board of Studies, University of California at Santa Cruz.

Gray, J. Glenn (1959) *The Warriors: Reflections on Men in Battle*. New York: Harper & Row.

Grier, Peter (1986) 'Aegis to put swagger in the Navy's step', *Christian Science Monitor* 21 August:3.

Haraway, Donna (1985) 'A manifesto for cyborgs: science, technology, and socialist feminism for the 1980s' *Socialist Review* 80:65-107.

Harding, Sandra (1986) *The Science Question in Feminism*. Ithaca, NY: Cornell University Press.

Hauty, G. *et al.* (1957) 'Effects of normal air and dextro-amphetamine upon work decrement induced by oxygen impoverishment and fatigue', *Journal of Pharmacology* 119:385-9.

Hudgens, G. and Holloway, W. (1971) *Behaviour Modification and Changes in Central Nervous System Biochemistry: An Annotated Bibliography*. Washington, D.C.: Human Engineering Laboratories/Department of Defense.

Hunt, James, and Blair, John, eds (1985) *Leadership on the Future Battlefield*. Texas: Pergamon-Brassey's.

Jameson, Fredric (1984) 'Postmodernism, or the cultural logic of late capitalism', *New Left Review* 146:53-92.

Kaldor, Mary (1987) 'The imaginary war', in D. Smith and E. P. Thompson, eds *Prospectus for a Habitable Planet*. London: Penguin.

Kaplan, F. (1983) *The Wizards of Armageddon*. New York: Touchstone.

Keegan, John (1976) *The Face of Battle*. London: Penguin.

Kennedy, William (1988) 'Why America's national-security planning process went awry: military mentality took control', *Christian Science Monitor* 12 January: 8.

Lyotard, Jean-François (1985) *The Postmodern Condition*. Minneapolis, MN: University of Minnesota Press.

McRae, Ron (1984) *Mind Wars: The True Story of Secret Government Research into the Military Potential of Psychic Weapons*. New York: St Martin's.

Mazione, Elton (1977) 'The search for the bionic commando', *National Reporter* 10:36-8.

Meyer, Rear-Admiral Wayne (1988) 'Interview', *U.S. Naval Proceedings* October: 102-6.

Miller, Marc (1988) 'New toys for robocop soldiers', *Progressive* July: 18-21.

Mumford, L. (1967) *The Myth of the Machine: I. Technics and Human Development*. New York: Harcourt Brace Jovanovich.

Payne, R. and Hauty, G. (1954) 'The effects of experimentally induced attitudes on task efficiency', *Journal of Experimental Psychology* 47:267-73.

Peters, Capt. Ralph (1987) 'The army of the future', *Military Review* September: 36-45.

Radine, Lawrence (1977) *The Taming of the Troops: Social Control in the United States Army*. Westport CN: Greenwood Press.

Sarkesian, Sam, ed. (1980) *Combat Effectiveness: Cohesion, Stress, and the Volunteer Military*. London: Sage.

Satchell, Michael (1988) 'The new U.S. military: pride, brains and brawn', *San Francisco Chronicle* 20 April, Briefing, p. 2.

Scientific American Staff (1987) 'Networking', *Scientific American* January: 67.

Skantze, General Lawrence (1987) 'AF science and technology - the legacy of forecast II',

Briefing at AIAA 'Aerospace' 87', Crystal City, VA. 29 April.

Squires, Sally (1988) 'The new army has gone New-Age', *San Francisco Examiner-Chronicle* 1 May. *Punch*. 3.

Stein, K. (1985) 'DARPA, stressing development of pilot's associate system', *Aviation Weekly & Space Technology* 22 April: 69–74.

Theweleit, Klaus (1987) *Male Fantasies* Vol. 1: *Women, Floods, Bodies, History*. Minneapolis, MN: University of Minnesota. Foreword by Barbara Ehrenreich.

Timmerman Jr, Col. Frederick (1987) 'Future warriors', *Military Review* September.

United States Government (1975) *Biomedical and Behavioral Research*. Joint Congressional Hearings, Ninety-fourth Congress, First Session, 10 September to 7 November. US Printing Office.

_____ (1983) *Strategic Computing – New-Generation Computing Technology: A Strategic Plan for Its Development and Application to Critical Problems in Defense*. DARPA.

_____ (1984) 'HEL Builds "Generic" Command Post Vehicle', *Army Research, Development & Acquisition Magazine* September–October: 15.

_____ (1986) 'Forecast II Executive Summary' and project list. USAF.

_____ (1987a) *AirLand Battle 2000*. August. US Army.

_____ (1987b) *Strategic Computing: Third Annual Report*. DARPA.

Weiner, Tom (1987) 'Black budget' (series), *San Jose Mercury News*, 13–16 February.

Wilford, John (1986) 'It's all in his head', *San Francisco Chronicle-Examiner* 13 July, *Punch* insert.

Zakaria, Fareed (1987) 'The colonels' coup', *This World* 2 August: 19.

GROUPS

'The Path of the Pagan Warrior as Revolutionary Activism today' and 'Defense of Mother Earth & the Web of Life' (1988) *Pagan Warriors* c/o *Pagansword*, St 432 (Dept R), 263A West 19th St, New York, NY 10011, USA.

'Why we need a nonviolent Peace Army and how it can happen' (1988) from the *First Strike Prevention Project*, PO Box 7061, Santa Cruz, CA 95061, USA.

'Warning: war cartoons increase childhood violence and behavioral problems' (1988) from the *National Coalition on Television Violence*. Monitoring & Newsletter Office, PO Box 2157, Champaign, IL 60182, USA.

Peace Brigades International, Life Center Association Inc., 4722 Baltimore Avenue, Philadelphia, PA 19143, USA.

'Peace Army Organizing' (1988) in the *Test Banner*, 7 November; paper of the *American Peace Test*, PO Box 26725, Las Vagas, Nevada 989126, USA.

3 THE CLOISTERED WORK-PLACE
Military electronics workers obey and ignore

DENNIS HAYES

The 4th of July air show at Moffet Field in Santa Clara County, California, provides a festive interlude during which Silicon Valley shows off its least understood and most silently birthed offspring: high technology, military issue. The jet fighters, assault helicopters, and spy planes attract half a million spectators – the largest public gathering of the year. Laden with computers and microchips, the military aircraft return to the Valley like prodigal sons. Estimates of the livelihoods that depend on military spending in the Valley run as high as 50 percent. The Valley's largest employers are prime military contractors. It is the hub for the $55–$60 billion military electronics industry, a development site for most missiles, a funnel for military artificial intelligence R&D, a design centre for Star Wars programmes and for the avionics aboard most combat aircraft and bombs.

Concerning its military preponderance, Silicon Valley is not so much boastful as resigned: without the military, the US electronics industry might never have been. In fact, there are signs of a timid but widespread resentment towards the military subsidy, which favours large corporations over the fabled entrepreneur, and which has made Silicon Valley an incubator of unwholesome technology.

Many people say they would rather not work for prime military contractors. Some refuse to. Stanford University students attend occasional protests at the Lockheed Space and Missile Company. A distinct minority, inactive politically in any conventional sense, display bumper stickers that proclaim 'A World beyond War' – the therapeutic message of a Palo Alto-based national organization that advocates peaceful thinking as the path to world peace.

The noisy 4th of July air show, which ties up traffic and closes down commuting channels, provides a rare focus for these resentments. The rest of the year the military presence is camouflaged. Unseen, like the $3 million underground bunker that is equipped with computers and two weeks of provisions for seventy Santa Clara officials who hope 'to keep the city running' after a nuclear holocaust. Or disguised, like the Lockheed engineers who periodically visit Valley grade schools to treat children to 'Mr Wizard' science shows – but who spend most of their time designing satellites and missiles for use in a nuclear holocaust.

The most enigmatic camouflage is that which keeps knowledge of military products from the producers themselves. It is woven from a decades-old tradition of work-place secrecy. At primary contractors, explicit policies forbid workers from knowing a product's final use. Instead, they are offered project nicknames, a technical language and a narrow way of looking at work; these obscure military purpose and, in the process, probably undermine product quality. Less formal but comparable policies produce similar results at military subcontractors. As a result, a special ignorance structures life in the classified cubicles and shops of military electronics. Those who prepare the battlefields of the future need not dwell on the horrors of war to perform their work. The air show's family entertainment format caters to this sensibility: there are airstrikes without casualties, exploding napalm bombs without burning flesh.

For those prone to troubled consciences, the secrecy is both functional and lonely. The prohibition of product application knowledge creates a 'black box' productive culture in which work's purpose is ignored or forgotten. When programmers write 'graphics display software' rather than missile performance reports, when rocket engineers hold back from discussing their work with friends, they shield themselves from responsibility for the horror their work makes possible. When fellow workers carry on like this, it imbues the work-place with odd loneliness. That which they share in common – work – creates that which they must avoid talking about – work's products.

The loneliness of military electronics workers often extends beyond their work-places. During an interview, I asked a Lockheed Space and Missile Company project co-ordinator what he worked on. He replied that he could not be specific. He paused and then said 'everybody knows that Lockheed make missiles and spacecraft. It says that on the door. And I am not working on missiles.' He then spoke of his wife, who also worked at Lockheed.

Because each had a separate security clearance, however, they could not, and did not, talk to each other about their work. Sometime after the interview, husband and wife separated.

The military electronics worker's silence and isolation are redolent of the medieval monastery, its monks busy transcribing those works of antiquity deemed worthy by the papal censors. By accepting that certain questions are forbidden, even certain phrases unutterable, military electronics workers take vows of ignorance as well as of obedience. In exchange, they can imagine they have relinquished responsibility for their work to a higher authority. In the military electronics cloister, these imaginings are undeterred, and the silence is welcome.

THE FORBIDDEN FRUIT

Behind a formica reception desk at a large microchip firm, a display case lists the day's special visitors:

WELCOME!

Litton Guidance
Hughes Aircraft
Lockheed
Raytheon

Inside, 'application engineers' help these and other customers design logic for military and business microchips. In its start-up days, the firm did little military work. But a slumping civilian market led first to military sub-contracting – designing chips for primary defence contractors – and then to classified work for the National Security Agency. One of the unclassified application engineers is Jeff, a Stanford electronic engineering graduate several months into his first electronics job.

The title 'application engineer' is peculiar. For 'security reasons', Jeff says, none can know their military customers' chip applications. This stricture does not impede their work. To design microchip logic for a Raytheon or Litton chip, Jeff need not know that it will store microcode for an on-board missile guidance system that may one day claim thousands of lives. 'I don't know what it's used for, what system it's part of – usually only the company's name,' Jeff says. Yet he is vaguely aware that Litton Guidance, Hughes Aircraft, Lockheed, and Raytheon are major military contractors. He also has informal access to project-specific information at his work-place. Away from work, over pizza and beer, Jeff acknowledges that his company currently has six Lockheed contracts. From gossip among fellow engineers he has gleaned that some of the chips are destined for a radiation-detecting satellite device. I suggest that it may be connected to the Milstar project – Star Wars. 'It's just a part to me,' says Jeff.

For Jeff, the moral or political implications of his work, its probable contribution to space-based missiles, the question of whether it increases the likelihood of war are *separate issues* from the tasks he performs every day. This separation between work and work's product does not create tension for Jeff – nor is his aloofness exceptional. On such issues Jeff stands with most of the other application engineers, steeped in a culture of collective avoidance that is officially encouraged by their employers and Pentagon sponsors.

Fred once worked as an auditor for an oil company but now works for Lockheed as a software programmer with a secret clearance. The security 'doesn't bother' him: 'Maybe I've just gotten used to it.' Fred has grown accustomed to other things at Lockheed:

> I'm not thrilled with the application. What I do nicely separates itself from the application though, because what our graphics system produces is nothing different from what you might see in a magazine if they were plotting the gross national product year to year. So where my thinking goes every day, it's got nothing to do with those big nasty missiles.

Fred writes system-level code for a graphics package that displays data in a time/history plot. The software is not classified, but the data it handles will be. The data comes from Trident missiles whose warheads are loaded with transducers and sensors that transmit in-flight performance records to Fred's software package. Aided by a work setting that divides programming assignments among fellow workers, his distance from the application is nearly infinite:

> It's very easy not to think about it [that is, the missiles] – the finished product for me is when they can take data and put it on the screen. I get to see all of that. I don't see where that data came from [that is, the missiles] ... my product is a very small piece of a large thing which includes submarines and all kinds of things [for example, missiles]. But the thing that I directly work on, I feel like I see the whole thing. That may be kind of unusual.

At Qubix, a start-up company, laughter and enthusiastic chatter punctuate a programmers' meeting. Before a white board bearing cryptic symbols, a presentation of Qubix software unfolds. The talk is sophisticated, specific, but makes no mention of Qubix's first customer – or the customer's use for Qubix work-stations.

When queried later on these topics, most Qubix workers acknowledge that the customer is General Dynamics. Asked if General Dynamics makes assault jets, airborne missile-and-gun systems, and cruise missiles, many plead ignorance. Their ignorance is hard to credit. At the time, front-page articles are breaking the story of General Dynamics' Pentagon scandal. Many of the articles describe General Dynamics' long line of military products. Uninformed or not, Qubix people are bothered by my entreaties. Their responses suggest that military products are unpopular topics of conversation.

The ethics of making war materiel constitute an unspoken dialogue among electronics workers. A widespread and informal self-censorship complements official boundaries on what workers can know, and this tends to pre-empt conversations. Of 'big nasty missiles,' Fred says he and his (approximately seventy) fellow employees 'don't talk much about that kind of thing. I think the people around me tend to feel the same way. Like I say, I stay away from politics.' The social silence sustains a contrived, if awkward, innocence. For example, Fred let on that he knew surprisingly little about Lockheed's operations. He wasn't sure what went on inside the Blue Cube (the US military satellite command centre adjacent to Lockheed Sunnyvale), or that Lockheed workers staffed the Blue Cube, only that 'I presumed, just the way people talked, that more highly classified work went on there.'

THE MANHATTANIZATION OF
MILITARY ELECTRONICS

The censorship, formal and informal, that pervades the contractor's workplace is a legacy of the military's tutelage of micro-electronics. The rationale is that the less workers know, the less capable they are of sharing secrets with hostile agents. The centrepiece of this world-view is the 'need-to-know' policy adopted by virtually all primary military contractors performing classified work since World War II.

The need-to-know policy is adapted from the hallowed tradition of the military mission. In the military, the concern is not so much that access to privileged information may result in loss of life, but that it may compromise the mission. (This is the spirit of the wartime slogan, 'loose lips sink ships', which reminded sailors and civilians to avoid discussing fleet destinations and embarkation dates that might reach enemy ears.) This policy implies that those who actually carry out the mission, that is, the subordinates whose lives are at stake, are kept in the dark by their superiors until the last possible moment.

The arms industry's need-to-know policies are thus an intrusion of military convention in the work-place, a tradition already apparent in the 'chain of command' and 'line' or 'staff' models for dividing work-place authority. We are reminded of this lineage by the policy's work-place début in 1942 during work on the Manhattan Project – the code name for the United States government's atomic bomb development. Then, as now, the need-to-know policy created an atmosphere approaching that of the Inquisition. The best possible work-place was one purged of all but the minimum amount of technical detail required to complete a project. Project managers denied workers knowledge of product research and fabrication processes that did not directly bear on their work tasks. Project information – especially regarding the project's destination and use – was strictly and hierarchically controlled. Of the 150,000 persons who worked on the Manhattan Project, perhaps a dozen were allowed a 'comprehensive overview of the project's plans and objectives' (Davis, 1984).

Four and a half decades later, a comparable minority of the workers who receive clearances are trusted with 'comprehensive knowledge'. For the rest, classified status does not, as popularly imagined, confer access to privileged knowledge. Instead, it means working more or less blindly.

If the public rationale for the need-to-know policy is minimizing espionage, its practical effect on employees' daily lives is to stifle awareness and discourage discussion of the hostile technology they create. This custom dates from the policy's first civilian application. Manhattan Project electrical engineer Robert Odell recalls working on the top secret project in Oak Ridge, Tennessee, that developed the radioactive material used in the first atomic bombs dropped on Hiroshima and Nagasaki:

> I was among those who thought we were developing a new kind of fuel. Others thought it must be an explosive. *You didn't ask questions* – We were having a meeting in July of 1945 and one of the supervisors got a phone call in an adjoining room. It was from New Mexico. He came back with a big smile on his face and said, 'It went off with a big bang.' That was the first time it really hit me. (Odell, 1985, emphasis added)

Today, the Pentagon continues to insulate the classified work-place with the need-to-know policy. In its *Industrial Security Manual for Safeguarding Classified Information*, the government sheds this definition of a worker's need to know:

> ... a determination made by the possessor of classified information that a prospective recipient, in the interest of national security, has a requirement for access to, knowledge of, or possession of the classified information in order to perform tasks or services essential to the fulfillment of a classified contract or program ... (US Government, n.d.)

The policy is variously implemented. At most primary contractors, including Lockheed (Silicon Valley's largest), the security classifications, in descending order of privilege, are 'top secret', 'secret' and 'confidential'. Workers who share a clearance status, for example 'top secret', are also often segregated by project-specific clearances. That means they cannot exchange work-related information or enter each other's project area unescorted. Improprieties are 'security breaches' whose implications may transcend the wrath of management, perhaps tripping the alarm of 'national security'.

What determines the level of clearance? Apparently, the Department of Defense (DOD) deems this question too sensitive to answer unequivocally lest the clearance title reveal the nature of a classified project. According to the *Safeguarding* manual, 'top secret' refers to information or material 'the unauthorized disclosure of which reasonably could be expected to cause *exceptionally grave damage* to the national security'. The disclosure of 'secret' material could be expected to cause '*serious damage*', while leaks of 'confidential' information could be expected to cause mere '*damage*'. Elaboration, as provided in the DOD *Manual*, is vague.

Working to classified military specifications means that workers always have a ready excuse not to discuss the content of their work with their families or friends, or even among themselves. The atmosphere also discourages discussion of the military contractor's product line. For example, classified Lockheed machinists, plumbers, carpenters, and composite workers cannot openly acknowledge, even if they suspect, that they build missile parts. Companies instruct employees that shop talk off the shop floor is forbidden, or worse – grounds for clearance revocation, which may mean job loss (if the firm cannot or will not find unclassified work for the offender). A worker whose record bears the demerit of a clearance revocation is an unlikely job candidate for civilian or military work, since the demerit creates a subversive aura that most employers find troubling.

Of course, there is scarcely a work-place in which work-related gripes and gossip can be stifled. This the classified work-place does not attempt. 'You can let off steam,' the Lockheed project co-ordinator observes – as long as the steam has been purged of overt references to the work's military nature. But the military gag rule constricts the boundaries of acceptable, spontaneous discussion among most workers, increasingly as the level of clearance moves from 'confidential' to 'top secret'. Among Lockheed programmers, the social implications of making missiles, not to mention the alternatives to doing so, are topics that fall outside the boundaries. 'Like I say,' Fred reminds us, 'I stay away from politics.'

THE FOREST FROM THE TREES

How it is possible for workers to create classified products without knowing what their products actually do?

One answer, suggested by the Pentagon's perennial acquisition of badly designed and malfunctioning equipment, is that workers cannot produce blindly without compromising quality. To the extent that classified production can proceed, it does so through a highly evolved division of labour that transcends, and is often at odds with, capitalist efficiency.

Since Charles Dickens and Friedrich Engels, the division of labour has been consistently reprimanded. These authors, and many since, decried the stunting of mind, body and soul on the assembly lines of capitalism, and later, of socialism. The critiques varied, but not in their essentials: workers feel alienated from their subdivided and boring work tasks and disconnected from products they do not freely choose to create or cannot control. This was the inevitable consequence of organizing the labour process to maximize production.

To meet project deadlines and to reduce notorious cost overruns, military contractors also attempt to 'rationalize' their work-places to maximize efficiency – and profits. But national security introduces a competing principle around which to organize the labour process: secrecy. In practice, the need-to-know policy conspires with the division of labour to perform a special role: *obscuring a worker's contribution to hostile technology*. This highlights a modern category of alienation, the separation of work from its final purpose.

The politically motivated need-to-know policy could not be implemented without a division of labour. As in civilian electronics, numerous job tasks separate military products from the raw materials and concepts they incorporate. Most of the workers performing the in-between tasks needn't know each product's intended use, only its translation into technical specifications. For example, the narrow focus of Jeff's workday is on microchip circuitry – clusters of 'on' and 'off' switches, several of which would fit across the width of a sheet of paper – and whether they perform to military specifications simulated in his company's design software. This makes possible Jeff's ignorance of the classified projects he contributes to. It follows that the Pentagon has a political stake in encouraging product ignorance – a stake it is not wasting any time claiming.

For decades, the Pentagon has issued specifications by which contractors classify, test and deliver work. Now, it is coming much closer to dictating the way in which work itself is organized. The DOD is positioning itself to demand from computer system and software vendors a work environment that is likely to deepen the gulf between job task and product use. The vehicle is Ada, the Pentagon's official computer language, and, upon examination, a Trojan horse bearing a management policy.

As of summer 1984, all new weapons and other 'mission critical' systems for the Pentagon must be written in the Ada programming language. As of January 1986, all systems built for Nato bear a similar requirement. These decisions affect an estimated 400,000 computer workers in the Pentagon's direct employ, and countless others in military contracting shops – eventually, anyone who sells software to the DOD and Nato. The goal, of course, is to reduce the large number of computer languages that currently run on the Pentagon's computers and those of its allies.

The message conveyed by the DOD and a growing number of boosters is that Ada is not just another programming language. 'Ada was developed to not only allow, but to encourage the use of sound engineering discipline,' observe two Ada consultants. There may not be much room for choice in this matter. Pentagon-approved Ada compilers (the devices that interpret and translate software instructions into a series of actions that computers perform) accept only those programs that can pass a battery of tests for 'configuration management', 'modularity', and much more. These tests 'will force people to use structured techniques', according to a spokesperson whose company makes Ada compilers. Army Colonel Dick Stanley of the DOD's Ada Joint Program Office asserts that 'it's virtually impossible' to write unstructured Ada programs.

Structured techniques imply breaking up the job of writing a software program into modules, groups of relatively simple, isolated, step-by-step job tasks. Managers and project leaders then assign modules to project team members, who work on them more or less simultaneously. Some programmers like this because it allows them to write ever more sophisticated and complex programs. Under various names, structured programming techniques have been adopted by civilian firms primarily as an attempt to introduce capitalist efficiency into the complex process of software engineering. But the principles of 'scientific management' are not easily adapted to the management of scientists. Software engineering is an inherently creative process, resistant to the subdivision and routinization implied by such techniques. With bootcamp finesse, the Ada environment, according to an advocate, attempts to 'enforce' structured techniques by changing the 'programming environment'.

Whether and how structured techniques improve software productivity is hotly debated. It's unlikely the Pentagon has overlooked the bonus such work methods will yield in the realm of security, however. By dividing and simplifying work, structured techniques may make complex programs easier to write and maintain, but they also tend to erect additional barriers between the programmer and his work's uncomfortable objective. This is so simply because structured programming does not compel programmers to acknowledge the program's purpose while they create it. Since programmers require less information about the application as a whole than about the internal requirements of the program's modules and submodules, managers can also use structured techniques to formalize a division of labour that is more conducive to the need-to-know policy. The sinister implication is that workers can – unwittingly – create and refine weapons of deadly sophistication.

The imperative to divide and subdivide military labour has remarkably obscured the connections between firms as well as within them. One hundred and fifty thousand subcontractors supply the Pentagon's approximately 20,000 prime contractors. The B-1 bomber, for example, is the work of 5,000 subcontractors located in every state except Alaska and Hawaii. Over 2,000 subcontractors participate in Lockheed's Trident missile program.

In the Valley, more than 500 firms receive primary military contracts in excess of $10,000. However, hundreds more receive subcontracts from the primary contractors. Subcontractors sell chips, boards, cathode-ray tubes, accounting programs, and so forth to other companies which, in turn, may sell to the Pentagon. This ripples the military connection, making it even more difficult to trace. When the subcontracting path to the Pentagon is several corporate layers deep, many employees simply don't know about the connection. For example, at Ramtek, a graphics display hardware company, only marketing, sales, management and a handful of key employees seemed to know that a frame buffer device sold to another firm was destined ultimately for military service. Several Ramtek employees said they were happy that they didn't work on military projects.

The maze of military subcontracting suggests the futility awaiting workers who escape a military contractor to find 'civilian' employment – only to discover there a subcontracting relationship to a military supplier.

SPEAK NO EVIL

Language is the most innocent accomplice to the military worker's ignorance.

Almost every work-place and occupation has its argot – technical language that serves as a shorthand for describing work problems and procedures. The advent of computers and micro-electronics, however, envelops the work-place in language several times removed from reality. Whether the work involves observing whales or tracking missiles, computers flatten and homogenize it into a colourless world of files, records, fields, reports, updates and processing. As a work-place tool, technical language has its place. But where hostile technologies are designed and brought to life, the computer vernacular and its legion acronyms have the cumulative effect of putting social conscience to rest.

It's not difficult to imagine what sort of work goes on at a facility such as the Air Force Weapons Laboratory in New Mexico. But you would never know by reading the 138-page government document that lists weapons-lab job descriptions.

What is required of the civilian computer workers at the laboratory? 'A high degree of specialized senior systems software engineering knowledge and experience in scientific/technical ADP computer processing applications.' What projects will employees work on? 'Computer systems which CDC's NOS/BE and NOS/VE operating systems and utility programs.' But what do the systems really do? 'These systems support a wide variety of technical R&D analysis functions and applications.' The specializations might as well describe a marine biology lab or a Federal Reserve Bank.

Of course, those who hire on at the weapons lab would know, in varying degrees according to their clearance levels, that their work involves bomb and missile development. But the Air Force's language suggests that their daily work culture will not remind them of their work's purpose. The job descriptions – 'system generation/installation', 'system software maintenance', 'documentation support task' – suggest nothing so concrete.

At Teledyne Microwave, workers make avionic subsystems for the HARM missile. A former worker describes how work is divided into project groups with titles such as the Switch/Attenuator Team, the Multiplier Team, the IRM (Integrated Receiver Module) Qual (Quality) Team, and the IRM Production Team. Neither the project titles nor the ambiguous microchips and circuit boards that the teams turn out suggest their ultimate destination. As a result, workers are not confronted every day by the fact that HARM warheads employ 146 pounds of explosives to scatter 25,000 shrapnel fragments, each of which is pre-formed to inflict maximum damage.

Language need not be technical to mislead. Lockheed employment advertisements in military electronics magazines and news-daily job classifieds sometimes conceal the military connection in plain language. 'Our Palo Alto Research Lab offers you a stimulating environment in a tranquil setting near Stanford University...[Lockheed] invites you to break away from established theories and venture out in new directions – creating new technologies that will take concepts and turn them into reality.' 'Reality' at the Palo Alto Research Lab is designing post-holocaust technology, such as the Pentagon's Milstar satellite programme. But to prospective recruits, the ad language is a cue that work does not unfold in the morbid surroundings that Pentagon projects might otherwise imply.

Some contractors help rehearse their employees' social conversations. When friends and other outsiders casually ask, 'What do you work on?' primary contractor Watkins-Johnson, according to an ex-employee, admonishes its workers to utter two words: 'electronic defence'. Further elaboration is considered – potentially – a security breach. As it is, 'electronic defence' is an impoverished characterization of the Watkins-Johnson line, which includes 'electronic warfare suites' and radar components for battleship, land and jet-launched missiles, including the HARM missile, whose primary role is offensive.

If a worker is not really making bombs and bombers, but instead constructing 'projectiles' or testing 'fuselage designs', then responsibility for the products of the worker's labour, too, is obscured. How much easier to motivate military programmers to perform 'data path analysis' to time and speed 'usage requirements' – especially if the 'data path' conveys heat-seeking missile trajectories for 'usage' by a jet squadron, none of which military 'software engineers' will need to know to complete their work. As a deference for computer terminology emerges in the high-tech military industry, the 'need-to-know' policy invades the domain of language. The jargon is a thicket that invites even curious programmers and engineers to lose sight of the implications of their work.

'A TOOL THAT CAN DO ANYTHING'

Doris is a production control expediter at the Teledyne Microwave facility that makes HARM missile circuitry and avionics modules. She feels badly about her contribution to the missile project. 'I want to be creative, in an artistic sense, instead of destructive.' Doris says she would rather solder stained-glass windows than expedite the soldering of war components, 'But I can't get to it,' she laments, in reference to a discouraging labour market.

By contrast, Fred sees his job as creative and challenging. He is vaguely disturbed about the implications of his work, but remains uninspired about brighter prospects and resorts to the private ploys of resignation and fantasy:

> We're making these big nasty missiles, and everybody hopes they'll never be used. It just seems like they could build bridges, help people someplace else... It's not just the US, it's not just Russia, it's a whole mental attitude that goes on that – maybe I just ignore it. I've got no interest in taking anything of theirs. I live in comfortable apathy about a lot of that. It would be nicer if it was all gone.

More often, military electronic workers tend to dismiss their responsibility by noting the distance between their job tasks and those that are more directly linked to a hostile product. Michael, a utilities software pro-grammer, worked on a log-in protocol for a computer system his company hoped to sell to the National Security Agency. (His company also sells computers to the Air Force.) According to Michael,

> I'm at ease a little bit 'cause I do know that I'm not putting the bomb together. My guess is that most people would not work directly for military applications, but would be comfortable working in an environ-ment [in which] they knew part of [their work] wound up in a military application – that they weren't *directly* fueling it. *That detachment is a sort of protection.* (emphasis added)

Victor, a systems software programmer, finds refuge in the ambiguity of micro-electronics technology. He insists that he 'wouldn't work for ... a company that does military work', but that working on 'a tool that can do anything' – that is, civilian or military tasks – is acceptable. 'If you're making a sewing machine to sew parachutes or wedding dresses [or] if ... you know you're sewing parachutes, that's the difference.'

'As long as I'm not working on weapons systems, that's fine with me,' says Stanford computer-science professor Thomas Binford. But Binford acknowledges that his research on stereo vision has direct relevance to cruise-missile guidance systems. 'If I chose not to do my favorite project because of that, I'd go to my second favorite project and I'd find the same thing. I'd keep going down the list and then I'd be left saying, "What is there left for me to do?"'

Peter Hochschild, a Stanford computer-science graduate student, is more to the point. 'A lot of people here don't even think about the issue. They look for a research problem that's technically challenging and intellectually interesting, and *they divorce it from its applications*' (emphasis added).

The reflections of Victor, Michael and Professor Binford are no doubt earnest appraisals. Is writing missile-performance analysis software less damnable than using it to perfect the missile's flight? How much less lethal is writing an accounting program that enables the Air Force to operate more efficiently than making chips that will guide its bombs to their targets? If there are obvious, unambiguous answers to such questions, they are lost in the everyday culture of the military electronics worker. Perhaps the experience of military electronics work is essentially ambiguous.

Reckoning moral responsibility by measuring the distance between one's labour and the product is a legitimate inquiry, but only if one can hope to measure reliably. The division of labour in military electronics suggests the interdependency and responsibility of all workers but – and this is the paradox – encourages profound distance between worker and product. This psychological distance is protected and extended by the cloistering – the need-to-know policy – that mystifies the military product and censors the product's ghastly purpose from the producer's daily life. As a result, workers can, in addition to military electronics, manufacture a naïveté about the impact of their labours and, at least among obliging fellow workers, escape ridicule for their ill-gotten innocence.

NOTE
This essay is based on the author's book, *Behind the Silicon Curtain*, Chapter 5.

REFERENCES

Davis, W. F. (1984) 'The Pentagon and the scientist', in John Tirman, ed. *The Militarization of High Technology*. Cambridge, MA: Ballinger, 1984.

Hayes, Dennis (1989) *Behind the Silicon Curtain: The Seductions of Work in a Lonely Era.* Boston, MA: South End Press/London: Free Association.

Odell, R. (1985) 'Reminiscence', *Milwaukee Journal* 5 August.

United States Government (n.d.) *Industrial Security Manual for Safeguarding Classified Information.* Washington, DC.

4   STRATEGIC OFFENCE
Star Wars
as military hegemony

VINCENT MOSCO

The military are largely responsible for the development of information technology. In the 1940s and 1950s, the US government, led by the Pentagon, provided most of the funding for computer research. Furthermore, the Pentagon gave big contracts to commercial firms to build the production equipment needed to create the microchips that have revolutionized the industry. The US military are also largely responsible for underwriting the development of computer software systems such as Cobol. To complete the cycle, the Pentagon has been the major consumer of computer products. The Pentagon funded the transition from large, unreliable vacuum tubes to transistors and eventually to semiconductor integrated circuits. So dependent was the electronics industry on military contracts that one 1957 business analyst worried that '"Peace", if it came suddenly, would hit the industry very hard...', though the analyst concluded that 'military electronics is a good business despite the "risk" of peace' (Harris, 1957, p. 216). The Pentagon continues to consume about 15 percent of the value of all integrated circuits produced in the USA (US Congress, 1987). Moreover, it funds 58 percent of all US government research in mathematics and computer science (Flamm, 1987, p. 46) and 87 percent of all Federal semiconductor research.

Though many people are aware that the military gave birth to information technology and continue to sustain its development, few comprehend how deeply the military influence what are generally perceived to be 'civilian' applications. People tend to separate the general use of information technology, even the information technology industry, from military use of the technology and from militarism generally. This essay begins by addressing briefly the general influence of the military on the 'civilian' sphere of social life. From this start, the essay investigates the wider social significance of the Strategic Defence Initiative (SDI) or 'Star Wars' project.

In order to examine the wider influence of SDI, it is necessary to depart from conventional views about the project. These either support the programme as a workable defence against nuclear attack or oppose it on the grounds that no such system can possibly provide such a defence and that, in any case, SDI is an enormous waste of valuable resources. My analysis departs from such views by starting from two fundamentally different premises. First, the technical characteristics of SDI need to be judged on how well Star Wars will work as an *offensive* military system or as sets of loosely coupled systems against selected targets, particularly recalcitrant Third World nations. Furthermore, my analysis challenges the current debate's premise that what matters most is whether SDI works in the strict technical sense. This view misses the numerous significant ways in which SDI is already working to extend military hegemony throughout the entire society, on an economic, political and ideological level. Indeed, beyond its capabilities as an offensive system, SDI's more profound offence may be its ability to institutionalize militarism even further in Western society.

THE 'CIVILIAN' AS MILITARY

As the historian of technology Merritt Roe Smith has shown, the US military have exerted a strong influence on the design, dissemination and management of new technologies. The military influence the design of technologies 'by establishing standards and specifications for various goods and contracting with private manufacturers for their production' (Smith, 1985, p. 6). Eventually these technologies, from dehydrated foods to nuclear power plants, enter the civilian economy. Military support, including the financial backing of government-funded research and development and the legitimacy of a government seal of approval, eases the process of technological dissemination. In some cases, such as 'instant' foods, the consequences are arguably benign. In others, such as nuclear power, the impact is quite different.

The military, particularly the US Navy, were a major force in the application of nuclear energy to civilian uses. In fact, in 1953, the Navy received the backing of the US Atomic Energy Commission to oversee the design and construction of the first civilian nuclear power plant built in the United States. According to Hewlett and Duncan (1974), the Navy won out because nuclear power, particularly systems based on light-water reactors, worked well on naval vessels. This success helped to inflate the hopes of reactor manufacturers, including such major defence contractors as General Electric and Westinghouse, and power companies. These interests used the US Navy's success to argue that energy costs would be reduced to a negligible fraction of a consumer's budget, if not 'too cheap to meter'. However, applying the relatively small-scale naval use of nuclear energy to large-scale commercial power generation raised enormous technical, managerial and political problems that continue to cause widespread harm.

In a similar fashion and at around this same time, the US Air Force promoted the dissemination of numerical control tools by going as far as paying prime contractors to learn how to use the new technology. This action was not only far out of line with cost-effectiveness, it contributed to the deskilling of the American machine-tool work-force (Noble, 1984).

This military influence on design and dissemination extends beyond the USA. Consider a recent example from Canada, where a newspaper photograph offered a benign view of the Minister of Communication standing in a pleasant-looking park; she was smiling admiringly in front of a small, remotely powered plane along with ministry bureaucrats and engineers. The portrayal, right out of a model aircraft show, gave no indication that this is the heir to a device that the Pentagon has worked on for years, a microwave-powered aircraft ideal for low-altitude surveillance.

Throughout 1988, the Canadian Ministry of Communication, with considerable fanfare, boasted about its own SHARP (Stationary High Altitude Relay Platform) aircraft, yet none of the boasting placed surveillance at the centre of SHARP's activities. In fact the Canadian government's draft request for development proposals from industry describes the project as one that 'could be used to provide services, such as communications and broadcasting, over an area on the ground up to 1,000 km in diameter' (Canada, 1988, p. 1). Since the range of existing means to disseminate telecommunications and broadcasting material is quite extensive – including ground microwave, coaxial, copper and fibre optic cable, and communications satellites – it is hard to comprehend the additional value of an aircraft operating in a continuous circle at an altitude of twenty-one kilometres.

The ministry's request for proposals does acknowledge the surveillance function, though it is presented in a peace-keeping mode.

The round-the-clock surveillance capability, combined with communications, could be effective in enhancing the safety and efficiency of fishing in Canadian territorial waters, as well as providing enhanced surveillance to control illegal activities. (Canada, 1988, p. 2)

Nevertheless, the inescapable conclusion is that the technology has little more than surveillance to recommend it. This is how forms of social control extend military hegemony outwardly from the Pentagon and inwardly within a society that sells military control to its people as just another gadget to serve our leisure or just another children's toy.

In addition to its influence on the design and dissemination of technology, the military has set the pattern for the structure and style of corporate management. According to Smith (1985), the centralized and hierarchical structure of the military arms industry was applied to the management of the earliest industrial enterprises such as development of a rail system. In fact, he contends that 'the history of every important metalworking industry in nineteenth century America – machine tools, sewing machines, watches, typewriters, agricultural implements, bicycles, locomotives – reveals the pervasive influence of military management techniques' (p. 11).

This influence deepened in the twentieth century with the application of military regimentation to Henry Ford's automobile plants and the development of 'scientific' management practices identified with the work of Frederick W. Taylor. Taylor was steeped in the management of the firearms and machine-tool industries. He drew on this experience for the development of time-and-motion studies and other techniques for measuring and monitoring work, deskilling craft workers, and concentrating skills in management. In recent times, military practice has funded and legitimized the use of survey research on large populations and the application of computer-assisted management systems.

The Pentagon has influenced the design, development and management of technology, particularly communication and information technologies. The Pentagon has also directly influenced industrial organization and practice through the use of government 'chosen instruments' or companies established by the State, with extensive military control, to develop technology in the interests of what the State defines as 'national security'. Over sixty years ago the US government formed RCA, complete with a naval admiral to represent the government's interests on the board. This chosen instrument was intended to overcome British dominance in international telecommunications. Over thirty years ago the government founded Comsat, the Communications Satellite Corporation, to overcome the Soviet lead in space systems. The military influence on Comsat was so extensive that one analyst dubbed it the 'old soldier's home' (Kinsley, 1976). In the last few years the Pentagon has spawned chosen instruments in the computer field to take on the challenge of Japan. MCC and Sematech are the latest organizations to bear the military stamp in the information-technology market-place.

In addition to shaping the commercial broadcasting, satellite, computer and related industries, the Pentagon controls a vast computer/communications system of its own. The Pentagon and intelligence agencies control about 25 percent of all radio frequencies used in the USA, Government agencies with primary civilian responsibilities control another quarter, and the remaining half of the total frequencies available are in private hands.

The Pentagon is the country's largest single user of telecommunications. Its yearly budget for communication and intelligence exceeds the total annual revenues of all the commercial radio and television stations in the USA. Through the Defense Communication Agency and the Defense Telecommunication and Command Control System, the Pentagon deploys a global system of communications satellites, submarine cables, computers and terrestrial telecommunications systems to operate perhaps the most powerful communications and data processing system. Furthermore, the National Security Agency, the largest and most secretive of US intelligence agencies, operates its own global telecommunications system with an estimated budget of $10 billion per year and 600,000 employees.

According to US Army Deputy Chief of Staff, 'Literally every weapons system that we are planning and bringing into development in some way employs minicomputers and microelectronics.' Battlefield computers are used primarily for remote sensing of enemy troop movements, precise targeting and firing, and damage assessment. Miniaturization has even taken the portable computer to the modern battlefield. GRIDSET is a briefcase-size computer, including a built-in modem for telecommunications. It has been tested in action in Lebanon and Grenada, on the Space Shuttle, and in a nuclear weapon retargeting exercise aboard an airborne command post. Computers are also used extensively in naval forces. A typical guided-missile cruiser – carrying nuclear warheads, antisubmarine rocket torpedoes and attack helicopters – is managed by sixteen on-board main-frame computers and twelve minis.

Military computers are integrated into systems of Command, Control, Communications and Intelligence (C^3I). These systems are integrated globally into the US Worldwide Military Command and Control System. Computers have expanded the range, speed and accuracy of weapons systems. Linked to communication technologies, particularly satellites and computers have expanded intelligence gathering, surveillance and reconnaissance. As the real size of the battlefield increases over the earth and into space, C^3I systems to acquire, process, communicate and issue commands grow more vital.

In 1983 the Pentagon began one of its more ambitious computer projects, an effort to apply expert systems to conventional and strategic nuclear weapons. With its promise of automated weaponry, this Strategic Computing Initiative is a vital complement to the Star Wars programme.

OUTER SPACE MILITARIZED

The military control of the space programme belies the view that the USA has been committed to the peaceful uses of outer space. Indeed, Star Wars is just the latest in a long series of space-warfare projects that began even before the USA was technically capable of launching a space satellite.

US military interest in space pre-dates the launch of Sputnik, the first Soviet space satellite, by over a decade. In 1946, the Air Force sponsored the study, *Preliminary Design for a World-Circling Spaceship*, which contained material on the military application of space satellites, including recon-naissance and communication (Rand Corporation, 1946). Subsequent Air Force projects on pilotless spacecraft for communications, early warning, navigation and reconnaissance grew out of this research. In the early 1950s, studies stressed the need to develop an accurate and reliable Inter-continental Ballistic Missile (ICBM). This expanded in 1956 to fully funded programmes for satellite reconnaissance, subsequently for climate assess-ment and, of particular importance, for military communication.

The growth of US military forces world-wide created enormous problems of co-ordination and integration that only a very sophisticated com-munication system could manage. Established systems for C^3I were inadequate, particularly in the event of a nuclear war. Space communica-tions systems anchored in satellites would meet this pressing need. Consequently, the Pentagon began a major programme to promote the development of communications satellites.

Though it was the Republican Eisenhower Administration that proposed them, military satellites received enthusiastic backing from the Democrats as well. A 1957 Democratic policy statement signed by former President Truman, Senators Adlai Stevenson and Hubert Humphrey, and New York Governor Averell Harriman reads:

> Let us not fail to understand that control of outer space would be a military fact of the highest importance... the air war of yesterday becomes the space war of tomorrow. We must do more than merely catch up. The all-out efforts of the Soviets to establish themselves as masters of space around us must be met by all-out efforts of our own. (Manno, 1983, p. 39)

And from Senator Lyndon Johnson, who would go on to become the President most deeply committed and closely identified with the space programme:

> [C]ontrol of space means control of the world, far more certainly, far more totally than any control that has been achieved by weapons or by troops of occupation. Space is the ultimate position, the position of total control over Earth. (p. 39)

In 1958 the Eisenhower Administration gave primary responsibility for manned space exploration to an ostensibly civilian agency, the National Aeronautics and Space Administration (NASA). Amendments to the NASA act subordinated the civilian programmes to military requirements. In this way, the military were able to influence programme decisions on the Mercury and Gemini flights that culminated in the Project Apollo lunar landings. In fact, the Air Force Systems Command won direct control over experiments on Project Gemini.

The Air Force co-ordinated its role in testing how to conduct manoeuvre and rendezvous operations in Project Gemini with its own programme to develop military space vehicles. The major early projects were SAINT (for SAtellite INTercept), the first anti-satellite spacecraft; Dyna-Soar, a rocket-launched space glider developed for the Air Force by two former advisers to Adolf Hitler, Walter Dornberger and Kraft Ehricke; and BAMBI (for ballistic missile boost intercept), the earliest version of the Star Wars defence. BAMBI would deploy hundreds of satellites armed with heat-seeking missiles. The missiles would fire at Soviet ICBMs during their ascent period. These programmes were cancelled in 1963 because of mounting budget constraints and the growing military commitment in Indo-China. Later on in the decade, a proposed Manned Orbiting Laboratory met a similar fate after $1.3 billion was spent on the project.

In the 1970s, US military and intelligence agencies built satellite systems to enhance ground-based military forces. The systems were used principally for reconnaissance, early warning, communication and navigation. In 1972, supporters of a strong military space programme applauded President Nixon's approval of the Space Shuttle project. They did so because the Shuttle was designed and managed according to military specifications. Its major characteristics – reusability, manoeuvrability, large carrying capacity – grew out of military objectives. Flight details are covered in greater secrecy than for other NASA space projects. Moreover, the military has made use of half the Shuttle flights, and is likely to require a greater percentage in the aftermath of the *Challenger* disaster. Most analysts agree that NASA had to pay the price of military control in order to keep the Shuttle under its formal aegis or, put more simply, to remain in existence.

According to a 1987 study by the Federation of American Scientists, the military account for roughly half of the 337 operational satellites world-wide and half of US satellites, including twenty-six satellites for intelligence alone. The Defense Department budget for satellites, which historically has lagged behind that of NASA, is now twice the NASA amount. The Pentagon now spends between $15 billion and $20 billion a year on military space activities, compared with only $8.9 billion for NASA.

Military designs on outer space have been openly acknowledged by General Bernard Schriever, who was put in charge of Air Force space programmes in 1954 and whose ideas have propelled the USA along its Star Wars track. It would be hard to disagree with his 1983 quip, 'Space for peaceful purposes – what a bunch of goddamned bullshit that was!'

STAR WARS

The Star Wars programme – the so-called Strategic Defence Initiative (SDI) – is a major step towards the further militarization of outer space. There has been a great deal written about SDI, but almost all of the analysis addresses a single technical question: can SDI provide a defence against a nuclear-missile attack? This question is often subdivided into such components as: Can SDI stop all or only a percentage of incoming missiles? Can it protect population centres or is it limited to a defence of Western nuclear facilities, the heart of the deterrent?

These are important questions. Critics make a good case that Star Wars, particularly as a total defence, is technically unfeasible, would cost astronomical sums, and would be likely to increase international instability because it would undermine existing arms-limitation agreements. Moreover, critics point out that SDI requires computing capabilities that can only be found in science fiction.

The Star Wars project has sparked one of the most significant debates of our time. Nevertheless, it suffers from the myopic view that SDI is *only* about what it officially says it is about; the debate has missed the wider military, economic, political and ideological significance of Star Wars. Although SDI may not work in the narrow technical sense of providing a shield against incoming missiles it may well work in the wider sense of deepening and extending a militarized information society.

Despite its title, SDI can work as an *offensive* military system, either as part of a first-strike nuclear attack or, more likely, to attack specific targets such as recalcitrant Third World nations. Moreover, SDI is pumping massive amounts of money into the high-tech sector. Concretely, SDI provides the State with the means to pressure the transnational micro-electronics industry to harmonize its objectives with the US government's definition of the national interest. The latter includes winning in international competition with Japan and drawing the Soviet Union into an unaffordable military spending race.

Finally, Star Wars and the Strategic Computing Initiative are powerful ideological weapons. Star Wars sustains the popular illusion of a *defence* against nuclear weapons and an end to the principle of Mutually Assured Destruction (MAD). Strategic Computing assures Americans that all this can be done, and their standard of living protected, without the need to rely on Vietnam-style troop commitments and the often faulty judgements of military commanders.

One is tempted to agree with Johan Galtung, founder of the International Peace Federation, when he concludes:

> By shrewdly selling it as a way of 'making nuclear weapons obsolete', the Administration has brainwashed the public, including the many who have wasted nearly four years debating the irrelevant question of whether a leak-proof shield is achievable. (Galtung, 1987, p. 249)

'Brainwashing' may be too strong a term. Yet, it is hard to disagree with the view that SDI has been marketed with expert salesmanship.

The sales pitch is helped by the arrival of computer graphics on television. In fact, television and SDI appear to be made for each other. The hyper-reality of these displays makes the reality of SDI more credible. As Nelson puts it:

> Inevitably, any television news reference to 'Star Wars' is accompanied by hyper-realistic animation of rays zapping incoming missiles, videogame-like explosions eliminating enemy blips: seductive imagery that fascinates, makes the product appear tidy and efficient, and also presents the technology as a virtual fait accompli. (Nelson, 1987, p. 148)

As the remainder of this chapter will demonstrate, then, the momentum for SDI comes from the benefits it provides to major power centres in the USA. This has little to do with providing a protective umbrella against a torrent of nuclear weapons. Rather it is because SDI will work, because SDI is working, to strengthen the US offensive capacity against the Soviet Union and the Third World, to provide an acceptable means of subsidizing the micro-electronics industry and assisting US companies to compete globally, to maintain the government's ability to influence US corporate behaviour, and to promote a public belief in the US commitment to automated defensive military systems.

HOW STAR WARS WORKS MILITARILY

Arguing that SDI strengthens the USA's nuclear capability, Johan Galtung has renamed the project the Strategic Offensive Initiative. In essence,

> whatever might destroy a Soviet missile right after liftoff might also destroy farmland, a forest, perhaps even a city. A stationary or slowly moving object, such as a human being, would be considerably easier to destroy than a highly mobile, rotating, mirror-coated, hardened object, such as a missile, especially one that has been launched under cloud cover, with decoys and multiple warheads. (1987, p. 248)

That view is supported by a study prepared by R&D Associates, a Pentagon consulting firm. According to R&D, a space-based laser system, though ostensibly established for defence against nuclear weapons, can 'destroy the enemy's major cities by fire. The attack would proceed city by city, the attack time for each city being only a matter of minutes' (*Harper's*, April 1986, p. 15). Caroline Herzenber, a physicist, argues that lasers 'have the potential of initiating massive urban fires and even of destroying the enemy's major cities by fire in a matter of hours' (*Physics and Society*, January 1986). According to a study prepared by the Library of Congress, Congressional Research Service,

> Most or all of the weapons concepts that do prove feasible could in principle be used either offensively or defensively. Military objectives would be the driving factors determining their purpose. (*Aviation Week and Space Technology*, 30 November 1987, p. 23)

At present, the simplest of the SDI arsenal, a homing rocket that destroys targets by smashing into them, is believed to be the most effective offensive force, more so than the lasers, particle beams, and other futuristic weapons that the Pentagon is studying. Such weapons could attack Soviet satellites and battle stations in space. They could also be modified to enter the earth's atmosphere to knock out Soviet planes, radars and perhaps even missiles in silos.

Critics maintain that these weapons will be very useful in fighting an offensive nuclear war. According to Stanford physicist Harvey Lynch, 'The most obvious one is to use them in conjunction with a first strike, use them to mop up the weakened response of your adversary.' Even some advocates of SDI see it as an offensive system:

> In private, some Star Wars advocates say space-based antimissile systems can be viewed as exclusively offensive, given that a leaky shield would work best for fending off a foe's ragged retaliation after a first strike destroyed as many enemy nuclear weapons as possible. (Broad, 1987, p. 88)

Nevertheless, supporters contend that because the West is 'fundamentally pacific', it is not likely to use these weapons offensively. State Department consultant Colin Gray is less hopeful. Given what he perceives to be Soviet expansionist tendencies, he concludes his book on nuclear strategy with the ominous view that 'It is likely that it will be the United States which first feels moved to threaten and execute a central nuclear strike' (1984, p. 56).

A US first strike would be co-ordinated by force-enhancing systems such as Milstar and IONDS which are hardened to survive a protracted nuclear war. In fact, Milstar is an Air Force communication satellite system whose chief advantage over its predecessor is a greater capacity to operate in a nuclear battle. IONDS is a surveillance satellite system that uses the network of Global Positioning System satellites to provide data instantaneously on the effectiveness of an initial nuclear strike in order to make a second-wave attack more productive. A first strike would be led by anti-satellite weapons to destroy the Soviet early warning and communications capacity. Land-based MX missiles and the submarine-launched Trident II would drop nuclear weapons on Soviet missile silos. An SDI system would be geared to the thousand or so warheads, chiefly from the Soviet submarine fleet, that manage to survive.

The development of precise surveillance, targeting and attack systems may not convince Washington officials to attack the Soviet Union, or even to rely on such a system for defence against Soviet attack, but it strengthens the case for use against recalcitrant Third World nations. A limited Star Wars system, one that need not operate flawlessly, could be used effectively as a means of controlling nations or groups labelled as supporting terrorism, the international drug trade, Communism, a combination of these, or some suitable alternative.

Such 'enemies' would face the threat of a precisely targeted, devastating attack of space-to-ground or ground-to-ground weapons: 'The advantages are clear. Recalcitrant third world nations could be intimidated, punished, disarmed, embargoed, silenced, rendered leaderless, or destroyed with little or no risk to American forces and, perhaps, much less protest and political difficulty at home' (Leemans and Luker, 1986, p. 44). Moreover, though officials in Washington, including President Reagan, have entertained the idea of sharing SDI technology with the Soviet Union, 'no one has offered any shields to the Third World' (Thompson and Thompson, 1985, p. 144). Analysts have been discussing the value of SDI as a weapon against Gaddafi (Broad, 1987, p. 88), though some of this may be just another part of the sales pitch. As critics puncture the argument that SDI will protect against the Soviets, proponents begin to talk about using it against Gaddafi and Khomeini in the same way that they talk about beneficial civilian spin-offs like curing cancer or stopping acid rain.

Nevertheless, since the end of World War II, US armed forces have been engaged in a continuing series of wars with Third World countries. One of the leaders of this offensive, Richard Nixon, has offered important insight on the USA's future combat activity in his book *No More Vietnams*. In the chapter given the heavy-handed title 'The Third World War', Nixon claims that we are likely to have seen the last of superpower combat for a long time. The world is entering a phase of protracted wars of low and high intensity throughout the Third World. He calls on the USA to prepare itself for this version of World War III.

In 1988 a Pentagon panel issued the Iklé–Wohlstetter report (US

Department of Defense, 1988). Comprising military officials and such leading strategists as Henry Kissinger and Zbigniew Brzezinski, the panel took up Nixon's view and called on the USA to make a major commitment to improve on its abilities to fight wars in the Third World. It is necessary to do this even though, while such wars 'are obviously less threatening than any Soviet–American war would be, yet they have had and will have an adverse cumulative effect on US access to critical regions, on American credibility among allies and friends and on American self-confidence' (Carrington, 1988, p. 16). The panel is particularly pleased with technological developments ('By the standards of a decade ago, the accuracies of current weapons are extraordinary') that make it possible to pinpoint Third World targets without risking troops or aircraft. The panel report reflects the significance that the highest US policy circles place on intervention in the Third World.

The physicist credited with inventing the neutron bomb, Sam Cohen, applauded the Iklé-Wohlstetter conclusions and extended them by suggesting specific uses of SDI technology in the Third World. These technologies, he said, 'hold the potential for considerably more discriminate and effective application in a large-scale Persian Gulf conflict'. Moreover, SDI lasers 'could eliminate US dependency on overseas bases' and 'might have value for counterterrorist operation in the Middle East' (Cohen, 1988).

As a loosely coupled set of weapons systems that would complement a first-strike nuclear offensive or attack an enemy in the Third World, SDI can work. In this respect, Star Wars resembles the other major Reagan Administration military buildup, the development of a massive naval force comprised of 600 ships and fifteen carriers. As one analyst put it, 'Aside from the Strategic Defense Initiative... the maritime strategy represents *the* major change in United States war planning by the Reagan Administration' (Beatty, 1987, p. 37).

Like SDI, the 'Maritime Strategy', as it has been called, is sold as a defence against Soviet attack. Critics, including conservative strategist Edward Luttwak and former CIA Director Admiral Stansfield Turner, say it won't work. Like the technical critics of SDI, they may be missing the point. According to Beatty, such a force would free the USA from reliance on Nato allies, who often try to restrain its intervention in the Third World. No one recognizes this more than former Secretary of the Navy James Webb, who singled out a relaxation in the US Nato commitment as the first reason for supporting the Maritime Strategy:

> First, although the Nato alliance is one of the keystones of our military structure, we need to remind ourselves that we are more than a European nation. Moreover, we should bear in mind that no region is better equipped to reassume a great share of the burden of its own defense than Western Europe. (1988, p. 14)

Table 1   Major private Star Wars contractors, 1983 to March 1987

Organization	Contracts awarded (millions)
Lockheed*	$1,024
General Motors*	734
TRW	567
Lawrence Livermore Laboratories	552
McDonnell Douglas*	485
Boeing*	475
EG&G	468
Los Alamos Laboratories	458
General Electric*	420
Rockwell International	369
MIT	353
Raytheon*	248
LTV	227
Fluor	198
Grumman*	193

*Indicates one of the top fifteen defence contractors, 1987.

Source: *High Technology Business*, December 1987, p. 24. *Aviation Week and Space Technology*, 4 March 1988.

Former Nixon aide William Safire put it more bluntly when he asserted that 'For Europe, today's talk is healthy if it leads to regional self-reliance; for America, worldwide action to defend freedom requires a new freedom of action' (*New York Times*, 7 April 1988, p. A27).

Freed from even the admittedly gentle pressure of its Nato allies, 'such a Navy would give teeth to what has been called the Reagan doctrine – the US effort to aid guerrilla fighters against revolutionary regimes in the Third World' (Beatty, p. 53). The fleet, with a total of 569 vessels by January 1988, has already been used off Nicaragua to terrorize the Sandinistas and stands ready to aid US-backed guerrillas in Angola. In that sense, the Maritime Strategy is already working 'not as a force to fight a conventional war with the Soviet Union but as a force for intervention in the Third World' (p. 53). Those who suggest that Star Wars doesn't compute might learn a lesson from the Maritime Strategy. They might learn to amend their calculations to include what have been the direct targets of US aggression, targets that US strategists have been searching for ways to hit rapidly, efficiently, and without the use of its own combat troops.

HOW STAR WARS WORKS ECONOMICALLY

Military projects such as SDI are the primary legitimate means of providing direct government funding for corporate research and development in the USA. If the object were the provision of non-military services the contracts with private companies that this funding makes possible would be criticized as improper government intrusion into the free market-place. In this sense, SDI and its associated information-technology programmes work well for major arms manufacturers such as Rockwell, McDonnell Douglas, Ford Aerospace, Hughes, and for major companies with a stake in robotics and artificial intelligence such as General Motors, Boeing, Martin Marietta and Texas Instruments.

As Table 1 suggests, many of the same companies that have benefited most from Pentagon contracts are the chief beneficiaries of Star Wars deals. In this respect, SDI is deepening and extending long-established relationships between government and business. Business pressures government to maintain a permanent war economy as a channel for stable flows of guaranteed profit.

Aside from the sheer size of the R&D budget that DOD has to dispense, companies benefit in numerous special ways from its contracting system. Firms in the military industries are practically free from competition; 96 percent of all Pentagon contracts are awarded on a non-competitive basis. Pentagon largesse also makes defence companies more profitable than their civilian counterparts; typically, defence contractors enjoy profit rates twice as high as their non-military counterparts. In addition, defence contractors more often than not pay little or no corporate income tax (Shaffer, 1987, p. 97). When profit rates are recalculated to account for taxes actually paid, return on equity for the years 1981–4 increases from 25 percent to 35 percent, almost three times the average for civilian industry (*Economic Notes*, July/August 1986).

The case of General Motors, the second leading SDI contractor, offers important insights into the wider economic value of Star Wars. For GM, SDI and other defence contracts provide public money for private investment in computerized design, manufacturing and robotics systems that will modernize the company and thereby contribute to its international profitability.

In 1984 GM spent $2.5 billion to buy EDS, a leading software producer with substantial government contract experience. Its first contract was a $656-million, ten-year deal to update the computer systems at forty-seven US Army bases, including a training programme for 60,000 US Army personnel. This was followed by major contracts with the Navy and US Postal Service (McClellan, 1984, pp. 15–17, 137–45). In 1985 GM bought Hughes Aircraft, at that time the eighth largest defence contractor, with military contracts in 1985 alone worth $3.6 billion.

This form of diversification is particularly attractive to investors because long-term military commitments mitigate cyclical declines in business activity, buttressing a firm from the effects of recession. Furthermore, in its own case as a major defence contractor, General Motors is guaranteed a steady flow of government investment that it can apply to the civilian workplace. Admittedly, there has been considerable press attention paid to the difficulties that GM is encountering in meshing its traditional operations with those of EDS and Hughes. Nevertheless, if GM can overcome its organizational problems, the company will soon enjoy the benefits of having bought more than a ticket to an expanded defence sector.

In EDS and Hughes, GM has bought the technical expertise that it will use to automate its automobile assembly plants and expand its international operations. The Strategic Computing component of the SDI is particularly significant here. According to the Pentagon's prospectus on the program, 'spinoffs from a successful Strategic Computing Program will surge into our industrial community'. Big winners here are 'the automotive and aerospace industries as they integrate intelligent CAD (Computer Assisted Design) into the development process and intelligent CAM (Computer Assisted Manufacturing) and robotics into manufacturing' (US, DARPA, 1983, p. 9).

Even allowing for the hyperbole that often fills such documents, SDI is working economically by providing stable funding to major corporations and by subsidizing their efforts to enter high-technology production. As one engineer in SDI described the hegemony exercised by the programme, 'No, it won't work, but we need the money for research; and no, it isn't an efficient way to fund research, but it's the only way we've got' (Reed, 1985, p. 43). By influencing how the US economy is restructured, SDI works to promote specific economic goals, regardless of meeting its stated defence goals.

HOW STAR WARS WORKS POLITICALLY

SDI gives the US government leverage to harmonize corporate activity with what the government perceives to be overall national interests. The need for such leverage increases as the power of transnational corporations increases, because the interests of such companies and the government are increasingly divergent. The government is interested in business activities that will increase domestic revenues, employment and the security interests of the State. Transnational businesses that look to opening advantages in a global market may very well take actions, such as joint ventures with non-US transnationals, not benefiting US employment, revenue or security. Defence spending can send a strong message to suspected corporate recalcitrants.

In the computer industry, the government has been concerned that IBM, the world's largest computer company, has been lukewarm to government-backed joint ventures such as MCC (Microelectronics and Computer Technology Corporation). MCC and artificial intelligence research may be high on the government's agenda, but not necessarily central to IBM's business plans. Why should IBM share secrets with lesser competitors? Why should it invest in research whose commercial potential is less than firmly established?

In this case, the Strategic Computing Initiative can work to bring IBM into closer line with US government policies. As the head of DARPA made clear in Congressional hearings on Strategic Computing:

> What we expect to happen is that as Darpa stimulates industry research efforts and university efforts in machine intelligence, either IBM will decide that it will be good to do research in this field and to have a capability in it for defense in the 1990s, or it will not.
>
> If it does not, there will be many others who will participate in those research programs and will spin off technology both for defense and commercial applications.
>
> If IBM does not see that, then in my opinion their market share will decline. (*Aviation Week and Space Technology*, 27 February 1984, p. 27)

The Pentagon's concern with commercial applications and the need to bring IBM into line is prompted to a great degree by Japanese advances in artificial intelligence research. In House hearings, DARPA identified the threat from Japan as a major reason for investing so much in strategic computing. DARPA expected that 'the commercial spinoffs will help the US computer industry to meet, and in fact surpass, the Japanese activities' (US Congress, House Committee on Science and Technology, 1984, p. 135).

Star Wars supporters are not as vocal about European competition as they are about the feared threat from Japan. Nevertheless, SDI promoters claim that by attracting European participation in Star Wars research, they will deter European efforts to develop independent high-technology research projects, such as the French Eureka, EEC Esprit and British Alvey. Star Wars can work politically against threats from Japan and Europe.

SDI and strategic computing also provide the State with substantial leverage over the course of R&D conducted in the USA. Indeed, Pentagon officials have been explicit about the sort of control that this provides. As the undersecretary of defense for research and development has warned,

> I am not enthusiastic about the idea of using defense resources to subsidize the work of people who are outspoken critics of our national defense goals or policies ... If they want to get out and use their roles as professors to make statements that's fine, it's a free country. [But]

STRATEGIC OFFENCE

freedom works both ways. They're free to keep their mouths shut ... I'm also free not to give money. (*Toronto Globe and Mail*, 12 August 1986, p. A7)

Thus Star Wars can work as an instrument to control the US research agenda and silence criticism of defence policy.

SDI can also work politically against the Soviet Union. Despite the publicity about Soviet advances in ballistic missile research and strategic computing, most analysts see little Soviet achievement in these areas (Gervasi, 1986). Given the consistent pattern of Soviet counter response to US military expansion (Table 2), one would expect that the Soviet Union would develop its own version of SDI. Yet the Soviet Union doesn't seem able to sustain the spending required to match the US commitment to SDI. Star Wars can work against the Soviet Union by drawing it into a spending spiral that will produce severe strain on its economy. Indeed, this strain was intended by President Reagan:

They cannot vastly increase their military productivity because they've already got their people on a starvation diet as far as consumer products are concerned. But they know our potential capacity industrially, and they can't match it. (Cited in Shaffer, 1987, p. 92)

Nicholas Lemann has put the 'spend them into the ground' scenario into sharper perspective:

The other scenario, which can be heard around the Pentagon and elsewhere in the Administration, is this: Of course we are in an arms race with the Soviets. Of course it won't end at the bargaining table. We can win it. Their society is economically weak, and it lacks the wealth, education, and technology to enter the information age. They have thrown everything into military production, and their society is starting to show terrible stress as a result. They can't sustain military production, the way we can. Eventually, it will break them, and then there will be just one superpower in a safe world – if, only if, we can keep spending. (Lemann, 1984, p. 94)

Or, as science fiction writer Isaac Asimov put it, 'It's just a device to make the Russians go broke' (cited in Thompson and Thompson, 1985, p. 1).

HOW STAR WARS WORKS AS IDEOLOGY

The Star Wars programme may seem to us merely an expensive, if dangerous, piece of science fiction. Yet, it strikes deep resonances with many aspects of our lives: the reshaping of our work; the manipulation of our yearning for security; even our nightmares, as well as the science fiction that

Table 2   The nuclear arms race

Device	Time of adoption	
	USA	USSR
Atomic bomb	1945	1949
Intercontinental bomber	1948	1955
Thermonuclear bomb	1952	1953
Intercontinental ballistic missile	1955	1957
Submarine-launched ballistic missile	1960	1968
Multiple independently targeted warhead	1970	1975
Long-range cruise missile	1982	1984
Neutron bomb	1983	?
New strategic bomber	1985	1987

we read. In the sense that it affects our behaviour and fears, it is already working.

SDI and the Strategic Computing Program work as ideology by promoting beliefs that resonate strongly with public desires about military activity. Americans would like their standard of living protected, even if it takes military action, but would prefer that it be done in the name of defence and without resorting to large troop commitments. Star Wars offers the powerful image of defence against nuclear weapons and, particularly with the investment in strategic computing, the prospect of automated warfare, of battles in which few soldiers are involved.

Reagan has been able to enunciate this belief system with religious fervour. Here is how he described his SDI discussions with Gorbachev, including God's role in the programme, to a group of high-school students:

> I told Gorbachev that SDI was a reason to hope, not to fear; that the advance of technology, which originally gave us ballistic missiles, may soon be able to make them obsolete. I told him that with SDI, history had taken a positive turn. I told him that men of good will should be rejoicing that our deliverance from the awful threat of nuclear weapons may be on the horizon, and I suggested to him that I saw the hand of Providence in that. What could be more moral than a system based on protecting human life rather than destroying it? I could no more negotiate SDI than I could barter with your future. (Smith, 1987, p. 23)

The power of Reagan's view lies very much in his belief in the vision. Indeed, a movie of his, *Murder in the Air*, featured the young Ronald Reagan protecting a primitive Star Wars device from enemy agents. According to the historian C. Vann Woodward, 'the implausible scheme is at one with Reagan politics and personality, a "nice" weapons system – defensive, not offensive; killing missiles, not people, another act of American altruism and a bonanza of billions for business' (Woodward, 1987, p. 29). He likens SDI to the Lone Ranger's silver bullet, used only to knock guns out of bad guys' hands.

The ideology of defence is highly visible among those directly involved in SDI research. For some, a commitment to defence seems to motivate their work. A common response from the physicists working at the centre of SDI research, the Lawrence Livermore Laboratories, is that they are actively devoted 'to eliminate nuclear weapons' (*New York Times*, 31 January 1984). The bulk of physicists at Livermore are young (late twenties and early thirties) and convey a youthful enthusiasm for their work:

> I don't think I fall in that category, of working on weapons of death. We're working on weapons of life, ones that will save people from weapons of death.
>
> There's almost an infinite number of issues to be pursued. The number of new weapon designs is limited only by one's creativity. Most of them have not been developed beyond the stage of thinking one afternoon, 'Gee, I suppose you can do so and so.' There's a tremendous number of ways one might defend the country. (*New York Times*, 31 January 1984)

Others simply get caught up in the details of research, separated from their wider political implications. Employment in Huntsville, Alabama, fuelled with $862 million in Star Wars contracts, has grown 23 percent since the start of SDI. Engineers there leave the politics to others: 'It's so easy to get caught up in the details,' said one, 'you don't think about the wider implications. You just hope that somebody else is doing that. If you're lucky, you wake up someday and realize that nobody's in charge' (Charles, 1987, p. 750). Engineer George von Tiesenhausen is a scientist brought to work in Huntsville with several hundred German scientists and engineers smuggled out of Europe after World War II. Taking a more sober view of SDI, he argues that the programme is 'money thrown out the window'. However, he adds, many engineers 'are overwhelmed with the technical challenge as we were during the V2 [Nazi rocket] era' (p. 750).

Supporters of SDI are well aware of the importance of selling Star Wars by seizing the language of peace. The influential Star Wars lobby High Frontier hired consultant John Bosma to organize its public-relations effort. Bosma acknowledges the significance of identifying 'Ballistic Missile Defence' (BMD) as 'a new approach to arms control':

A primary objective is to force a drastic reorientation of the arms control debate in such a way as to make it politically risky for BMD opponents to invoke alleged 'arms control agreements' against an early BMD system. In fact, the project should . . . seek to recapture the term arms control and all the idealistic images and language attached to it . . . BMD proponents should stress nuclear disarmament as their goal. (*Harper's*, June 1985, pp. 22-4)

Robert Jastrow, founder of NASA's Goddard Space Institute and professor at Dartmouth College, offers an excellent example of Star Wars public relations in action. In an article for the popular magazine *Science Digest*, Jastrow argues that precision-guided weapons will end the nuclear arms race, 'It is one of the paradoxes of our time that the remarkable accuracy of the smart warhead, applied to nuclear tipped missiles, may lead to the virtual disappearance of these terrible weapons' (June 1984, p. 39).

Few critics of Star Wars have acknowledged the ideological force contained in the promise, however contrived, of a technologically guaranteed, nuclear-weapon-proof world. One who does is the Canadian historian Robert Malcomson:

Star Wars proposes that Americans can, in a sense, repeal the nuclear age. It has a powerful nostalgic appeal to the American public, which looks back to the good old days when geography did provide genuine security for the US . . . Star Wars is an attempt to escape from the present realities and for many . . . this escapist vision is hopeful and comforting. (1986, pp. 121-2)

Television helps to make this vision all the more comforting by presenting SDI news stories in what Gitlin calls a 'cheerful visual language'. The general viewer is presented with the vivid, colourful language of animated progress telling us that

what can be drawn can be planned, what can be planned can be built, and what can be built can protect. The diagrams helped confer upon SDI the force of the feasible; the opposition looked like progress-bashing grumps. (Gitlin, 1987, p. 29)

For those who have their doubts that SDI can provide real hope and comfort, there is the ideology of the spin-off, or what computer scientist and former Star Wars consultant, David Parnas, calls, 'the Jello theory' of defence spending. Even if the guns don't work, research gets you a better-tasting dessert. This is a common defensive strategy among military supporters. Since the military benefits of SDI await the next century, short-term spin-offs are a particularly important selling point.

Playing on American fears for its educational system and the future of work, Colorado Congressman Ken Kramer boasts that SDI will 'lay the foundation for an education-vocational renaissance for the American labor force, particularly the unemployed in the smokestack industries' (Hartung and Nimroody, 1985, p. 202). A science writer for the *New York Times* holds out the promise of an end to acid-rain pollution, improved patient diagnosis, better weather forecasting, improved shop-floor production and an electron-beam weapon that will ultimately be used to fight cancer, in financial terms $5-$20 trillion in private-sector sales of spin-off items (Browne, 1986).

The SDI office operates its own spin-off programmes. One makes available a technology transfer data base of unclassified materials that contain some profit potential. SDI officials report on a number of biomedical and industrial uses. These include research by US and Mexican agricultural interests that uses SDI laser technology to track African killer bees, medical company interest in the use of carbon-fibre ceramics for prosthetic devices, and tiny cooling devices used for SDI sensors that may be of use in microsurgery. The SDI office is also setting up a classified spin-off programme for companies that the Defense Logistics Agency certifies to be acceptable. For access to this data base covering technologies in nineteen 'militarily critical' areas, companies have to agree not to transfer data to a foreign entity (*Aviation Week and Space Technology*, 23 November 1987, p. 84).

The ideology of the 'spin-off' is part of a wider process that Boot refers to as 'techno-patriotism'. He uses the idea to explain how the American mass media could miss the warning signs of an impending Space Shuttle disaster, including engine shutdowns, brake failures, fuel leaks and cost overruns. Boot argues that, for the news media, the space programme 'became a symbol of US technological redemption following an era of American malaise' (Boot, 1986). Wayne Biddle, who covered technology for the *New York Times* until he resigned in frustration in September 1985, claims that 'it was always an uphill battle to get articles critical of the shuttle into the paper. There was a great deal of resistance' (Boot, 1986).

It is easier to understand the resistance when one comprehends the significance of the space programme in the minds and spirits of Americans. Consider the startling results of a survey that Peter Hart Research Associates conducted for *Rolling Stone* magazine on the attitudes and values of Americans aged eighteen to forty-four. When asked what event had more effect on them than any other in their lifetime, the most frequent response was the explosion of the Space Shuttle *Challenger*. The Shuttle disaster was ahead of the Vietnam War, the Aids epidemic and the taking of the American hostages in Iran, the next most frequently chosen events (Sheff, 1988).

Popular writers, particularly those who produce science fiction, have their own brand of techno-patriotism. In his analysis of science-fiction ideology, Thomas Disch writes that the genre serves 'as a debating society, moral support system and cheerleading section for the present and future personnel of space-related industries and military services' (Disch, 1986). According to Disch, the enormously popular work of Robert Heinlein is especially significant here because Heinlein considered space, not as the realm of imagination, but as the next frontier, 'and he was its recruiting sergeant'. More recently, people like Jerry Pournelle, a former Rockwell International executive, take up the issue explicitly, by writing about space-age Rambos piloting Star Wars to American supremacy. Pournelle's *There Will be War* sees the only hope in victory coming from total US mobilization. His non-fiction *Mutually Assured Survival* is a defence of the Star Wars programme that features a supportive dust-cover letter from President Reagan thanking Pournelle for 'assisting us in achieving a safer and more stable future for this country'.

Just as the Star Wars programme is wrapped in the ideology of a world without nuclear weapons, the Strategic Computing Program is packaged by its defenders as war without American soldiers, the automated battlefield. By giving computers some decision-making power, we take away responsibility from human commanders.

Automated warfare can be understood as a major outcome of the Indo-China War:

> As the Vietnam War ... demonstrated, Americans – be they soldiers or civilians – are hesitant to support wars of intervention in which the lives of American troops are threatened. (Siegel and Markoff, in Edwards, 1984, p. 12)

Automated weapons of the sort proposed in the Strategic Computing Initiative make it easier to justify a future Vietnam, Grenada or Nicaragua. Moreover, whether or not such weapons systems are militarily effective, as Edwards concludes,

> From the history of war after World War II, it seems apparent both that Third World nations will become dumping grounds for intelligent weapons systems they cannot afford, and that machine intelligences may eventually play decisive roles in armed political struggles. (p. 13)

CONCLUSION: STRATEGIC OFFENSIVE AND MILITARY HEGEMONY

When one takes into account the technological history, funding, research, development and applications of advanced communication and information technology, it is not difficult to draw the conclusion that we are moving toward the creation of a military information society. At its leading edge is Star Wars – leading not for how the programme promises to work, but because it is already working as an offensive economic, political, ideological and military strategy.

SDI leads an offensive against international competitors in the high-tech market-place and against workers who would oppose the application of military control principles to the computerized work-place. SDI leads a political offensive against companies whose allegiance to the national effort is questioned and against a Soviet Union whose ability to keep up with an enormous spending binge is questionable. SDI leads an ideological offensive against our real need for security by providing us with a false technical fix that can only lead to greater insecurity.

Moreover, it may not be long before we see SDI systems or their real spin-offs used against some recalcitrant Third World nation or as part of a nuclear offensive. In fact the attack of the cruiser *Vincennes* on a commercial airliner, prompted as it was by commands from a radar system that is central to SDI planning, may be considered the first literal Star Wars offensive.

There is no doubt a price to be paid for making Star Wars work in this fashion. The logic of military technology is a poor substitute for much-needed economic and social planning. And patriotism, even techno-patriotism, has its limits. Nevertheless, Star Wars critics have been working under the well-meaning but misguided assumption that by giving the programme a sound technical thrashing, it would go away.

There is little doubt that such a thrashing has been delivered. Even the *New York Time*'s Malcolm Browne, who boasts of SDI providing a cure for cancer and acid rain, had to admit to the strength of the opposition, expressed in part by petitions signed by 6,500 scientists and science educators who pledge not to accept SDI funding. More recently, the American Mathematical Society, with 7,000 of the Society's 20,000 members voting, passed a resolution calling on members to refuse SDI research grants. In this way, Star Wars may also be working to develop an important oppositional force within the scientific community.

Yet one also has to wonder about how many of these would sign anti-Star Wars petitions if the programme were presented not as a defensive umbrella but as a set of loosely coupled weapons for selective use against those accused of promoting 'terrorism' or the drugs trade. One need not wonder. The scientific community has shown far less opposition and considerable support for the development of every major weapons system deployed since the end of World War II, many of which have been used in combat against Third World nations.

The point is not to discourage technically based opposition to SDI, but to acknowledge that it is not stopping Star Wars. The budget has grown substantially in each year since Reagan announced the programme in March 1983. Technical criticisms have not even made substantial inroads in the Democratic Party opposition. Though opposition exists, it is mainly applied to differences in how SDI ought to develop, not in whether it should continue at all. The leadership of the Democratic Party approves continued SDI funding. It simply does not want to see SDI undermining existing international agreements such as the ABM treaty. Moreover, it favours funding in line with overall defence growth and a commitment to long-term research rather than early deployment. (Johnston and Proxmire, 1987) One of the Senate's leading Democratic spokesmen on defence, Sam Nunn, has proposed rapid deployment of a limited shield against nuclear missiles that has won the praise of the right-wing Hoover Institution (Fossedal, 1988). This is consistent with the Democratic Party's long-standing commitment to the militarization of outer space. In addition, some Democratic opposition to SDI, including that of Michael Dukakis, stems from a desire to expand US conventional forces to better enable the USA to respond unilaterally to global problems. Even if this were implemented, it would do nothing to stem the shift towards electronic command over the military and industry. As it is presently constituted, the Democratic Party holds little hope for a decline in the military information society and the military uses of outer space.

Criticism of Star Wars would be more useful if it were linked to the ways the programme is already working to achieve Washington's wider goals of military hegemony, both at home and abroad. Opposition to Star Wars would be more useful if it were to show the programme's connection to the US effort to restructure its economy, control its labour force and emerge as the most powerful economic force in the international division of labour. Star Wars opposition would be strengthened by linking SDI to US government efforts to control the production and distribution of scientific research and information world-wide.

Opposition to Star Wars is better spent subverting the notion that the world's leading imperial power can even speak of defence, much less provide a technical fix for it. With such a perspective, the programme can be opposed for its hidden agenda of total control over all those forces – be they factory workers, scientists or Third World countries – who resist US government aims.

NOTE

This essay is based upon the author's book, *The Pay-Per Society: Computers and Communication in the Information Age*, Garamond, 1989, chapter 6. Both draw on material published in 'Star wars/earth wars', *Radical Science* 17, 1985 and 'Star wars is already working', *Science as Culture* pilot issue, 1987.

REFERENCES

Beatty, Jack (1987) 'In harm's way', *Atlantic Monthly* May: 37–53.

Boot, W. (1986) 'NASA and the spellbound press', *Columbia Journalism Review* July/August.

Broad, William J. (1987) 'Star Wars is coming, but where is it going?' *New York Times Magazine* 6 December.

Browne, Malcolm (1986) 'The Star Wars spinoff', *New York Times Magazine* 24 August.

Canada (1988) *The Development of Sharp: A Proposal to Industry.* Ottawa. 3 June. (Draft).

Carrington, Tim (1988) 'Pentagon panel urges better strategies to deal with conflicts in Third World', *Wall Street Journal* 12 January.

Charles, Daniel (1987) 'Star Wars fell on Alabama', *Nation* 19 December.

Cohen, Sam (1988) 'Use Star Wars weapons in ground wars', *Wall Street Journal* 20 April.

Disch, Thomas (1986) 'The road to heaven: science fiction and the militarization of space', *Nation* 10 May.

Edwards, Paul N. (1984) 'Border wars: the science, technology and politics of artificial intelligence', working paper of the Silicon Valley Research Group, University of California, Santa Cruz, December.

Federation of American Scientists (1987) *What's Up in Space.* Washington, DC: Federation of American Scientists.

Flamm, Kenneth (1987) *Targeting the Computer: Government Support for International Competitiveness.* Washington, DC: Brookings Institution.

Fossedal, Gregory A. (1988) 'Nunn's sensible shield', *New York Times* 28 January.

Galtung, Johan (1987) 'The real Star Wars threat', *Nation* 28 February.

Gervasi, Paul (1986) *The Myth of Soviet Military Supremacy.* New York: Harper & Row.

Gitlin, Todd (1987) 'The greatest story never told', *Mother Jones* June/July.

Gray, Colin (1984) *Nuclear Defense and Strategic Planning.* Philadelphia: Foreign Policy Research Institute.

Harris, William B. (1957) 'The electronic business', *Fortune* April: 137–226.

Hartung, W. and Nimroody, R. (1985) 'Cutting up the Star Wars pie', *Nation* 14 September.

Hewlett, Richard and Duncan Francis (1974) *The Nuclear Navy.* Chicago: University of Chicago Press.

Johnston, Bennett and Proxmire, William (1987) 'SDI's broken promises', *Wall Street Journal* 28 August.

Kinsley, Michael (1976) *Outer Space and Inner Sanctums.* New York: Wiley Interscience.

Leemans, Dirk and Luker, Bob (1986) 'Star Wars – the other agenda', *Canadian Dimension* Spring.

Lemann, Nicholas (1984) 'The peacetime war', *Atlantic Monthly* October.

McClellan, S. T. (1984) *The Coming Computer Industry Shakeout.* New York: John Wiley.

Malcomson, R. (1986) 'Exposing nuclear fallacies: an interview with Robert Malcomson', *Studies in Political Economy* 20 (summer).

Manno, Jack (1983) *Arming the Heavens.* New York: Dodd, Mead.

Nelson, Joyce (1987) *The Perfect Machine: TV in the Nuclear Age.* Toronto: Between the Lines.

Nixon, Richard (1986) *No More Vietnams.* London: Comet/W. H. Allen

Noble, David (1984) *Forces of Production: A Social History of Industrial Automation.* New York: Alfred A. Knopf.

Rand Corporation (1946) *Preliminary Design for a World-Circling Spaceship*. Santa Monica, CA: Rand.

Reed, F. (1985) 'The great Star Wars swindle', *Harper's* May.

Shaffer, Ed (1987) 'Militarism and the economy', *Studies in Political Economy* 24 (autumn): 87–104.

Sheff, David (1988) 'Portrait of a generation', *Rolling Stone* 5 May.

Smith, Jeff (1987) 'Reagan, Star Wars, and American culture', *Bulletin of the Atomic Scientists* January/February: 19–25.

Smith, Merrit Roe, ed. (1985) *Military Enterprise and Technological Change*. Cambridge, MA: MIT Press.

Thompson, E. P. and Thompson, B. (1985) *Star Wars: Self-Destruct Incorporated*. London: Merlin.

United States: Congress, House Committee on Science and Technology (1984) *Japanese Technological Advances and Possible United States Responses Using Research Joint Ventures*. Congress, First Ninety-eighth session. 29, 30 June. Washington, DC: Government Printing Office.

———— Office of the Budget (1987) *The Benefits and Risks of Federal Funding for Sematech*. Washington, DC: Congressional Budget Office.

———— Office of Technology Assessment (1988) *SDI: Technology, Survivability and Software* Washington, DC: OTA.

———— Defense Advanced Research Projects Agency (1983) *Strategic Computing*. Washington, DC: DARPA.

———— Department of Defense (1988) *Discriminate Defense*. Report of the Commission on Integrated Long-Term Strategy, Fred C. Iklé and Albert Wohlstetter, co-chairmen, Washington, DC: GPO. January.

Webb, James H. Jr (1988) 'US military: strength through flexibility', *Wall Street Journal* 18 January.

Woodward, C. Vann (1987) 'The President – and us', *New York Times Book Review* 11 January.

5 ARTIFICIAL INTELLIGENCE, WISHFUL THINKING AND WAR

TOM ATHANASIOU

> Confronted with the unexpected and unaccepted unravelling of their short-lived empire, Americans are now clinging to their epic myths of national identity and destiny, hoping for yet another revival. And central to these myths is a collective fantasy of technological transcendence. Whatever the question, technology has typically been the ever-ready American answer.
> (Noble, 1984)

It has become almost tiresome to hear of 'advanced' US weapons systems that work poorly. The list is long: Divad, the easily evaded computerized anti-aircraft gun; Pershing, deployed without adequate guidance systems; Cruise, likewise unable to pass its flight tests; Awacs, pushed through Congress with faked demos and easily jammed; the Main Battle Tank (M-1), twice as expensive as its predecessor, with less range and twice the breakdown rate; the Aegis automatic-battle system, useless against low-flying missiles; the A-6, F-14 and F-18 aircraft; even the over-designed Hummer, which failed to replace the lowly Jeep; and the immensely failure-prone M-16 rifle.

Some of these weapons are quite low-tech, so the problem of their dysfunctionality (if indeed it is a problem) must involve more than the injudicious use of advanced technology. Still, the inappropriate reliance on high technology seems a common element in most recent weapons-system failures. And since technological exuberance characteristically takes its most extreme forms with regard to computer technology, so we should not be surprised to learn that many weapons systems currently in the development pipeline rely heavily on speculative computer technologies like artificial intelligence (AI).

Star Wars is such a system, as are the 'demonstration technologies' being patched together under DARPA's Strategic Computing Program (SCP). The services are establishing their own AI programs at a breakneck pace, setting up labs and dreaming of new 'brilliant' bombs, missiles, and C³I systems – some of their ideas are even wilder than those coming out of DARPA. Newsletters like *Advanced Military Computing* swarm with ideas for military AI applications. Eventually, weapons systems that incorporate AI technology may even be deployed. If and when they are, we can expect them to fail to work as intended.

It seems then, that the forces compelling the automation of war are something other than simply pragmatic and rational. Although they may have a certain strained logic, it comes in a rather perverse organizational and ideological package, as in the Star Wars initiative. And we should remember that the system that brought us Star Wars is far from exhausted.

ARTIFICIAL INTELLIGENCE GOES TO WAR

Though the term 'artificial intelligence' resounds with technological aspiration, AI programming techniques are closely related to those of other, less pretentious branches of computer science. All computer programs, AI programs included, consist of rules, precise rules written in unambiguous formal languages, and of mathematically encoded descriptions of objects, situations and relationships designed to be manipulated by those rules. AI programs are sometimes written in special languages (LISP, PROLOG or whatever), and they differ in structure from regular programs, but these differences are, at bottom, minor and stylistic. In general, what regular computer programs can't do – and there is much in this category – AI programs can't do either.

That we might think differently is testimony to a long tradition of hype and dreams. The very term 'artificial intelligence' was coined – in 1956 by John McCarthy – as a marketing ploy. McCarthy also invented the AI language LISP and helped to develop time-sharing, but his early move to replace terms like 'cognitive simulation' with the more flashy and fundable 'artificial intelligence' may well be his most crucial contribution to computer science.

AI's founders were unusually savvy in the positioning of their new enterprise. They looked far into the future, and refused to accept the limitations of their time. (Indeed, their impatience helped spur the development of more powerful and interactive computer systems.) They were ambitious and, from the very beginning, married to the military research agencies that had birthed computer technology – and whose budgets could alone support their research. Unfortunately, their flashiest projects consistently failed. The trouble started with one of the first major AI research programmes, which aimed at developing systems capable of automatically translating between 'natural' human languages (for example, between German and English). Machine translation turned out to be far more difficult than the AI optimists had imagined. By 1966 it was clear, to the National Research Council if not to the AI community, that further funding was futile.

Today, machine translation, along with machine vision, parallel programming, adaptive robotics and a variety of other AI subgoals, is recognized as beyond the capacities of existing techniques. The AI community, however, has more than survived; its government funding is at record levels. Accordingly, the goals of AI research are increasingly given in explicitly military terms – the Pentagon now seeks battle management instead of machine translation. This shift, it should be noted, is wholly inexplicable if, as is often claimed, the military's support for AI is simply an aspect of its support for high-tech research.

In fact, the US military is increasingly pursuing AI as a technology with real battlefield applications. The immediate roots of this shift can be found in three events, all of which occurred in the early 1980s:

> First, the Defense Department's advanced-research division came under Congressional fire. DARPA had been founded in 1958 to finance 'blue sky' research after Sputnik's launch fanned fears that the USA was losing its technological edge. But now Congress was grumbling that DARPA wasn't pursuing research that led to weapons the military could use.
>
> Second, in 1981 the Japanese Ministry of Trade and Industry unfurled an $850-million, ten-year Fifth-Generation Computer Project, a government-financed blitz to pioneer *commercial* uses for AI.
>
> Third, in March 1983, President Reagan said he wanted to build a computer-manned space dome over the USA. (Faludi, 1986)

The politics of military R&D, the dynamics of international technological competition, the delirium of Star Wars – all cast light on the dynamics of the AI buildup. In all this, Star Wars is the true sign of the times. Only marginally more practical than perpetual motion, it is nevertheless funded, and debated, as one rational option among others. And from the stream of Star Wars funding, the AI community has drawn much of its recent largess. This is perhaps as it should be, for the technological optimism of the AI community was a precursor to the Star Wars faith, and remains a key element of its litany.

This essay is not about Star Wars, but we cannot proceed without reference to it. (This, despite the fact that, with the West sinking into a deep fiscal crisis, the chances of Star Wars ever being built are slim.) Star Wars would require computerized battle-management systems for control, and the hope that AI will provide these systems has radically increased its cachet within the military. The debate over Star Wars, in its turn, has increased public awareness of military computerization, and of the hopes which military planners, even non-nuclear planners, have come to hold for magical high-tech solutions to their problems.

As Star Wars would require automated battle management, autonomous tanks would require machine vision, and computerized pilot's associates would require mechanized speech understanding. None of these capacities exists today, nor is there reason to believe that they'll be realized in the near future, yet all are being funded, researched and prototyped, and all are having their impacts on military doctrine.

In this AI is not so unique; the impact of technology on military doctrine is already great. Ballistic-missile defence, for example, would require hair-trigger responses and thus the decision – in fact if not in name – to 'take humans out of the loop'. The implications of such a development are quite frightening (witness the movie *War Games*) and, stated explicitly, the full automation of nuclear-fire control would be opposed even by military men and politicians. Yet crucial historical developments are seldom chosen explicitly, and it's difficult to imagine short-term political changes significant enough really to ease the pressure for automated nuclear response. Similarly, the pressure to automate non-nuclear battlefields is unlikely to abate, despite increasing awareness of the virtually intractable problems posed to computerization by chaotic battle environments.

There are many reasons for computerization in the military, just as there are for automation in the civilian economy. The cases differ considerably, to be sure, but in both the pressures of competition make it impossible, at the least very difficult, to slacken the pace of innovation. And warfare, like capitalist economic competition, is its own justification – technologies of survival and dominance are beyond price. The differences, of course, are equally crucial, especially in the nuclear age, where weapons are built to brandish, and not to use.

RESEARCH, DEVELOPMENT, DELUSION

For various reasons the Pentagon is not very good at developing complex weapons. The fault lies not in the nature of military men but in the circumstances in which they work. The test of the marketplace does not exist. If a civilian company makes a poor product, no one buys the thing, whereupon the engineers fix it so as to remain employed. If a weapon performs poorly, nothing happens until the war, which no one expects anyway... Star Wars will be particularly prone to this sort of thing because it will be secret and, unlike a fighter plane, won't be flown by hundreds of pilots who would notice if the wings fell off. (Reed, 1986, p. 44)

The extent of current military support for AI is quite startling. The Strategic Computing Program alone has already quadrupled the annual Federal funding for AI R&D, and if the five-year Program is extended, the Pentagon will have spent $1 billion on AI by the end of the decade. The SDI office is spending another $200 million per year on the Star Wars battle-manager, and then there are the dozens of AI programs being run directly by the services.

Most of this is new, the result of initiatives that began after the Japanese launched their drive to build 'fifth-generation' computers and the subsequent flurry of concern over a Japanese threat to the nascent American AI industry. Indeed, the SCP is often defended – by computer scientists uneasy at seeing their field become dominated by the military – as a covert, even enlightened, means of supporting advanced computational research. And though it may be exaggerated to claim 'enlightenment' for a military-managed industrial policy based exclusively on advanced technology, there certainly are those within DARPA who hope for commercial spin-offs, and who doubt that they'll see real robot tanks in the near future (Athanasiou, 1987).

This is a dangerous game. Today, about 75 percent of the USA's computer-science research is funded by the Pentagon, nearly double the level of ten years ago. The military has made an immense commitment to AI, and thus AI thrives. As Gary Martins, former manager of advanced software R&D at the Rand Corporation, recently put it: 'When DOD takes a big bag of money and paints "AI" on it, this instantly creates a lot of believers in artificial intelligence' (Martins, 1986). It does not, however, create a working technology where there is mainly smoke and mirrors.

AI boosters often point to the turn towards 'practicality' that characterized their industry during the early eighties. Then, AI entrepreneurs were only too happy to turn away from the 'overclaiming' of their academic brethren, and to focus on the fat profits to be made selling so-called 'expert' systems. Such systems, however, are truly successful in only narrowly limited areas, and the boom years of commercial AI inevitably ended. Commercial AI stocks dropped hard in early 1986, and haven't been the same since. Meanwhile, the Pentagon, never noted for its ability to adapt to new conditions, has increased funding for AI. In Martins's words: 'Four years ago, AI was going to conquer the world, and the SCP was its lift-off booster. Today, SCP is frankly described by its own managers as a vehicle for nurturing the faltering AI industry.'

The Japanese initiated their Fifth-Generation Computer Project with an uncharacteristic publicity blitz. Or, perhaps, the blitz was not theirs at all, but Edward Feigenbaum's, who used the Japanese Fifth Generation as his foil in a well-publicized book by the same name. Feigenbaum, professor of computer science at Stanford, AI entrepreneur and one of AI's most tireless backers, wrote his screed – subtitled 'AI and Japan's Computer Challenge to the World' – as a means of promoting US research. In this, he certainly succeeded.

Today, the SCP, America's militaristic response to the Japanese, has taken on a life of its own. In the vicissitudes of US politics, the economic threat from Japan conveniently alternates with the supposed military threat from the USSR. It's clear that, commercially viable or not, AI will be subsidized by way of the military budget.

In the interim, and in marked contrast to events in the USA, Japan's AI managers have come to regret the publicity with which their research was launched. According to Mike Harrison, editor of *Future Generation Computer Systems*, the Fifth Generation project was 'overhyped' and 'is not delivering breakthroughs and surprises'. SRI's Frank Kuo, who tracks the Japanese research rather closely, describes a project which has been adapted to the needs of the civilian economy: 'The blue-sky days were some years ago; now the project is oriented towards a far more limited set of goals.' What goals? To 'find viable commercial applications' (which have proven elusive) and to 'establish AI programming languages and techniques' in Japan.

The technological demands of Star Wars and the SCP prototypes are, everyone agrees, beyond the capacities of present-generation computer technology. What everyone does not agree about is whether a major R&D programme can reasonably be expected to produce the theoretical and technological advances necessary to make such systems workable, and to produce them on schedule in the near future. This question, like all such questions about advanced technology, is immediately complicated by politics, hype and strategic deception. DARPA officials, for example, are compelled by the exigencies of their relations with Congress to at least say they believe that their talking jets and computerized battle-managers will soon be practical. And with the bulk of the AI community now slurping from the SDI/SCP pork-barrel, few rise to contradict them.

AI's critics are up against more than money and ambition; they face as well the challenge of convincing a nation of technological optimists that, this time, a crash development programme will not make the difference. The optimists, contemptuous of such defeatism, point to their successes, the Manhattan Project and the race to the moon. It's left to the critics to split hairs, to argue that atomic bombs are relatively easy to build, to explain that when President Kennedy declared that we would stand on the moon in a decade, NASA scientists already knew how to get there, and that only engineering problems remained. When DARPA's Robert Cooper declared that autonomous machines would tour battlefields in only five years, the situation was different: his predictions rested not on scientific theory, but on an ideological commitment to advanced technology. Knowing new theory to be necessary, he based his prediction on what DARPA officials now call 'scheduled breakthroughs'.

Unfortunately, AI researchers have been striving to make these breakthroughs since the 1950s, and they have never met their schedules. Progress has been narrow and piecemeal, and is best characterized as learning how to make do with the limited techniques that have proved workable. The situation is not analogous to, say, the design of ever more complex integrated circuits or statistical data-processing techniques; in both these cases, basic theory is understood and hence rapid improvements can be reliably predicted, provided only that steady money is made available. Current AI theory does not work, and huge amounts of money will only obscure the fact that progress is not being made.

THE LIMITS OF COMPUTATION

The autonomous land vehicle project resulted in the construction of a handsome test track and a huge, lumbering van stuffed with computers running expert-systems software. If it travels slowly enough (under 3 miles per hour), the van is sometimes able to make it all the way around the brightly lit, carefully marked, optically smooth course without serious mishap...

The pilot's associate project aims to produce a refrigerator-sized computing system, having functionality comparable to a 3-inch by 5-inch checklist card, to remind future F-16 pilots of the obvious. (Martins, 1986)

Nothing is more common, in the AI debate, than the claim that advances in computer technology will lead to a thousandfold increase in computer speed, and, in so doing, make qualitatively new kinds of software possible. In fact, one of the real goals of the SCP is to produce high-speed computers containing dozens, if not thousands, of processing elements. These computers will, so their proponents claim, decompose problems into smaller subproblems, each of which will be allocated its own processor. The subproblems will then be solved simultaneously, in parallel, and their results aggregated to yield final answers at lightning speed.

About fifty such machines, of various kinds, already exist or are being built. Unfortunately, no one has any idea how to program them. The wrinkle, as always, is software, a wrinkle which parallel machines just worsen by introducing the problem, some would say the impossibility, of automating the process by which arbitrary problems can be fruitfully presented to multiple processors. Once again, reality intrudes on the artificial intelligentsia – since problems must be understood before they can be decomposed into little pieces, run, and recomposed into a final result, machines cannot do the job themselves. Everything, every little thing, still must be specified in advance.

The limits on AI are ultimately imposed not by the limits of hardware, but by the nature of computer programs themselves. Like regular programs, AI programs are collections of statements in formal computer languages. These statements are not about the real open-ended world, where the wars of the future will be fought, but about artificially tidy worlds – 'microworlds' or 'toy worlds' in the AI lexicon – as they have been constructed by computer programmers. AI programs do not 'understand' what they do, they just make the manoeuvres they've been told to make. They have only the stiffest kind of 'surface knowledge' and their reasoning mechanisms, such as they are, are limited to the straightforward channels of logical inference.

Teknowledge, a large commercial AI firm, has a toy system which demonstrates the flavour of such mechanical reasoning. Called Wine-Advisor, it solves one of the most vexing problems of modern life: what should we drink? Wine-Advisor asks what you're having for dinner and then uses its rules to select an appropriate wine. *If* fish *then* white wine, and so on.

DARPA's battle-management systems will work in essentially the same way. They may have more rules in their 'knowledge bases' than does Wine-Advisor, they may run on faster machines and have fancier user interfaces, but they will proceed by way of the same basic process of 'structured selection'. They may cost billions, but they'll still be trapped in special-purpose microworlds, microworlds only as complete, consistent and bug-free as their programmer creators made them.

These matters may be rather abstract, but they have been noticed in Washington, at a late 1986 DARPA meeting on automatic planning systems. There, one after another, AI researchers spoke of the so-called Block's World: 'How do you get a program to put block B on block C when block B is already under block A?' According to one AI researcher, 'The government folks who called the meeting were beginning to get very disturbed.' As well they should, for classical AI is at a dead end. Knowledge systems simply can't cope with the complexity of the real world: they can't learn, break their own rules or determine for themselves the relevance of new information. They can't know the limits of their own knowledge, nor can they reorganize it. They can't understand natural human language, and they can't see.

Even within well-structured microworlds, computer programs don't always do as well as humans. We might expect, for example, that the procedures necessary for playing good chess would be more easily automated than the procedures necessary for, say, diagnosing illnesses – for the world of chess is completely specified by a finite and well-defined set of rules and descriptive features. We would be wrong, however, if we inferred from the formal tidiness of the chess world that the cognitive activities of expert chess players were of necessity tidy as well, and thus amenable to formal specification. In fact, years of research into chess have failed to reveal the mechanisms by which human experts operate, though they have indicated that these mechanisms are qualitatively different from those used in chess-playing computers. And, not incidentally, they have failed as well to produce a machine that can defeat the best human players (Dreyfus, 1986).

There is, of course, always the possibility of a theoretical breakthrough. For the last decade or so, the great hope has been parallel computing, but now that its problems are becoming known, its lustre has begun to fade. Fortunately, a new great hope has emerged, one known as 'connectionism' or 'neurocomputing'. Here an attempt is made to design circuits that emulate neural networks, and to 'teach' these circuits to perform pattern-recognition tasks that have eluded traditional AI logic machines.

Connectionism has had some surprising successes, but it's simply too new to evaluate. Clearly, it differs fundamentally from traditional AI, and must be judged on its own terms. In the words of Stanford computer scientist Terry Winograd, an AI pioneer who has since abandoned the field, 'There's something in those tea leaves.' Connectionism may even lead, as some of its developers hope, to workable machine-vision systems. A bit of scepticism, however, is still in order – 60 percent of the human brain is involved, by some estimates, with vision. It will be a long time before connection machines can duplicate the functionality of that much grey matter.

Connectionism may improve pattern-recognition technology, but it will not make automated battle management possible. Humans inhabit an unstructured world of goals, actions and chance events; machines are trapped in tidy spaces of number, fact and logic. They can never know the real physical and social worlds, the worlds of accidents, tensions and battlefield chaos. They cannot reason about the nature, purpose and destination of previously unknown objects, nor can they reason about the intentions of an adversary. They can't use analogy to adapt existing plans to new situations.

This is not to say that an AI-based battle-manager couldn't be built. However, it would be a special-purpose system unable to cope with unforeseen circumstances. A Star Wars manager could, for example, be built by souping up existing expert-systems technology: it would be inflexible, unreliable and dangerous, but it could be built.

War is not a predictable, programmable activity. For this simple reason we can safely predict that computerized battle-management will never really work. That this is not immediately obvious to Pentagon planners is a sign that, under the spell of their organizational and ideological imperatives, they have forgotten what Clausewitz called 'friction' – the difference between plans and reality, between war as it's imagined and war as it actually occurs. Clausewitz already understood, in the early 1800s, the reasons for the impossibility of automated battle-management:

As long as we have no personal knowledge of War, we cannot conceive where the difficulties lie. All appears so simple, all the requisite branches of knowledge appear so plain, all the combinations so unimportant...

Everything is very simple in War, but the simplest thing is difficult. These difficulties accumulate and produce a friction which no man can imagine exactly who has not seen War. Suppose now a traveller, who towards evening expects to accomplish the two stages at the end of his day's journey, four or five leagues, with post-horses, on the high road – it is nothing. He arrives now at the last station but one, finds no horses, or very bad ones; then a hilly country, bad roads; it is a dark night, and he is glad when, after a great deal of trouble, he reaches the next station and finds there some miserable accommodation. So in War, through the influence of an infinity of petty circumstances, which cannot properly be described on paper, things disappoint us and we fall short of the mark. (From Clausewitz, *On War*, quoted in Fallows, 1981, p. 17)

'Friction', said Clausewitz, 'is the only conception which in a general way... distinguishes War from War on paper.' In other words, 'friction' is a military view of the unpredictability that characterizes all human activity, an unpredictability with which machines lack the ability to cope. It is, then, as important a concept for today's technobureaucratic officers as it was for the Prussian cavalry officers whom Clausewitz was addressing.

SO WHY THE DRIVE TO AUTOMATE WAR?
Evacuation of dead and wounded could also be accomplished by robotic vehicles similar to those which provide urgent logistical support to close combat forces. When evacuating dead, these vehicles, programmed to designated close combat units, could be loaded and by merely activating a switch dispatched to the nearest mortuary. (Crumley, 1982, p. 20)

From my point of view, Strategic Computing is already a success. We've got the money. (Mizell, 1985)

Any catalogue of military technology initiatives quickly overflows with absurdity. Even the Star Wars movies didn't relegate the actual battles to machines, yet the Reagan administration proposes SDI, inconceivable without almost total automation, as a means of seizing the moral high ground in the arms-control debate. The Autonomous Land Vehicle is confused by breezes blowing across its manicured test track, yet military planners still speak of battlefield robots as 'force multipliers' for the short-handed, post-baby-boom army of the not-too-distant future. Robots will even, by some accounts, collect the human dead.

Are these serious proposals? Are they even serious fantasies? Is it simply that fantasy pays well? Has the weapons procurement process become so corrupt that military planners no longer care if their schemes work? Are military planners enthralled by the same industrial models that lead civilian managers through their automation planning? Or is there a method to the madness? Are there real military and political benefits to be gained by pushing military technologies that cannot reasonably be expected to work?

Such questions are difficult to answer well. There are many reasons, and many kinds of reasons, for military technological excess. Some are rooted in the structure of military organizations, others are characteristic of capitalist society, still others grow from the deep past of the scientific culture. Some are common to the civilian and military worlds, some distinctly martial. Some reduce to ideology, some to fantasy, some to ambition, some to *realpolitik*. In the end, it's possible only to give many reasons, and to gesture at those which may be key. This strategy may seem odd, for the organizations and ideologies within which military technologies are created cannot be separated from the larger society, and in seeking to explain the automation of war, too much else may be hinted at as well. This is, however, the nature of the case.

In any event, a number of interlocking sets of factors can be distinguished within the tangle, all linked together by the interlocked civilian, governmental and military interests that are the post-World World II American military apparatus.

Ideological factors

George Lucas, an admirer of mythologist Joseph Campbell, intended his Star Wars saga as, in part, a high-tech version of the ancient myth of passage into manhood. President Reagan, adrift in different myths, saw it differently.

In 1940, Reagan starred in *Murder in the Air*, a B-movie pot-boiler which featured a proto-SDI secret weapon called the Inertia Projector, with mysterious rays capable of destroying enemy aircraft from miles away. Years later, it seems fair to conclude, his memory of this film returned buried in an eagerness for ballistic-missile defence. Yet one man's decline into senility cannot explain the Reagan-era emergence of the Star Wars faith. Here, we have to look at the opportunism of the ideological apparatus, and at the problems which Star Wars helped the Right to solve.

We should not forget that the peace movement was doing well, and the Reagan administration was suffering from images of bellicosity, when Star Wars first emerged as a major governmental initiative. It allowed the Right to seize the moral high ground with one magnificent stroke. SDI would be a 'defensive' system, one that hard-headed politicians could counterpoise to the irresponsible idealism of the peaceniks. It would serve as well as any tank or fighter as a vehicle for the military Keynesianism that sustains the US economy. It would serve, too, as a bulwark against the rising pressures for arms control, for it would be a 'weapon of peace', not of war. In this it was tailor-made as a vehicle for imperial ideology, which always prefers the role of 'defender' – witness the US 'defence' of South Vietnam, or the Soviet 'defence' of Afghanistan.

Star Wars could exist as such an ideological master-stroke only because, as a vehicle for the technological transcendence of a social crisis – in this case the nuclear arms race – it was easily dovetailed into a pre-existing ideological and political strategy. The mobilization for technological omnipotence is a role well established in the anti-Communist soap-opera that dominates US politics, as is the device by which the exaggeration of Soviet military strength is used to justify ever more military technology as a means of 'catching up' with the USSR. And it was easy to frame the debate over Star Wars in technological terms: to be taken seriously as an anti-SDI critic, it helped to have a PhD in computer science.

Technological factors

It is important to realize that high-technology systems are often perceived, by their promoters, as absolutely necessary. This is especially true of military systems, which develop within the closed dynamics of competitive arms races, but it is also true of advanced technology in general, and AI systems in particular. These systems tend to be justified as means of coping with the exploding 'complexity' engendered by earlier generations of technology, a complexity which traditional computer technology has failed to contain. In this sense, AI systems are explicitly conceived as technical fixes, albeit technical fixes of a rather extreme variety.

Technofixes usually fail. That is to say, they usually displace problems rather than solve them. Yet for this very reason, they can be politically expedient. Technological problems invariably reflect social problems, and managers rarely possess either the will or the inclination to address social problems at their roots. Technofixes can buy time, and thus help avoid facing politically and ideologically unacceptable realities. Hair-trigger nuclear systems, for example, have made world war too dangerous to be used as a routine instrument of policy – even as new explosives and delivery systems have made limited war complex, chaotic and deadly beyond all precedent. On the high-tech battlefield, too much happens too fast for humans to exercise any real control over it. AI holds out the possibility of business as usual: robots will augment humans on the terrestrial battlefield; AI systems will command space. Everything will change, that it might stay the same.

According to Steve Sloan, a retired naval captain, now an assistant professor of government at St Mary's College and a careful student of the military:

The thing that's unique about AI is the way it fits into the modern battlefield environment, where things happen very fast and where attack comes simultaneously from many different directions. Battle is just too fast, and involves too many events. The desire for machines that can make it manageable is great.

Thus the military's insatiable desire for AI image-processing, sensor-fusion and battle-support systems able, in the words of one representative report, to 'assist human operators in targeting, navigation, and situation assessment functions, and to replace the human under high vulnerability or weight/volume constrained conditions'. As Sloan says,

> Maybe the real danger of AI is that the desire to know what can't be known makes you vulnerable to the snake-oil salesmen. If you have cancer and someone tells you they have a cure, you're going to believe them. And, in battle, the information explosion is cancer.

Organizational factors

Whenever Reagan's confusion of wish with reality has been noted, it's usually assumed that, in this, he has been atypical. In fact, the military R&D process – with its inter-service rivalry, classified testing procedures, cost-plus contracting and career-sensitive development paths – encourages a systematic confusion between technological fantasy and serious research, as any objective evaluation of the SCP funding process would show.

Defenders of the high-tech faith argue that the military has a responsibility to fund fringe technology and basic research, that DARPA is America's MITI, its key to global economic competitiveness. Perhaps, but this does not explain the confusion between cutting-edge research and the sophistic hype that characterize the AI community.

Again, Star Wars is a fine example – this time of the ways in which organizational forces generate systematically distorted analysis of controversial weapons systems. There's a great deal of opposition to it within the military, some very strongly held. Yet, when the disputes go public, they are softened by institutional *realpolitik*. Everyone in the Pentagon knows that calling Reagan's programme lunatic is not the optimum in career management.

Once impelled into motion by politicians or contractors, peacetime weapons programmes are dragged along by bureaucratic inertia. How many programme managers, confronted with the evidence of rot and corruption, will speak up and risk their own careers? What are the incentives to do so? If it's early in a programme, they'll answer critics by saying it is too early to tell what will happen. If it's late, they'll plead not to waste the money that has already been spent. With AI, of course, it's always too early.

Scientists and engineers can be very cynical about all this. It's not really that difficult to find scientists who admit to laughing when they get military AI grants, but who gladly take the money. They do so because they need the jobs, support the research goals, hope for civilian spin-offs, because working on military-funded projects can be exciting, and because the whole system seems so inexorable and corrupt that it seems pointless to apply everyday ethical standards on the job.

Economic factors

AI would not be what it is today without its military subsidies, and it wouldn't receive those subsidies if the great bulk of public R&D money were not controlled by the military bureaucracy. It's no accident that the USA, with an economy structured by the desires of the military, is the home of the most overreaching and impractical AI projects in the world. In Japan, where the post-World War II industrial culture is oriented not to military production but to old-fashioned production for private consumption, computer science is more practical and less dangerous.

The high-tech sector isn't evolving in a vacuum; it's the whole US economy that is growing stiffer and more dependent on military Keynesianism. The high-tech sector, in particular, is coming to bear a more than passing resemblance to its counterpart in the Soviet Union. It's by now a quasi-civilian extension of the military State, in which ideological, bureaucratic and political forces take the lead in determining research priorities and development paths. Certainly the details differ; the USSR, for example, has no precise equivalent to the cost-plus contract. But the basic dynamics are remarkably similar. So we shouldn't be surprised if US bureaucracies prove to be almost as incompetent as Soviet ones.

Geopolitical factors

There are often real political advantages to technological posturing. Star Wars, and by extension, AI, seem almost designed to prove that crackpot ideas can serve real political masters. The clearest case in the whole sleazy saga probably began in late 1986, when Secretary of Defense Weinberger made a push for the deployment of 'early generation' SDI systems that no competent observer believed would work. Still, Weinberger seriously proposed their deployment, with the aim of undercutting the ABM treaty and increasing SDI's budget-item momentum.

The Pershing II story is similar. Unable to pass its flight tests, it was nevertheless deployed, with the immediate geopolitical benefits of strengthening Nato and demoralizing the European peace movement. Nato planners knew the Pershings didn't have to work as advertised to be useful to them – as a palpable symbol of nuclear brinkmanship, they served to cement the Cold War system and keep the Iron Curtain closed, as the Americans wished. The peace movement, for its part, tended to take official claims about the Pershing's accuracy at face value. Reports of its failed tests were available enough, but their significance failed to be appreciated against the larger terror of the nuclear arms race. In this the peace movement was not entirely unjustified – some of the Pershings would work, not as well as advertised but well enough to add instability to an already shaky configuration of forces. Besides, there was always the possibility that the generals would believe their own propaganda, and attempt to use the Pershings as first-strike missiles.

Military factors

This last point is crucial. High-tech systems can be militarily useful even if they fail to meet their original design objectives. Military power is a relative thing, always conditioned by the strength of the opposing force, the morale of the population and the nature of the battlefield. Air-to-ground missiles, justified as necessary to defend against Soviet tank attacks in Eastern Europe, will almost certainly not work as well in reality as they do on the drawing-board. Still, they'll be effective enough, especially when used not against the Soviets but against the Third World.

Military systems can be dangerous even when they don't work much at all. This is especially true at the nuclear level, where threats and posturing are of greater immediate significance than actual force. And high-tech systems, fragile and unreliable though they be, still have an impact on doctrine and planning, sometimes in destabilizing ways. Star Wars, the obvious example, has fed the atavistic military desire to see nuclear war as survivable, as a kind of war that can be 'fought' and 'won'.

In the end, many forces compel military automation. The military hopes that advanced technology will allow it to pursue its ever-widening agenda; the civilian polity, committed to the same agenda and the same high-tech faith, cannot effectively oppose it. The AI/high-tech solution is popular because it solves, or seems to solve, so many problems, and to do so without rocking the boat. Managers, civilian and military, love their dreams of automation; AI assures them that they may keep dreaming. Technologists love their toys; AI buys them billion-dollar sand-boxes. Politicians love their easy answers; AI grants them their mystic defence shields. All this and cost-plus contracts too!

MILITARISM AND MILITARY REALISM

Every war is fought, every army is maintained in a military way and in a militaristic way. The distinction is fundamental and fateful. The military way is marked by a primary concentration of men and materials on winning specific objectives... It is limited in scope, confined to one function, and scientific in its essential qualities.

Militarism, on the other hand, presents a vast array of customs, interests, prestige, actions and thoughts associated with armies and wars and yet transcending true military purposes. Indeed militarism is so constituted that it may hamper and defeat the purposes of the military way. Its influence is unlimited in scope. It may permeate all society and become dominant over all industry and arts. Rejecting the scientific character of the military way, militarism displays the qualities of caste and cult, authority and belief. (Vagts, 1967)

Mark Stefik, a senior scientist at Xerox's Palo Alto Research Center, is not worried about the deployment of unworkable military AI systems. In an overview of the Strategic Computing Program, he notes that:

Although the Strategic Computing Program may have seemed like a cover story to academics in its preliminary planning stages . . . it appears that DARPA takes the program quite seriously as stated.

But he then goes on to assert:

The alleged 'overselling' of machine-intelligence technology to the military is an issue vis-à-vis technology that the military contends with all the time. Furthermore, there are technological conservatives in the military that provide perspective and a balancing caution . . . Too many promising new things have been tried and broken down at critical times in completely unexpected ways; and whenever a weapon fails, the news sweeps through the military community. (Stefik, 1985)

In Stefik's view, the government and military as a whole are less technologically enthusiastic than DARPA. Faced with evidence of DARPA's excesses of zeal – for example chief Robert Cooper's 1984 Congressional testimony that 'We might have the technology so that the President couldn't make a mistake' – Stefik might regret the extravagance. But it's safe to assume that he would cite the subsequent anger of Cooper's Congressional critics as evidence that technological conservatism is alive and well in the government.

Alive and well it may be, but can it stand before the complex of forces, outlined above, that compel faith in high-tech warfare? The brute fact is that, despite the road-blocks put before it by conservatives, technology has come to dominate military affairs. This has occurred in the conventional arsenal, where planners have been unable to resist the desire for 'technological leverage', and it has occurred in the nuclear arsenal, where launch control has shifted, by virtue of a sort of technobureaucratic drift, from humans to machines. Thus, while we can accept the assertion that DARPA's zealotry is uncharacteristic of the military establishment as a whole, it's

difficult to agree that the military is, on balance, technologically conservative. We need a more precise and more specific understanding of the conservative forces in the military, and of their standing in relation to the forces which compel not only technological excess, but military excess as well.

According to Steve Sloan, there is, indeed, a great deal of resistance to computerization within the military, at least within the Navy. His research shows how this resistance extends from the ship's bridge to its air-traffic control tower and reactor room. Sloan recounts his experiences on the USS *Carl Vinson*, the newest of the US Navy's nuclear carriers:

Captain Good [*sic*] explained that he could run the ship from his seat on the bridge assisted by various installed computer systems. He could call up color pictures of various charts of the world... By using the Spatial Data Management System, which was still in the process of development,

Good might look at a display of the tactical picture. This would include friendly forces as well as whatever was known about a threat in the area. Captain Good could also read various schedules or any other information programmed into ZOG [an AI information management system], potentially the specification of all tasks on the ship... Having demonstrated the use of the computerized Commanding Officer's station on the bridge of the ship, Good made the comment that he 'did not use this stuff much, if at all.' In fact he never turned on the equipment described.

Sloan locates the source of the military's technological conservatism in what he calls 'professionalism' and bases his analysis on the operational demands of ship duty (as opposed to shore duty). He agrees that the military can be technologically conservative, but he adds an all-important proviso. Military organizations, according to Sloan, are conservative only to the extent that they concern themselves with operational tasks: delivering bombs, flying planes, communicating with distant ships. Shore organizations are largely spared such real-world concerns, and within their dominion the dynamics of cash and power overcome the logic of military effectiveness. Success, in shore organizations, depends first of all on spending money.

For Sloan, it's not the military, but the operational military – where 'some "rubber" meets some "road"' – that has the good sense to be conservative. And since the concerns of the military power structure are more political and bureaucratic than practical, he thinks such good sense unlikely to prevail at the higher levels of the military hierarchy. In the strategic nuclear area, where encounters with the real world are mediated by stage-managed tests and computer simulation, the odds against realism are steep indeed.

Not that there aren't some signs of realism within the non-operational military. The 'military reform' movement of recent years has raised the critique of military technological excess in both volume and sophistication. As far as AI itself goes, the grumbling has definitely increased. *Advanced Military Computing* abounds with articles like 'Overhype Bad for AI, Says Expert', 'AI Not Ready for Electronic Warfare' and 'Are AI Market Forecasts Accurate?' Even Lt-Col. Robert Simpson, head of expert-system funding at DARPA, has, on occasion, played the critic, though his criticism has been limited to distinguishing 'knowledge' systems (which he considers workable) from 'expert' systems (which even he admits cannot match the abilities of human experts).

Any officer will resist computer systems that he perceives as threatening his autonomy, or as endangering his ability to carry out his tasks. However, the simple fact of such resistance does not imply its eventual success. Likewise, the pressure to bring the military budget under control will strengthen the case of the military reformers, but it's still difficult to imagine their case carrying the day. In the end, the question is simple enough. Will internal military dynamics like Sloan's 'professionalism' succeed in undercutting the pressure to rely ever more heavily on advanced technology? It seems unlikely.

The ultimate source of military technological excess, like military excess in general, is that we find too many uses for military power. The 'American century', that short post-World War II time of American industrial and atomic monopoly, lasted barely ten years. Yet there are those in the military, as in government, who see in advanced computer technology a chance to re-establish it. Whatever compelling, nuanced cases we may make against placing faith in machine intelligence, they are confident that, even if AI itself remains elusive, its pursuit will generate spin-offs of military benefit. Without technological leverage, the American military cannot hope to pursue their global aspirations. For this reason alone, and against all logic to the contrary, military planners will remain committed to their high-tech pursuits.

MILITARIST THREAT

There is no technological reason why the Pentagon should not achieve its goal of an automated battlefield (Barnaby, 1986)

The peace people, like people on the left, tend to disbelieve everything that they read in military journals except the ads. They have a touching faith in high technology. (Cockburn, personal communication, 1987)

The immediate danger, as Star Wars has shown, is the emergence of a military policy based upon corruption and hype. But, in the end, the danger is militarism, as it draws together and crystallizes economic, institutional, technological and ideological elements of American society. It is militarism, 'a vast array of customs, interests, prestige, actions and thoughts', that made AI into the financially viable enterprise it is today, and it is with militarism that we conclude this essay.

Military technologies are always shaped to political purposes; critiques of them which abstract their technical properties (how well they work) from their institutional matrices must necessarily fail. Advanced military technology is ridden with the consequences of wishful thinking, but it will not do to criticize it on this ground alone. The pressure to continually expand the capacities of weapons systems, a pressure that ultimately manifests itself in the search for robot soldiers, reflects first of all the logic of the overall military project, that is, the logic of empire. Ultimately, it is that logic which lies behind the receptive hearings that the high-tech dreamers receive in the halls of power.

How could this change? Consider a world in which the real purpose, as opposed to the ideological purpose, of American military power was defence. What shape would a military apparatus appropriate to defence take? Would advanced technologies be crucial to it? Would dreams of computerized perfection corrupt it?

This is no idle thought experiment. There is a mounting body of theory relating to non-provocative military strategy, and a widespread suspicion that, in the high-technology age, the military edge is shifting to the defence. For example, it's now clearly possible to equip territorial defence forces with cheap, yet extremely formidable precision-guided missile systems designed to help prevent invasions by radically increasing their costs. Such territorial defence would, in effect, be designed as forces of defensive deterrence (Evangelista, 1983).

Scepticism is certainly in order here, but not dismissal. Obviously, there can be no defence against nuclear ICBMs, but nuclear ICBMs are only the last, and perhaps the least usable, tools of military intimidation. 'Alternative defence' strategy, which seeks to appropriate new military technologies for the cause of peace, is an important, and welcome, addition to the disarmament debate. It seeks realism, and realism in these matters cannot be overvalued.

Unfortunately, realism is not the only current flowing in these waters. Alternative defence makes much of technology, and in so doing, it seems to make itself vulnerable to the same sorts of technological optimism that stalk the halls of DARPA. Frank Barnaby has demonstrated as much. Barnaby, a former director of the Stockholm International Peace Research Institute and now co-director of Just Defence, recently published *The Automated Battlefield*, in which he predicted that all SCP goals would soon be realized, that AI will be 'much used in military decision making', that autonomous robots able to 'not only walk but also climb, hang, swim and roll' will soon be used by the military 'for reconnaissance and surveillance, transporting ammunition, sentry duty and clearing mines'.

Barnaby's concern is for peace and, given the chance, he would abolish military robots with invasion armies and nuclear missiles. He argues at length that computerized missile technology has changed the realities of defence and offence, made tanks and aircraft-carriers obsolete and expanded the importance of territorial defence. He makes this argument to legitimize defensive deterrence and thus to promote peace. Unfortunately, his logic is too tidy. It carries him along to a land where every missile, every computer, every sensor, works as advertised. In a time when the dysfunctionality of advanced military hardware is a matter for opinion-editorial pages and jokes, Barnaby's techno-optimism serves as an embarrassment and a warning.

Technology has a role to play in opening paths out of the militarist maze, but its role is not the central one, and we should not exaggerate its potential. Defensive military strategies and their associated tools, important though they may be, cannot substitute for the social and political changes which must underlie any real movement away from the militarist brink. Technology cannot solve the problems of the Star Warriors; neither can it solve the problems of the peace movement.

Yet surely talk of an end to militarism is hopelessly Utopian. Has it not become difficult to take meaningful social change, and even diplomacy, seriously? Indeed it has, but we must remember that realism, in the nuclear age, has become crackpot realism, and that if it has become Utopian to hope for change, it has become quite impossible to believe that matters can continue in their present course without eventual catastrophe.

REFERENCES

Athanasiou, Thomas (1987) 'High-tech politics: the case of artificial intelligence', *Socialist Review* 92.

Barnaby, Frank (1986) *The Automated Battlefield*. New York: Free Press.

Cockburn, Andrew (1983) *The Threat: Inside the Soviet Military Machine*. New York: Vintage.

Crumley, Dennis V. (1982) *Concepts for Army Use of Robotic-AI in the 21st Century*. US Army War College Strategic Studies Institute, Futures/Long-Range Planning Group. 1 June.

Dreyfus, Hubert and Drefus, Stuart (1986) *Mind over Machine*. New York: Free Press.

Evangelista, Matthew A. (1983) 'Offense or defense: a tale of two commissions', *World Policy Journal* Fall.

Fallows, James (1981) *National Defense*. New York: Vintage.

Faludi, Susan (1986) 'The billion dollar toy box', *San Jose Mercury News West Magazine* 23 November.

Feigenbaum, E. and McCorduck, P. (1983) *The Fifth Generation: Artificial Intelligence and Japan's Computer Challenge to the World*. London: Michael Joseph.

Martins, Gary R. (1986) 'AI: the technology that wasn't', *Defense Electronics* December.

Mizell, David (1985) Talk at a conference on SCI organized by the Silicon Valley Research Group.

Noble, David (1984) *The Forces of Production*. New York: Knopf.

Reed, Fred (1986) 'The Star Wars swindle – hawking nuclear snake oil', *Harper's* May.

Sloan, Steven (n.d.) 'Organizations as communities of professionals'. Unpublished PhD dissertation, Department of Political Science, University of California, Berkeley.

Stefik, Mark (1985) 'Strategic computing at DARPA: overview and assessment', *Communications of the ACM* July.

Vagts, Alfred (1967) *History of Militarism*. New York: Free Press.

6 THE CLOSED WORLD
Systems discourse, military policy and post-World War II US historical consciousness

PAUL N. EDWARDS

Until the early 1960s, the US armed forces were the single most important influence on the development of digital computers. Their research organizations, both public and private, sponsored technical progress. Military use of many kinds of computer systems provided both a proving ground and a market-place. In this essay I argue that these computer systems formed a support for the USA's dominant post-war ideology and military policies, through a closed-world discourse whose profound effects persist today.

After the emergence of mature commerical computer markets by about 1960, US military and other agencies continued to invest heavily in advanced computer research, equipment and software. Artificial intelligence (AI) was nurtured by the Advanced Research Projects Agency (ARPA, now called DARPA) throughout the 1960s and 1970s. ARPA also supported such other important innovations as time-sharing and large-scale computer networks. During those decades, however, the Department of Defence (DOD) allowed commercial manufacturers and independent university researchers to take the lead in most areas of computer R&D. In the early 1980s, even relatively esoteric AI began to find major backing in the commercial world. Starting in 1983, with the Strategic Computing Initiative and the Strategic Defense Initiative, the Pentagon began a deliberate attempt to regain control over certain critical fields of leading-edge computer research in America, and to guide them in particular directions favourable to its own larger goals (Edwards and Gordon, forthcoming; Flamm, 1987).

Why has the American military maintained such a deep and intimate involvement with computer research? The most obvious answer is that computers are simply the right tools for important military tasks. The speed and complexity of high-technology warfare have created control, communications, and information demands that completely defy the capacities of unassisted human beings (Forrester, 1962). Computers improved military systems by 'getting man out of the loop' of critical tasks – tracking the enemy, analysing data from remote electronic sensors, piloting missiles, handling complicated command-control-communications-intelligence (C^3I) networks, and many others.

On the whole, computerized systems have been highly beneficial in military terms. They act as 'force multipliers', reducing the numbers of necessary combat personnel. In general, computers have limited rather than expanded the chances for human error, made possible more sophisticated and accurate intelligence information, and increased military capacities for speed and co-ordination. An explanation in terms of automation, communication and co-ordination partly accounts, then, for the US military's historical drive to computerize its forces.

However, some critics have disputed the conclusion that computers are a technological necessity and a clear-cut advantage. There are trade-offs between complexity and efficacy in all technological systems, and computer-based military technology is no exception. Many commentators have noted the devastating problems that may be caused by mechanical failures or organizational rigidities in computerized systems. For example, the US BMEWS – Ballistic Missile Early Warning System – has produced a number of relatively serious false alerts due to hardware, software and operator errors (as documented by Aldridge, 1983, p. 245). Because of the extreme complexity of the computer-centred BMEWS system, detection of these errors can be quite difficult. As the difficulty of error detection increases, so does the level of uncertainty about the correct interpretation of an alert. The stakes, obviously, are very high (Borning, 1987).

The early 1980s, in fact, saw the rise of the so-called 'defence reform movement', a loose-knit but influential coalition of members of Congress, disgruntled Pentagon analysts and non-affiliated investigators. The movement centred around a cost-effectiveness critique of high-technology weapons. The critique suggested that the extreme complexity of 'loaded' high-technology weaponry, such as fighter aircraft and computerized tanks, led to a kind of brittleness and fragility that might make such weapons liabilities on the battlefield. At the same time, the geometrically increasing costs of such weaponry – not only capital costs, but maintenance and training costs as well – meant that the armed forces were able to purchase fewer units of any given weapon. The result was a situation in which outnumbered troops relied on too few high-tech weapons, with dangerously high failure rates, in the vain hope that the weapons' extreme 'capabilities' would carry the day (Fallows, 1981; Spinney, 1985).

Soon after the defence reform movement arose, a strong ground swell of criticism emerged against the use of computers to control nuclear weapons, led by a coalition calling itself Computer Professionals for Social Responsibility. This group argued that the increasing confidence of Defense Department planners in computerized early warning and control systems was unjustified. They cited massive evidence of system failures, breakdowns and false alerts. Furthermore, they suggested that these problems were not gratuitous, but endemic to computer control. In the face of shrinking 'time windows' for nuclear alert, temptations to place increasing reliance on computer control systems would rise, creating a potentially critical danger of accidental nuclear war. The group also presented important technical arguments to the effect that a computerized controller for the proposed space-based missile defence system could not, even in principle, achieve an acceptable level of reliability (CPSR, n.d., 1984–8).

The technical armature of the critique and its source within the ranks of computer professionals were relatively new. But the basic points – that computers are intrinsically prone to unpredictable failures, and that they rely on preconstituted representations that may not fit unpredictable situations – were old ones. In the 1950s and 1960s they frequently served as the vehicle for fictional renderings of Armageddon. One example is Stanley Kubrick's film *Dr Strangelove*, in which a US nuclear attack ordered by an insane Air Force commander is called off at the last moment. One plane cannot be recalled, and succeeds in delivering its nuclear payload to an obscure Soviet missile silo. The attack leads to global holocaust despite the recall of forces, because a Soviet computer has been programmed to explode a massive nuclear device, whose fall-out will choke the entire globe, in the event that it detects even a single nuclear explosion. The 'Doomsday Machine's' programming is irreversible and automatic.

Within the military itself, an undercurrent of opposition to computerization emerged at the outset. Those strategists who felt the necessity and promise of automation described by Jay Forrester were opposed by others who saw that the domination of strategy by preprogrammed plans left no room for the extraordinarily contingent nature of battlefield situations. By 1964, Air Force Colonel Francis X. Kane reported in the pages of *Fortune* magazine that '... much of the current planning for the present and future security of the US rests on computerized solutions'. It was, he wrote, impossible to tell whether the actual results of such simulated solutions would occur as desired, because 'we have no experience in comparing the currently accepted theory of predicting wars by computer with the actual practice of executing plans' (Kane, 1964, pp. 146–7) Also in the early 1960s occasional articles in the armed forces journal *Military Review* began warning of 'electronic despotism' and 'demilitarized soldiers' whose tasks would be automated to the point that the men would be deskilled and become soft (Miksche, 1962; Nusbaum, 1962). The view that computers could provide an optimal solution to major military problems thus faced both external and internal opposition from the start. Therefore, utility alone explains neither the urgency nor the magnitude of the US effort in computing.

Nor does utility explain the pervasive fascination with computers that may be detected in many elements of the US armed forces. This fascination is epitomized by General William Westmoreland's concept of the 'electronic battlefield'. From his experience of high technology applied to warfare in Vietnam, he visualized a 'battlefield of the future' and applauded 'developments that will replace wherever possible the man with the machine' (Westmoreland, 1969). Such fascination has repeatedly led Defense Department planners to overestimate the capacities of computers and to contemplate for them entirely inappropriate roles, for example as an ultimate decision system for nuclear defences or as 'natural language' interfaces to computerized weapons systems (Bellin and Chapman, 1987; CPSR, n.d.; Pullum, 1987).

Computer as symbol

Looking beyond the relationship of tool to task, the historical and cultural analysis I will sketch seems to me to provide an accessory, but indispensable explanation of US military involvement with computers, for two reasons. First, the technologies available to a military force both influence and reflect its internal sense of its own capabilities. As the foundation of force, military technology has profound political effects, since it largely defines the ultimate limits and parameters of national power. The world-view of military institutions and their technological choices develop under strongly reciprocal influence.

The second reason is that, within US strategic thinking in the post-war period, it is possible to trace the development of what I will call a closed-world discourse or, alternatively if less precisely, systems discourse. A 'discourse' is the social product of a cultural subgroup. It involves a language, a set of shared values, a world-view and a political or institutional structure. Closed-world discourse is characterized by tools, techniques, practices and language which embody an approach to the world as composed of interlocking systems amenable to formal mathematical analysis. As one of

its exponents describes it, systems sciences allow their practitioners to 'discern systems of organized complexity wherever [they] look'. As they are engineering approaches designed to solve real-world problems, systems theories tend in practice to assume the closure of the systems they analyse.

But this is not the main reason for the name 'closed-world discourse'. I chose that label because the mathematical theories and engineering methods of systems analysis and its related disciplines interacted strongly with military and political practices during the 1950s and 1960s. Together they generated a model of the world as politically closed. Global politics became a system that could be understood and manipulated by methods modelled on – or at least justified in the language of – systems engineering. The computer provided a core around which a closed-world discourse could crystallize.

Computers affected the rise of systems analysis not only as tools but even more so as symbols of power and metaphors for scientific precision. At the same time, as the language of systems analysis was approaching its zenith of power in the worlds of business and government, the computer was also 'putting muscles' on military command-and-control processes. The military environment – with its standardized procedures, hierarchical controls and insatiable demand for faster, better technology – was a friendly one for the growth of computer technology as well as for the disciplines of systems science.

Closed-world discourse can be understood as an 'apparatus of power' (to use Foucault's terminology), comprised of the following elements:

Techniques, drawn from engineering and mathematics, which involve modelling aspects of the world as closed systems.

Experiences of the political and social world as closed and manipulable, for example by means of the apparently absolute power conferred by nuclear weapons or by the economic power of immense wealth.

Tools, especially the computer, which make systems analysis practical on a very large scale. The computer made possible the creation not only of enormously complicated models of any system, but of detailed simulations. Weapons and military technologies such as the atomic bomb and the SAGE integrated nuclear defence system are also important elements of closed-world discourse.

Practices of systems manipulation in business, government and the military. Systems analysis was used to increase efficiency in many kinds of processes, often with excellent results. Practices of simulation brought forth a sense of power over the future, at the same time as the expansion of nuclear forces created a sense of future war as existing only in the unreal world of simulation.

Languages of systems and strategy that relied on formalism, to the detriment of experiential and situational knowledge. This formalism relied particularly on metaphors of gaming.

As computerized control systems crystallized the power of systems thinking, computers themselves became an icon of the approach to the world as a formal machine subject to manipulation and control. As I will argue, post-World War II US strategic throught had – and still has – deep affinities with systems theory that knitted the two together into a closed-world discourse. Their confluence became particularly prominent in 1950s strategic planning and during the Vietnam War (Bellin and Chapman, 1987; Gibson, 1987; Van Creveld, 1985). Under the Reagan administration's regime of 'strategic initiatives', computer influence has undergone a renaissance. Let us, then, examine the historical development of a military culture oriented toward computerized solutions to strategic problems.

SAGE: THE CONCEPT OF TOTAL DEFENCE

During the post-war years, digital computers' main military effects were indirect, through scientific and engineering problems they helped solve. For example, computers were a significant aid in the physics of both the atomic bomb and the hydrogen bomb, and they assisted the National Security Agency in decoding increasingly complex and voluminous cryptological traffic. By 1950 digital computers began to find their first direct roles in weapons systems.

One line of digital computer evolution emerged at Harvard in 1944 with Jay W. Forrester, whose group was responsible for the developoment of an analogue computer, called the Whirlwind, to be used in an aircraft training simulator. In late 1945 Forrester abandoned the analog approach and shifted his work towards a real-time digital computer. The Special Devices Division of the Navy agreed to continue funding the aircraft simulator project.

By 1949 Forrester's group had outspent every other government-funded computer project in the country by almost an order of magnitude, and they were planning to commit at least $5 million for flight simulation technology (Redmond and Smith, 1980, p. 166). As conflicts over funding increasingly approached a critical phase, Forrester moved to defend the Whirlwind project by making it yet more ambitious. 'The original justification for the computer, as the controller for a flight simulator, was rapidly replaced by the broader concept of a computerized real-time command and control system' (Flamm, 1988, pp. 54–5).

In the same year, the United Nations discussions of international control of atomic energy collapsed. Then, in August 1949, the Soviet Union detonated its first atomic weapon. The Cold War began in earnest. Proposals like Forrester's advanced defence technologies came into the limelight. Finally, in the summer of 1950, US forces became involved in the Korean War. 'Immediately the funds to be overseen by the Research and Development Board [of the armed services] for that fiscal year doubled, topping a billion dollars, and thereafter all areas of military R&D continued to grow rapidly' (Forman, 1987, p. 158). Research funding of a magnitude matched only by World War II itself was once again available, and the applications-hungry services once again came looking for technology to supply defence needs.

The World War II experience with air defence – especially the Pearl Harbor disaster, anti-aircraft gunnery problems, Japanese kamikaze attacks and the dangerous German rockets – had sensitized the US armed services to the future possibility of air attack on the continental United States. Even before the war's end, in February 1945, Army Ordnance and the Air Force had commissioned Bell Laboratories to study continental air defence against high-altitude, high-speed bombers. The result was the Nike anti-aircraft missile project. The original plan called for ground-based computers and radar, along the lines of Bell's analogue gun directors, to guide the missile to its target, where it would be detonated by remote control. Nike R&D was completed in 1952, and by 1954 thousands of Nike-Ajax missiles were installed throughout the United States (Fagen, 1978). Still the overall air defence system was considered inadequate, based as it was on obsolescent radar technology and a decentralized command system (Redmond and Smith, 1980, pp. 172–3).

By mid-1950 the Air Force had developed new long-term plans to defend the USA against Soviet atomic attack via long-range bombers. The plan called for centralized, computerized command-and-control centres able not just to respond to an attack, but to co-ordinate the responses of every sector to the massive offensive foreseen as coming from the USSR. The job of the air-defence system, eventually christened SAGE (Semi-Automatic Ground Environment), was to link together radar installations around the USA's perimeter, analyse and interpret their signals, and direct manned interceptor jets towards the incoming foe. It was to be a total system, one whose 'human components' were fully integrated into the mechanized circuit of detection, decision and response. Discussions with Forrester led to the choice of Whirlwind as the computer for the analysis and co-ordination task. This change of sponsorship and defence justification kept Whirlwind alive at just the point the ONR might have abandoned the project.

As we will see, it was no lucky accident that military computing was the chosen application: not only the political events, but the political and military culture of the time made it the most likely choice. Whirlwind's resurrection by the Air Force was extraordinarily important to the future of computing. The work of Forrester's group on the SAGE project was responsible for many crucial advances in computer technology, including the magnetic core memory, new methods of preventive hardware maintenance, and 'duplexing', or hardware redundancy.

A single, co-ordinated and automatic system to defend an entire continent was an immense project. Rapid changes in weapons technology during the 1950s made it doubly difficult. By the time the manned interceptor control system was operational, new guided missiles such as the Bell Nike and

BOMARC (Boeing-Michigan Aeronautical Research Center) were available, as were mobile, aeroplane-based early warning radars. The interceptors themselves had also evolved. These and other new technologies had to be integrated into the control system. This happened again when ICBMs and satellite surveillance were developed in the late 1950s (Jacobs, 1983). The ongoing problem of integration was one reason SAGE was never fully trustworthy, despite its major role in national defence.

Over the nearly fifteen years of its development, the SAGE system accordingly went through many changes. When SAGE was finally fully deployed in 1963, it encompassed twenty-three air defence sectors. Each of these had its own computerized direction centre. The centres received and processed not only radar data but weather reports, missile and airbase status, and flight plans of friendly aircraft. They also communicated with other centres, automatically co-ordinating activities across sectors. The vast system worked well enough to continue as a central component of American air defence well into the 1970s. Six SAGE centres were still operating in 1983, though by 1984 all had finally shut down.

In the 1950s, SAGE was less important as an actual defence system than as a symbol of things to come. Its fully integrated command-control network came to represent the future of advanced military forces, with computers at its heart. President Reagan's Strategic Defence Initiative hangs on command-and-control technologies rooted in the SAGE system. The ripple effects of SAGE development continue today, through the still-thriving institutions originally created to construct it, such as MIT's Lincoln Laboratory, the MITRE Corporation, the System Development Corporation, and the Air Force Electronic Systems Division (Everett, 1983).

Because of the ideas embodied in the SAGE project, the importance of computers to the modern military goes far beyond their role in any specific weapons system. It is the idea of automated control and information processes – the concept itself – that has shaped, more than any technology, the contemporary US armed forces. Since World War II, automation has replaced the skills and judgements of soldiers – and altered the nature of the risks they face. Beyond individual projects, there has been a steady trend toward total integration of all military systems within what Westmoreland called the 'electronic battlefield'.

Computers have been the catalyst in this integration. Increasingly, the battlefield has become the domain of weapons, not men. The measures and countermeasures of the electronic battlefield have become so complex, so rapid and so interlocked that the human element in war is increasingly difficult to discern. The speeds and sensory capacities of machines are now the critical factors in military success. All approaches to battlefield tactics and improvements must take them into account, on their own terms.

US HISTORICAL CONSCIOUSNESS
AFTER WORLD WAR II

What was the wider cultural context within which the 'electronic battlefield' developed? What were the factors above and beyond utility that brought about the gradual saturation of contemporary American arsenals with computerized equipment? In the rest of this essay I want to explore several political and ideological trends that were well served by computerization, and to identify a number of reasons why not only computer technologies but also the broader world-view I call 'closed-world discourse' became such an important military tool.

The Cold War: transference and apocalypse

World War II was a 'good war', justified in the eyes of most US citizens as a war not only against greedy aggressors, but against an anti-democratic ideology as well. This nearly universal sentiment was vindicated, after the war, by the revelations of Nazi atrocities. But the aura of biblical struggle that surrounded the fight against Nazism and Italian Fascism did not simply fade away after the war. Soviet manoeuvring in Eastern Europe, as well as the openly expansionist Soviet ideology, provided a means for a transition into a Cold War. Stalin was equated with Hitler; Communism replaced Fascism as a kind of total enemy. It was seen not just as another human order with its own goals and interests, but as a completely inverse and implacable system, opposed to the USA on military, political, ideological, religious and economic grounds.

This transition also carried with it the World War II sense of a global and total scale of conflict. The partitioning of Europe, revolutionary upheavals across the post-colonial world, and the global contest for alliances encouraged US perceptions that the world's future balanced on a knife edge between the USA and the USSR. With the Truman Doctrine of world-wide US military support for 'free peoples who are resisting attempted subjugation by armed minorities or by outside pressures', global conflict was permanently codified as 'a struggle between light and darkness... a universal conflict between freedom and slavery' (Ambrose, 1985, p. 87).

As the only combatant nation to come out of the war more or less unscathed, the USA also emerged from the economic depression and political isolationism of the 1930s into a sudden role as world leader. The only immediately available models for action in this new role were those of the war itself. The key events of the war thus became basic icons in the organization of American foreign policy and military strategy. The Munich pact symbolized the danger of appeasement. Pearl Harbor's lesson was always to be prepared for surprise attack. Hiroshima taught that total victory was possible through technologies of overwhelming force.

The unfolding political crises of the Cold War were always interpreted in those terms. The Berlin blockade was perceived as another potential Munich. US forward basing of nuclear weapons, in positions vulnerable to surprise attack, was likened to the risk of another Pearl Harbor. The growing nuclear arsenal was a reminder of Hiroshima, both horror and symbol of ultimate power. Thus, in many respects, the Cold War was not a new conflict with Communism but the continuation of World War II, the transference of the apocalyptic struggle on to a different enemy.

US antimilitarism

Another element of post-war cultural politics was the long history of antimilitarist sentiment in US politics. The authors of the US Constitution drew a distinction of principle between national self-defence and the unruly European standing armies of the seventeenth and eighteenth centuries. Victors in a war fought by future citizens, but anxious not to re-create the social abuses of the British armies long quartered on American soil, they understood both the importance of military power in international conflict and the dangers it posed in domestic political life. Later generations carried with them this ambivalence towards military force – a dangerous if necessary evil, but also a source of patriotic pride.

The disappointing aftermath of World War I, when dreams of world unity through a final defeat of nationalist aggression were shattered, added force to the antimilitarist impulse. Americans responded to the failed efforts at world political co-operation with withdrawal and wishful thinking. Between the wars 'most Americans believed in a natural harmony of interests between nations, assumed that there was a common commitment to peace, and argued that no nation or people could profit from a war' (Ambrose, 1985, p. xiv). The USA approached the widening second war in Europe with extreme caution. Congress and President Roosevelt were very reluctant to grant aid to US allies outright, despite the growing desperation of the military situation. America delayed its entry into the war even after American shipping had been attacked. In 1941 Japan and Germany forced a reversal of that attitude. Thereafter the US war effort was virtually unlimited. The ability of the United States to reverse gears almost immediately, after years of extreme restraint, pointed to the ambivalence of the antimilitarist ethic in American politics. Once war was joined, the USA took to it with the unmatched enthusiasm of patriotic pride.

In the post-war years a number of factors changed the national perception of the need for a powerful armed force in peacetime. The totality of Allied military success created a new over-confidence in the ability of military force to solve urgent political problems. The rapid transition from World War II into the Cold War left little time for a retrenchment into pre-war isolationist values: the apocalyptic conflict simply continued. The occupations of Germany and Japan meant an ongoing US military presence on other continents. The relative insignificance of the country's suffering in the war was responsible for an inflated sense of ease about military victory, for the idea that the USA, at least, could buy a lot for a little with military strength. Its full-blown emergence as a world power created new economic interests across the globe. Explicitly or implicitly, business – especially imperialist business, of the sort developing in Asia and Central America – required the US military to protect its investments.

Finally, technological factors, such as the bomb and the maturation of air warfare, made it possible to conceive of a new military role for the USA in world affairs outside its traditional North American sphere of influence. Ocean barriers had hitherto separated the USA from other nations possessing the technological wherewithal to mount a serious military challenge. These barriers were now breached: aircraft and, soon afterward, guided missiles could pose threats at intercontinental range. In effect, the : very concept of national borders was altered by these military technologies: : the country's northern boundary, in terms of its defence perimeter, now lay at the limits of radar vision in the Arctic Circle.

The Cold War marked the first time in its history that the USA maintained a large standing army in peacetime. But its geographical situation, combined with its antimilitarist tradition, ensured that the institutional form taken by a more vigorous US military presence would differ from the more traditional European and Soviet approaches of large numbers of men under arms. Instead of universal conscription of young men, the USA chose the technological path of massive, ongoing automation and integration of humans with machines.

'Big science'

A third component of the post-war political/cultural situation was the rise of 'big science' and engineering, linked to the increased prestige, presence and ambitions of the military. Science and engineering were, it was widely believed, largely if not entirely responsible for the ultimate Allied victory. The defeat of the Luftwaffe at the Battle of Britain was credited to the crash development of radar. British computers cracked the ciphers of the German high command. US radar and anti-aircraft technology played crucial roles in the Pacific war and in the defeat of German V1 bomb attacks on London. Finally, of course, the atomic bomb represented the military apotheosis of science. In the eyes of many these weapons – and their creators – became part of the war's pantheon of heroes (Baxter, 1948).

This coincided with a more general increase in the number, prestige, and activity of US engineers through the science-based industries that rose to prominence just before World War I, such as the chemical, electronics and telephone industries. Engineering academies like MIT and Cal Tech played major roles in the war effort, vastly increasing their base of political power and prestige in the process. American culture had always valued pragmatic enterprise. During the war, the engineers got a chance to show what they could do given virtually unlimited resources, and it was indeed impressive.

The post-war consequences were the emergence of a powerful, self-conscious science and engineering lobby and a permanent governmental association with science, largely mediated through the military. The wartime science/engineering community, organized around military problems, had been an exhilarating experience for many of those involved. It had provided invigorating interdisciplinary contacts, vast amounts of money, equipment and research time, and the euphoria of rapid success. It had also opened up a multitude of new and intriguing research problems. The post-war scientific community therefore enjoyed an unprecedented sense of community, and its wartime miracles had opened the ears of political and military leaders to its voice.

The world as a closed system

Perhaps the most significant feature of the polarized world that rose from the ashes of the war was its truly global character – at least from a US point of view. World War I, despite its world-wide staging ground, was essentially the last in a long series of local European wars. But the import of the partitioning of Europe after World War II was the USA's perception that the world was now closed, fully occupied by the apocalyptic struggle between the US and Soviet superpowers. The frontier mythos had reached an impassable limit in the form of the Eastern bloc; it was no longer possible to imagine the world as a gigantic America waiting to be explored or awakened. Colonialism was dying, and the Soviet Union and China had supposedly achieved near-parity with US military power.

This perception of closure was soon reinforced by the US intervention in Korea and by the other Asian upheavals of the 1940s and 1950s. Under the Truman Doctrine and the Marshall Plan, the world had become a system to be protected – and manipulated – by the US government. In its quasi-religious mythos, no ideological space remained for other conflicts. Bilateralism created a systematic vision of the world by reducing all Third World conflicts to surrogates for the real death struggle between the Free World and its Communist enemies (Baritz, 1985).

The atomic bomb, with the vast scale of conflict it implied, and space flight – also born of the events of World War II – completed the sense of closure. A world that could be completely annihilated was a new truth. As the doctrines of nuclear war developed, it became increasingly clear that there was no escape; no military solution would make nuclear war just a more vicious form of conventional war. The notion of apocalyptic struggle took on an increasingly literal cast. This was a kind of limit never before experienced in politics, a power so total it was useless. At the same time – since it was, after all, power – the temptation to approach that limit was almost overwhelming.

Military preparations in the post-war world both responded to and magnified the sense of a closed system. If Americans gained anything from World War II, it was the dual sense of awesome national power and compelling national responsibility. Yet, in the relief that followed the war's end, US military force, the instrument of that power, was rapidly and thoroughly demobilized. By 1947 the US Army stood at only one million men – a vast contrast to the USSR's post-war conventional military strength. What remained of the USA's decisive wartime role was technology – especially the bomb.

The scientific and technological successes of the war, and the great geographical distances involved in conflict with the Soviet Union, served both to justify and to exaggerate the focus on high technology. The Los Alamos experience held out the promise of unlimited military power through American know-how. At the same time, the policy of containment required an ability to intervene with force anywhere in the world (Gaddis, 1981). 'Truman and his advisers wanted to meet the Communist challenge wherever it appeared, but except for the atomic bomb they had nothing with which to meet it . . . Truman wanted a balanced budget and was enough of a politician to realize that the public would not support higher taxes for a larger military establishment' (Ambrose, 1985, p. 80).

Antimilitarism, too, thus helped to focus strategic planning on technological solutions. The Strategic Air Command (SAC) rose to prominence in the post-war defence establishment, despite bitter inter-service rivalries, largely because it controlled the technological means for intercontinental nuclear war. It was the USA's primary threat against the USSR – yet it required mainly money and equipment, not large numbers of troops. The Army's massive manpower seemed less impressive, less necessary, even a political liability when compared to minimally manned or even automated forces. As the Soviet Union acquired long-range bombers, nuclear weapons, and then ICBMs, the role of the US Air Force and its technology continued to expand in both defence and offence.

The technological threat of atomic war – total, global war, without front lines, in which millions of civilians would perish – brought with it demands for a total technological defence. The SAGE air defence system was only the first in a long series of responses to this felt need. It was the first large-scale demonstration of digital computers in a real-time military command-and-control operation. It was also the first role in which computers were the critical core of an entire military system. In a technical sense, SAGE was necessitated by two factors: the sheer numbers of aeroplanes and quantities of data to be co-ordinated, and the very high speed of the anticipated attacks. But SAGE was also a response to the sense of global closure: it was a true system, an all-encompassing, totally integrated management of continental US airspace. Indeed, SAGE was more than a weapons system: it was a dream, a myth, a metaphor for total defence.

MILITARY SYSTEMS DISCOURSE

Thus the USA's rapidly evolving geopolitical concerns as a nuclear power shaped a strategic discourse involving a closed but complex system, accessible to technological control. Immediately after the war, computers were integrated into that discourse, both as tools in the solution of strategic problems and as models of the strategic situation itself. While a political discourse of 'containment', bipolarity, and closure developed around nuclear strategy and the 'domino theory', computer scientists were developing their own discourse about systems, communication and control. Digital computers were seen as universal machines, theoretically able to solve any problem that could be formulated precisely enough – that is, that could be systematized, mathematized, modelled, reduced to an algorithm.

At the same time, disciplines such as cybernetics, information theory, game theory, systems analysis, operations research and linear programming succeeded in isolating algorithms for difficult problems in communication, social interaction and the control of highly complex systems. This extension of mathematical formalization into the realm of social problems brought with it a sense of new-found power, and hope for a technical control of social processes to equal that achieved in mechanical and electronic systems. What I am calling 'systems discourse' included not only the formal techniques and tools of the systems sciences, but also this ideology and language of technical control.

Rand's systems

Strategy, especially nuclear strategy, seemed to some military planners to fit the systems mould. At the Rand Corporation, the Air Force think-tank, game theory and systems analysis became central paradigms for strategic thought. Founded in 1946, Rand was a private research group with a broad Air Force mandate to study 'techniques of air warfare'. Like the ONR, it was a way for the military to continue the extremely fruitful interdisciplinary team efforts in science and engineering that had achieved so much success during the war. Rand's staff included social scientists, economists, and mathematicians as well as physicists and engineers. It became a major locus of advanced hardware, software and systems analysis development in the 1950s.

Rand's most important contribution was not any specific product or idea but a whole way of thinking – a systems philosophy of military strategy. Many of Rand's brightest minds were mathematicians; von Neumann, for example, was a Rand consultant. Others had been trained in the techniques of operations research – mathematical analysis of complex logistical problems, such as the optimum number of ships in a protected convoy – during the war. Rand soon began to apply statistical analysis, systems analysis, game theory (invented by von Neumann and economist Oskar Morgenstern), and other formal and mathematical techniques to the burgeoning problems of nuclear strategy. Computers were an important element of the Rand environment, dominated by the formalistic approaches of the 'hard' social sciences such as economics. But it would be an exaggeration to say that computing was the centre or the focus of Rand style systems discourse. (Rand's advanced computers, programmers and engineers could not, of course, have advanced immediately to the levels of sophistication achieved later.) Computers were not necessary to much of Rand's formal modelling of strategic problems; it could have been done anyway, with calculators, pencils and paper.

Although computers were not the sole causal basis for the rise of systems discourse, they did serve as a support for it, as they did for the entire complex of formal modelling techniques developing in science, business and the military during the period between 1945 and 1960. Computers added prestige, high-technology glitter and a scientistic appearance of infallibility to the process. As fast as the technology improved, it was incorporated into the process of analysis. As Weizenbaum observed,

> ... the crucial transition, from the business computer as a mere substitute for work-horse tab machines to its present status as a versatile information engine, began when the power of the computer was projected onto the framework already established by operations research and systems analysis ... As the prestige of systems analysis was fortified by its successes and as, simultaneously, the computer grew in power, the problems tackled by systems analysts became more and more complex, and the computer appeared an ever more suitable instrument to handle great complexity. (Weizenbaum, 1976, pp. 33–4)

Thus by the late 1950s computers had become firmly entrenched as icons of systems discourse. Rand was one of the reasons.

The Rand analysts' results led to a series of shifts in US military strategy. One example was the finding of mathematical logician Albert Wohlstetter that the Strategic Air Command's forward bomber bases could be annihiliated by a surprise nuclear first strike. Wohlstetter's alternative was an intercontinental bomber force based in the USA, relying on forward bases only for refuelling. Inter-service rivalry, and the military's traditional suspicion of civilian armchair generals, almost prevented turning Wohlstetter's analysis into accepted strategy. But after this initial achievement, Rand became a central force in military planning. In the history of Rand's influence, Fred Kaplan has argued that the Rand forward-basing studies were the goad behind the US nuclear buildup of the 1950s and 1960s. Rand analysis also lay behind flexible-response strategy, the no-cities doctrine of counterforce, and other key elements of US nuclear strategy. The Rand analysts' formal models, assisted by computerized data processing, rapidly became the standard for military thinking in the era of high technology.

The result was a gradual shift away from traditional military philosophies of command and towards a management-oriented style (Herken, 1983; Kaplan, 1983). This importation of scientific and industrial methods into military policy became such a powerful trend that by 1961 a lieutenant-colonel of the US Army could write that 'every professional military man in recent years has read or heard the theory expressed that management and command are essentially the same thing. Chances are better than even, in fact, that he has never heard any serious dissent from the proposition that the terms command and management are synonymous, or nearly so' (Ramsey, 1961, p. 31).

Vietnam as system

This new rationalism, supported by computers, played direct and significant roles in the Vietnam War. President Kennedy's Secretary of Defense, Robert S. McNamara, had been a professor at the Harvard Business School, as well as a general manager and president of Ford Motor Company. McNamara was known as a mathematical whiz. He had developed systems analysis techniques for the Statistical Control Office of the Army Air Corps during World War II. At Ford, he had introduced these same techniques into business management with astounding success. Like many other intellectually oriented managers of the 1950s, he found mathematical modelling techniques far superior to traditional wisdom or intuitive approaches to management based on shop-floor experience.

His experiences in the war and at Ford provided McNamara with the confidence that he could gain command of any situation and that he could do so more quickly and proficiently than the conventional experts in the field, whether they be auto executives or Air Force generals. McNamara was coldly clinical, abrupt, almost brutally determined to keep emotional influences out of the inputs and cognitive processes that determined his judgments and decisions. It was only natural, then, that when Robert S.

McNamara met the Rand Corporation, the effect was like love at first sight. (Kaplan, 1983, p. 251)

McNamara established an Office of Systems Analysis within the Department of Defense and staffed it with Rand Corporation defence analysts and others of a similar persuasion. After McNamara's own group at Ford in the late 1940s, the systems analysis group within the DOD came to be called the 'whiz kids'. They created an atmosphere of sober, 'scientific' analysis of military problems, often divorced from a political and historical understanding. Trained within the Rand preoccupation with global nuclear confrontation, and largely innocent of military or diplomatic experience, the whiz kids' perspective ignored Vietnam's special features. They applied doctrines of limited nuclear war, developed at Rand using the techniques of game theory, to counter-insurgency. Each military manoeuvre was conceived as a political message about the costs of continued war to the other side. It was partly because of the influence of systems discourse, through the medium of Rand, that the Pentagon came to view Vietnam as a token in a political game played between the two superpowers, instead of seeing it for the much more complicated, local, historical situation it actually was. (Gibson, 1987; Van Creveld, 1985; Wilson, 1968).

It is important to note, however, that the systems analysis approach to military policy was met by powerful resistance within the armed forces themselves. By the time the Office of Systems Analysis became fully operational in 1963, it was necessary for its head to publish a defence of its technique in *Military Review*. His words reflect the negative reaction of the military services and the public at large:

'Computers are replacing military judgment.' 'Weapon systems are being computed out of existence.' 'Computers are running the wars of the future.' These and similar statements are being published in prominent American newspapers and magazines ... these statements are ... worse than wrong, they are dangerous. (Enthoven, 1963, pp. 7–8)

Whatever the reality, by now the role of computers in military strategy had clearly risen to the status of a major controversy. The Joint Chiefs of Staff reacted to the intrusions of civilian strategists and computerized formal analysis with both disgust and accommodation. The Joint Chiefs and each service individually created their own systems analysis departments, to turn the techniques as far as possible to their own ends (Baritz, 1985, pp. 240–1). But they still felt, as one SAC general put it, that 'computer types who were making defense policy don't know their ass from a hole in the ground' (in Gaddis, 1981, p. 251n).

While the systems analysts themselves remained under suspicion, the discourse they generated, and the computers that were their tools, ultimately won acceptance at the highest levels of power, signified by Westmoreland's vision of the 'electronic battlefield'. As systems discourse gained power and prestige, it merged with the closed-world view of world politics to form what I named above 'closed-world discourse'. A historian of the Vietnam War has written,

> As the possessor of an advanced technological system of war production, the United States began to view political relationships with other countries in terms of concepts that have their origin in physical science, economics, and management. A deeply mechanistic world-view emerged among the political and economic élite and their intellectual advisers.
>
> The Vietnam War should be understood in terms of the deep structural logic of how it was conceptualized and fought by the American war-managers. Vietnam represents the perfect functioning of [their] closed, self-referential universe. (Gibson, 1987, pp. 14, 27)

The 'deep structural logic' of the 'war-managers' of Vietnam was closed-world discourse. Modelling techniques drawn from engineering and mathematics were used to design strategies for the war and to project the results of campaigns. Experiences of the closed, manipulable political world of the late 1940s, when the USA was still the sole possessor of atomic weapons, had shaped the thinking of men then at the peak of their political and military careers.

For managers like McNamara, who had seen entire industries revamped by operations research techniques, more recent experiences of the social world as manipulable were salient. Computer tools had reached a plateau of maturity and could serve powerful roles in data analysis. They had already – for example, in the SAGE system – become the crucial core of major weapons systems. Practices of manipulation of systems, for example in business, had achieved wide currency through the ongoing evolution of operations research and systems analysis.

The goal of the Vietnam effort was couched in terms of systemic manipulation: the USA would 'strike to hurt but not to destroy, and strike for the purpose of changing the North Vietnamese decision on intervention in the south' (McGeorge Bundy, in Kaplan, 1983, p. 333). A formalistic language of systems and strategy tied these elements of the discourse together. It was one that saw the war as a game or a bargaining situation, as a rational problem rather than a struggle with its roots in ancient feelings of patriotism, desire for justice, and resentments of foreign intervention that might not respond to a 'rational' challenge.

Military microworld

Within computer science artificial intelligence, notorious for its active imagination with respect to the potential of computers in human affairs, participates perhaps most fully in the characteristic technical and ideological elements of closed-world discourse. The 'microworld' approach to AI illustrates both. Microworlds are internally consistent, complete environments with their own private ontologies, simpler than the open universe of which they are a partial model. They are true closed worlds, in the sense that they cannot recognize or address entities or processes beyond those that are given or taught to them. The assumption of many AI workers is that the limitations of microworlds simply reflect inadequate complexity. Given enough processing power and a sufficiently sophisticated model, they believe that the AI microworld could simply be expanded to reflect reality itself.

Yet there are good reasons to believe that this is not the case. For most complex social interactions, it may be fundamentally impossible to achieve the kind of complete specification of entities and processes required by algorithmic problem-solving techniques. As Winograd and Flores observe, 'the essence of intelligence is to act appropriately when there is no simple pre-definition of the problem or the space of states in which to search for a solution' (Winograd and Flores, 1987, p. 98). One of the primary criticisms of computer control of military systems is precisely this ontological closure. The performance of computer systems, unlike that of human experts, degrades very rapidly once entities or processes outside the programmed field of expertise are introduced (Dreyfus and Dreyfus, 1986). Thus, for example, battle-management computers based on expert systems are likely to suffer from the same inability to recognize unfamiliar objects that caused nuclear early warning systems to raise alerts at the rising moon and at flocks of geese. Their much greater sophistication may prevent gross errors like these – but at the same time it opens such systems to failures much more subtle and difficult to detect (Jacky, forthcoming).

This objection to computerized weapons systems applies on a larger scale to all strategic thinking based on a systems approach. Part of the lesson of Vietnam was precisely that their 'simple pre-definition of the problem' had obscured the realities of the situation to US military and political leaders.

> The analysts could analyze a question, but could not pose the question in the first place and could not ask a different question. They were trapped by their useful technique into accepting the given framework. Like other bureaucrats, they wanted to please the boss, their only audience, and did not want to offer him recommendations which they knew he would reject. They were therefore trapped by considerations of power and influence.

They could analyze what the US could do better than they could analyze what the enemy could do. One critic said that systems analysis 'discourages the study of one's opponents, his language, politics, culture, tactics, and leadership'... Systems analysis reinforced the traditional American assumption that the enemy, or anybody else, is just like us. This ignorance made it even more difficult to take the insurgency seriously... (Baritz, 1985, p. 241)

The dawn of this realization partially rectified the tendency to rely on formal analysis. 'Vietnam... exposed something seamy and disturbing about the very enterprise of the defence intellectuals. It revealed that the concept of force underlying all their formulations and scenarios was an abstraction, practically useless as a guide to action' (Kaplan, 1983, p. 336). The frustrations of the world's most highly computerized and technology-based extended war brought home – at least to some – the hard lesson that the closed world of military force could not prevail alone in the open-ended world of political struggle. Even Secretary of Defense McNamara ultimately regretted the 'almost ineradicable tendency to think of our security problem as being exclusively a military problem... We are haunted by this concept of military hardware' (Kaplan, 1983, p. 336).

Yet for others, the lesson was in fact the opposite: that US technology simply had not yet matured. Westmoreland's vision of the 'electronic battlefield' was actually *based* on his Vietnam experience. Drawing on his favourable experiences of the military promise of high technology, he contemplated a future war zone 'under 24 hour real or near real-time surveillance of all types... an Army built into and around the integrated area control system that exploits the advanced technology of communications, sensors, fire direction, and the required automatic data processing' (Westmoreland, 1969). Computers were the heart of Westmoreland's vision, which echoed Forrester's proposal twenty years previously.

The vision has transformed the thinking of modern military planners. For example, DARPA's second annual report on its Strategic Computing initiative, begun in 1983, stresses that

commanders must have automated systems that can deal consistently and accurately with the complex interrelationships of the many variables inherent to battle management during combat and crisis action... Machine intelligence technology... will provide capabilities to dramatically reduce the time required for planning and monitoring operations, support the development of early offensive postures, identify sensitivities in key strategic and tactical decisions, and demonstrate the implications of complex combinations of events and decisions. (DARPA, 1987, p. 7)

The original proposal for the Strategic Computing Program noted that in '... the projected defense against strategic nuclear missiles ... systems must react so rapidly that it is likely that almost complete reliance will have to be placed on automated systems' (DARPA, 1983, p. 3). On the nuclear battlefield, according to this vision, computer control will be more than a virtue – it will be a necessity.

The parallel between the microworlds of AI programs and the blinkered strategic thinking of the Vietnam War points to the fundamental comparison I am trying to make. Computers are the basic tools of high-technology war, without which command, control and communications under modern military conditions would be difficult or impossible. They have made it possible to link other technologies together into a smoothly functioning, co-ordinated system. Yet computers also represent a particular way of understanding reality through formal techniques. This style of thinking is crystallized in proposals for total defence such as SAGE, WWMCCS, the Strategic Computing Program and the Strategic Defence Initiative. It assumes the possibility not only of complete, consistent surveillance and comprehension of inherently unstable, dangerous situations, but of controlling them by technical means. Seen in this light, terrorism and guerrilla war, the major forms of conflict the USA has had to face since World War II, are a logical response to systemic closure. They are a refusal to fight by the 'rules of engagement', to accept the fixed set of entities and actions of a systems discourse. Their randomness, their failure to distinguish 'civilian' from 'military' targets, the ability of their perpetrators to fade into the general population, and the vast frustration they have caused US armed forces across the globe are all marks of the realization that the military microworld is a closed system.

Systems discourse created the pre-conditions for the ascendancy of the rationalistic, bureaucratic, formal-analysis tradition of military strategic planning in the post-war years. In consequence an older, competing tradition of individual leadership, soldierly creativity in strategy, and heroism went into decline – though it is far from disappearing (Gray, 1988). This happened not because of something inherently militaristic in systems discourse, but because systems thinking fits so neatly into the cultural niche formed by post-war American Cold War, technology-based military power and computerization. In the nuclear age, strategic thought has become amenable to formal modelling.

Thus military interest in advanced computing stems not just from practical demands, but from the larger strategic mentality that the military operates. It is an integral part of the closed world constructed in post-World War II political discourse.

NOTE

An earlier version of this essay appeared in the journal *AI and Society* 2: 2, July 1988.

REFERENCES

Aldridge, Robert C. (1983) *First Strike! The Pentagon's Strategy for Nuclear War.* Boston, MA: South End.

Ambrose, Stephen (1985) *Rise to Globalism.* New York: Penguin.

Baritz, Loren (1985) *Backfire.* New York: Ballantine.

Baxter, James Phinney 3rd (1948) *Scientists against Time.* Boston: Little, Brown.

Bellin, David and Chapman, Gary eds (1987) *Computers in Battle.* New York: Harcourt Brace.

Borning, Alan (1987) 'Computer system reliability and nuclear war', *Communications of the ACM*, February 1987. (Includes an extensive bibliography of other sources.)

CPSR (Computer Professionals for Social Responsibility) (n.d.) *CPSR Newsletter*, PO Box 717, Palo Alto, CA 94301.

DARPA (1983) *Strategic Computing – New Generation Computing Technology: A Strategic Plan for Its Development and Application to Critical Problems in Defense.* Washington, DC: Defense Advanced Research Projects Agency.

———— (1987) 'Strategic Computing: Second Annual Report'. Washington, DC: Defense Advanced Research Projects Agency.

Dreyfus, Hubert and Dreyfus, Stuart (1986) *Mind over Machine.* New York: Free Press.

Edwards, Paul N. and Gordon Richard, eds (forthcoming) *Strategic Computing: Defense Research and High Technology.* Santa Cruz, CA: Silicon Valley Research Group.

Enthoven, Alain C. (1963) 'Systems analysis and decision making', *Military Review* 43:7–12.

Everett, Robert E. (1983) 'Epilogue', *Annals of the History of Computing* 54:402–6.

Everett, Robert E. *et al.* (1957) 'SAGE: a data-processing system for air defense', *Proceedings of the Eastern Joint Computer Conference.* Washington, DC: Institute of Radio Engineers. Reprinted in *Annals of the History of Computing* 5: 4 (1983).

Fagen, M. D. ed (1978) *A History of Engineering and Science in the Bell System.* Bell Telephone Laboratories.

Fallows, James (1981) *National Defense.* New York: Random House.

Flamm, Kenneth (1987) *Targeting the Computer: Government Support and International Competition.* Washington, DC: Brookings Institution.

———— (1988) *Creating the Computer.* Washington, DC: Brookings Institution.

Forman, Paul (1987) 'Behind quantum electronics: national security as basis for physical research in the United States, 1940–1960', *Historical Studies in the Physical and Biological Sciences* 18:149–229.

Forrester, Jay W. (1962) 'Managerial decision making', in Martin Greenberger, ed. *Computers and the World of the Future.* Cambridge, MA: MIT Press, p. 53.

Gaddis, John Lewis (1981) *Strategies of Containment.* New York: Oxford University Press.

Gibson, James (1987) *The Perfect War: Technowar in Vietnam.* New York: Atlantic Monthly Press.

Gray, Chris Hables (1988) 'Artificial intelligence and real postmodern war: the shaping of postmodern conflict in the United States military today', unpublished qualifying essay, History of Consciousness Board of Studies, University of California at Santa Cruz.

Herken, Gregg (1983) *Counsels of War.* New York: Knopf.

Huntington, Samuel P. (1961) *The Common Defense: Strategic Programs in National Politics.*

New York, Columbia University Press.

_____ (1981) *American Politics: The Promise of Disharmony*. Cambridge, MA: Belknap.

Jacky, Jonathan 'Software engineers and hackers: programming and military computing', in Edwards and Gordon (forthcoming).

Jacobs, John F. (1983) 'SAGE overview', *Annals of the History of Computing* 5:323–9.

Kane, Colonel Francis X., USAF (1964) 'Security is too important to be left to computers', *Fortune* 69:145–50.

Kaplan, Fred (1983) *The Wizards of Armageddon*. New York: Simon & Schuster.

Laszlo, Ervin (1972) *The Systems View of the World*. New York: George Braziller.

Miksche, Ferdinand Otto (1962) 'The soldier and technical warfare', trans. LaVergne Dale, *Military Review* 42:71–8.

Nusbaum, Major Keith C. US Army (1962) 'Electronic despotism: a serious problem of modern command', *Military Review* 42:31–9.

Pullum, Geoffrey K. (1987) 'Natural language interfaces and strategic computing', *AI and Society* 1:47–58.

Ramsey, Lt-Colonel David M. Jr, US Army (1961) 'Management or command?', *Military Review* 41:31–9.

Redmond, Kent C. and Smith, Thomas M. (1980) *Project Whirlwind: The History of a Pioneer Computer*. Bedford, MA: Digital.

Spinney, Franklin C. (1985) *Defense Facts of Life: The Plans/Reality Mismatch*. Boulder, CO: Westview.

Van Creveld, Martin (1985) *Command in War*. Cambridge, MA: Harvard University Press.

Weizenbaum, Joseph (1976) *Computer Power and Human Reason*. San Francisco, CA: W.H. Freeman.

Westmoreland, General William, US Army Chief of Staff (1969) address to the Association of the US Army, 14 October. Reprinted in full in Paul Dickson, *The Electronic Battlefield*. Bloomington, IN: Indiana University Press, 1976, pp. 215–23.

Wilson, Andrew (1968) *The Bomb and the Computer*. New York: Delacorte.

Winograd, Terry and Flores, Fernando (1987) *Understanding Computers and Cognition: A New Foundation for Design*. Norwood, NJ: Ablex.

7 TOWARDS A MILITARY INFORMATION SOCIETY?

LES LEVIDOW and KEVIN ROBINS

All of us are already civilian soldiers, without knowing it. And some of us know it. The great stroke of luck for the military class's terrorism is that no one recognizes it. People don't recognize the militarized part of their identity, of their consciousness. (Virilio and Lotringer, 1983)

The notion of a 'military information society' may seem a contradiction in terms. After all, the Information Age promises us greater freedom, while things 'military' suggest orders to be obeyed. As we shall argue, there is an inner connection between the two, regarding the kinds of discipline involved. It is not simply a hierarchical command exercised by high-tech managers and military officers alike. It is also an internalized self-discipline, geared to making a system operate more effectively. Through the mediation of computer simulation, such a system seeks total control over a world reduced to calculable, mechanical operations.

As we shall also argue, this involves disavowing human qualities not so easily reducible – or, rather, redefining them according to computer metaphors. Through infotech, military models of reality appeal to widespread illusions of omnipotence, of overcoming human limitations, even as they conceal our relative impotence. Computer-based models of war, work and learning can promote military values, even when they apparently encourage the operator to 'think'. In all those ways, we are presently headed towards a military information society, which encompasses much more of our lives than we would like to acknowledge.

This essay draws connections between military-based discipline and people's experience of infotech. Our argument here proceeds by way of surveying those writers who have most contributed to such a critical approach or who have expounded the agendas that most warrant criticism. We begin by suggesting how military paradigms have served to shape our society. Then we describe how an emerging military-cybernetic complex influences forms of automation, at the same time as futurologists promise us a cybernetic liberation fulfilling our basic nature, or even improving upon it. In theory and in practice, such schemas reduce the individual to the 'human component', the 'vigilant operator' of a system – a role for which we are being prepared by recent educational reform and training programmes. Lastly the essay explores the psychic, unconscious dimension of the resulting 'cyborg self', and asks how we might find a way out of this possible future.

MILITARY PARADIGMS

Most social-science research ignores the profound effects of war and war preparation upon our culture. Military activities are considered to be exceptions or interruptions. Some commentators, however, have treated the military paradigm as the key to understanding social development.

As Max Weber observed (1948), 'The discipline of the army gives birth to all discipline.' The military serves as a model for the organizational imperative 'that the obedience of a plurality of men is rationally uniform'. From that base, Weber argued, it has developed a pervasive impact upon the broader social order: 'No special proof is necessary to show that military discipline is the ideal model for the modern capitalist factory, as it was for the ancient plantation.' The scientific management of both army and industry requires rational calculation and impersonal regulation. In both spheres, 'the psycho-physical apparatus of man is completely adjusted to the demands of the world, the tools, the machines – in short, to an individual "function"'. Discipline aspires towards the rational conditioning of performance, towards uniform and predictable behaviour.

Lewis Mumford (1964), too, assigned a central role to the military, particularly its development of 'authoritarian technics', which 'created complex human machines composed of specialized, standardized, replaceable, interdependent parts'. Work armies and military armies 'raised the ceiling of human achievement: the first in mass construction, the second in mass destruction'. Mumford (1967) argued, moreover, that coercions of a military character permeated and shaped all social activities. The whole social structure was organized as a megamachine, 'composed of living, but rigid, human parts, each assigned to his special office, role, and task, to make possible the immense work output and grand design of this great collective organization'. And the army was the fundamental model for this generalized megamachine. The system is devoted to control, above all else.

Mumford saw the modern fulfilment of that control mission in the form of cybernetic systems. 'Through mechanization, automation, cybernetic direction', he wrote (1964), 'this authoritarian technics has at last successfully overcome its most serious weakness: its original dependence upon resistant, sometimes actively disobedient servo-mechanisms, still human enough to harbour purposes that do not always coincide with those of the system.' The centre of authority is shifted from human operators to the system itself. And the objective of this 'systems-centred collective, this Pentagon of power... is to displace life, or rather, to transfer the attributes of life to the machine and the mechanical collective, allowing only so much of the organism to remain as may be controlled and manipulated'.

As Anthony Giddens (1985) argues, it is not just that the modern nation State has depended upon the military for its control over the means of external and internal violence. It is also the case that war and war preparation have been both the stimulus and paradigm for the State's organization of resources, as well as for industrial organization: 'The merging of industry, technology and the means of waging war has been one of the most momentous features of processes of industrialization as a whole.' More than simply serving military needs, industry tends to model itself after the military.

The technological mediations are explored by Paul Virilio and Sylvere Lotringer (1983), who raise questions about the technics and culture of warfare, about military logistics and control, about the space and speed and time of war. Labelling this process the 'military/scientific/economic complex', they argue that we have now arrived at 'pure war', the total militarization of society; after all, hasn't the war machine's technology invaded the heart of industrial society? Such an inquiry evokes emotional resistance: 'to be interested in technology through war already makes people suspicious: war is generally considered a negative phenomenon, and technology a positive one'. Yet the war machine is inscribed with a powerful 'technologic' of rationality and cold efficiency, of 'unbridled intelligence which gets its absence of limits from technology, from science'.

War is significant not only in its execution, but also in its constant preparation. As Virilio further argues (1986), it is about 'setting in place a series of automatisms, reactionary industrial and scientific procedures from which all political choice is absent'. Although he goes too far in attributing total success to the control project, and too far in attributing that success to automated systems replacing humans, he rightly emphasizes the role of military models in narrowing political choices throughout all our institutions.

Indeed, the military has had a totalitarian impact on our society. It has colonized both physical and psychic space. The economy's orientation to war preparation, its methods of incorporating people into a technological system, and its models of social organization: all these levels embody a

military-based authority, which becomes extensive, intensive, invasive. Moreover, the authority operates, if at all, by becoming internalized – not only in technological systems, but also in the self-discipline of each human entrusted with operating them.

THE MILITARY-CYBERNETIC COMPLEX

As is well known, the new technologies involved in this grand social project have gained impetus from enormous military expenditure. David Noble (1984) has documented how, in the period after World War II, 'the permanent war economy and the military-industrial complex affixed the military imprint on a whole range of heretofore industrial and scientific activities, in the name of national security'. Research and development, science and technology policy, economic and industrial policy: all have been shaped by military imperatives.

Most recently, since the late 1970s, the US Air Force has funded a programme for Integrated Computer-Aided Manufacture (ICAM). Earlier programmes, for numerical control of machine tools, had degraded shop-floor workers' skills by automating machines and transferring judgement to management level, in the name of enhanced efficiency. ICAM extended that logic in order to solve the resulting problems, perceived as managerial inefficiency. ICAM promised 'to free management from executing routine duties to do creative work' – apparently unlike the deskilling of manual workers. By reducing paperwork as well as shop-floor power, ICAM sought to fulfil the dream of push-button omnipotence in 'the factory of the future' (David Noble, 1984). And this programme was intended to serve as a model for all of US industry, to free production from the need for constant human intervention.

Developed into software packages by Honeywell and IBM, ICAM-type systems are designed to translate new information automatically into altered instructions for production, on a 'real-time' basis. In the case of General Electric's plant at Lynn, Massachusetts, dubbed the 'Factory of the Future', management personnel started doing all the computer programming, and all production was to be centralized through a computer positioned on a mezzanine overlooking the shop-floor operations (Centre for Productivity Enhancement, 1987). This type of automation encountered much worker resistance, expressed through the local union. It has been suggested that the Lynn plant's problems arose also from middle management's refusal to co-operate with its own demise, in a new system which assumes that everything works perfectly (Emspak, personal communication, 1989).

Such difficulties in increasing productivity hardly slow the advance of automation, however, as many US firms accept the dictum: 'automate, emigrate or evaporate'. Some attempt to cut costs through military assistance for high-tech investment, rather than risk winning no contracts at all.

From the early 1980s, the US military has won industrial recruits by offering firms direct subsidies to modernize their technology, in return for providing military supplies at lower costs. Set up by the Air Force's Electronic Systems Division (ESD), the deal has been called 'Productivity Realized through Incentivizing Contractor Efficiency', or GET PRICE for short. It stipulated that either side could propose ways for the other to help unleash productivity. The ESD's ex-Commander, Lt-Gen. James Stansberry, has proclaimed, 'Every time I look at an area, there's something that can be improved. It isn't just not enough automation or too much material. It is attitudinal more than anything else.' On the other side, a General Electric plant manager noted, 'Rather than just buying a new machine, we developed a holistic management style. We asked if the solution was in equipment, or process, or people, or management, or computers' (Ball, 1984).

Through a militarized version of holism, GET PRICE leads a relentless drive for management to discipline itself and its work-force to a system's automatic logic. In the USA, at least, military funding pushes firms to pursue the chimera of total control in the 'factory of the future'.

Beyond the USA, the war industry is becoming a multinational military-industrial complex. John Lovering (1987) describes the formation of a new 'Atlantic arms economy', with a whole new global system of military, administrative and industrial institutions: 'On the side of demand this apparatus is an instrument for harmonizing military strategies, thereby creating massive unified arms markets. On the side of supply, it is the framework within which huge international concentrations of capital are being forged out of formerly fragmented national units, to exploit those markets.'

For example, when the British helicopter firm Westland was declared inviable and came up for sale in 1985, government ministers divided over rival bids from US and European firms. The strange public split becomes more intelligible when one critic, Richard Ennals (1986), observed that Westland's sale to the US bidder Sikorsky would make it more attractive for SDI contracts, in a pattern that the government might apply to British Leyland as well. These manoeuvres coincided with a secret 'Memorandum of Understanding', dated December 1985, under which the British government agreed to keep SDI-related research 'secret in perpetuity'. Although the leak of the document resulted in the Memorandum's demise, this episode illustrates the military pressures exerted upon the direction of infotech research and industrial restructuring.

The great expenditures involved are continually justified by a military logic of total control over uncertainty, indeterminacy and insecurity. Its systemic model is C^3I – 'command, control, communications and intelligence' – a philosophy of struggle to shape reality through surveillance and information gathering on those labelled the enemy. This authoritarian technics is turned not only against other countries but also against the internal population.

In a context of continuous mobilization lacking popular enthusiasm, the State must fear and discipline its own population in the name of protecting it. Surrendering our freedom appears the unavoidable price we pay for accepting State protection from those who supposedly threaten that freedom. This totalitarian logic of security lies at the heart of political rule; it extends widely across social systems and deeply into human experience.

CYBERNETIC LIBERATION?

The security syndrome has been extended to the point of modelling the entire society as a system needing more sophisticated management of its technical parameters. Like the military terrain itself (analysed in this book by Paul N. Edwards), society becomes a closed world in which the enemy is inefficiency, disorder, dysfunction. The projected solution, cybernetics, promises to overcome all such instabilities.

Accordingly, Richard Wolin (1984/5) has described late capitalism as a 'brave new world of systems theory cybernetics', a bureaucratic-technocratic colonization. The scientistic turn of Enlightenment rationality has brought us to the point of a cybernetic society, where individual autonomy is seen to threaten chaos, disruption. In search of order and stability, administrative-technical imperatives are handed down to the cybernetic citizen, thus programming the individual's contribution to the society.

Lest this fate be resisted as totalitarian, futurologists have sought to persuade us that systems logic guarantees real freedom and democracy. Rooting his work ultimately in the 'cybernetic laws of nature', cybernetician Stafford Beer developed a massive computer model of the social system – 'the Liberty Machine'. How was it to work?

> There ought to be a set of operation rooms, strategically placed in relation to the spread of the system concerned. These rooms would receive real-time data from the systems which they monitor, and they would distil the information content. Using this input to drive models, the people inside the rooms would formulate hypotheses, undertake simulations, and make predictions about world trajectories. The meta-control is of course constituted by the linkage of these rooms across the subsystems – using colour television, and a network of fast-acting real-time computer terminals. (Beer, 1971, p. 347)

His vision draws its inspiration from military systems:

> Do we not already have systems looking very much like this – which were built in the cause of defence [sic]? Do we not have 'hot lines' – installed on the premise that the organizational stereotype called diplomacy will not

work in the face of the fast-acting thermonuclear threat, and that knowledge must constitute action? (pp. 347–8)

Is it a coincidence that he takes his model of liberty from the management of superpower nuclear confrontation? As the military system becomes paradigmatic, so do the Enlightenment ideals of freedom and progress become appropriated as technocratic expressions of the new cybernetic vision. For Beer, 'liberty may indeed be usefully redefined for our current technological era. It [liberty] would say that *competent information is free to act* – and that this is the principle on which the new Liberty Machine should be designed . . . [it is] the frustration of competent information, inhibited from action, that forestalls progress.' In this Newspeak, control is freedom.

Here individual freedom is redefined through an information system. People become bearers, transmitters and agents of 'information'. As analysed in Marx's critique of commodity fetishism (1976), the products of human labour become invested with superhuman powers and take on a life of their own: information becomes the subject of history. And the 'hot line' analogy serves as threat and promise, warning us of the terrible consequences if we fail to let information act, in real time.

A more recent schema, James Beniger's *The Control Revolution* (1986), similarly models society as a system, also rooted in nature. According to him, industrialization precipitated 'a crisis of control, a period in which innovations in information-processing and communication technologies lagged behind those of energy and its application to manufacturing and transportation'. As economic and political control was lost at the local level, this crisis called up new forms of communication 'to control an economy shifting from local segmented markets to higher levels of organization – what might be seen as the growing "systemness" of society'.

Here society becomes a cybernetic machine, a programmed and programmable processing system. Control is defined as 'purposive influence towards a predetermined goal', understood in a purely technical sense, acknowledging no possibility of contrary goals, partisan goals. For fulfilling the system's unitary goal, salvation lies in more technology: 'Because both the activities of information processing and communication are inseparable components of the control function, a society's ability to maintain control – at all levels from interpersonal to international relations – will be directly proportional to the development of its information technologies.'

For Beniger, moreover, these particular human activities provide the universal basis of organizational coherence; they are rooted 'in the nature of all living systems . . . in individual cells and organisms no less than in national economies or any other purposive system'. After all, he observes, 'All living systems must process matter and energy to maintain themselves counter to entropy, the universal tendency of organization toward breakdown and randomization.' The cybernetic model is naturalized, that is, projected from capitalist society on to nature. Once the model is discovered to be the prerequisite of any society, information-processing devices – be they microchips or bureaucracies – become great leaps forward in evolutionary progress.

The concept of countering entropy was also a reference point for Norbert Wiener when he coined the term 'cybernetics' (from the Greek term for pilot or, latterly, governor). In his book *Cybernetics: Or Control and Communication in the Animal and the Machine* (1948), he compared animals and machines by their similar methods of controlling the tendency for entropy to increase. 'Feedback loop' could describe the homoeostatic processes of warm-blooded animals, as of a thermostat. Later he called these 'locally antientropic processes, which perhaps may also be exemplified in many other ways which we should naturally term neither biological nor mechanical' (Wiener, 1954). His schema allowed a space for ambiguity between nature and artifice, rather than reduce one to the other.

Having refused to continue his war-related research into the Cold War era, Wiener intended cybernetics for human liberation, through such applications as prosthetics to compensate handicapped individuals for a lost sensory mode, and even biochemical prosthetics. Like any science, Wiener's involved anthropomorphic projections, but he did not go as far as to reduce the human mind or social organization to mechanical models. When cyberneticians soon did precisely that, they foreclosed the broad issue of human purposes, in favour of the inhuman use of human beings, against which Weiner warned.

As Steve J. Heims has noted, '... the subjective – an individual's cumulative experience, sensations and feelings, including the subjective experience of being alive – is belittled, seen only within the context of evolutionary theory as providing information useful for survival to the organism... If shorn of Wiener's benign philosophy, what remains of cybernetics can be used within a highly mechanical and dehumanizing, even militaristic, outlook' (in Wiener, 1989). Thus cybernetics can reduce people to an anti-entropic teleology, supposedly embodied in command-and-control systems, as in the human mind and nature itself.

The computer metaphor exerts great power over the late twentieth-century social imagination. As one enthusiast observed, even before the Information Age was officially declared, 'notions that the brain is like a computer, that man is like a machine, that society is like a feedback system, all reflect the impacts of cybernetics on our idea of human nature' (Neisser, 1966). As new technologies increasingly structure organizational rationalization and impersonal social regulation, the computer metaphor becomes invested with illusions of omnipotence. Meanwhile people are reduced to a 'human component', as epitomized by the military weapons system.

THE HUMAN COMPONENT

Do not metaphors illuminate in both directions? As nature came to seem more like a machine, did not machines come to seem more natural? (Harding, 1986)

In the military weapons system we find the most extreme expression of a system that reconstitutes human subjectivity as 'human materiel', not entirely distinguished from equipment. As Douglas Noble (1988) has argued, the weapons system has been paradigmatic for a 'new view of man', one in which 'a person is regarded as a 'human component' within the 'personnel subsystem' of complex 'man–machine systems'. Human and machine components, operating in programmed interaction, are seen as interfacing parts of an encompassing psycho-technological network.

Mary Kaldor (1980) suggests that the concept of weapons system may be likened to the replacement of tools by machines: 'Whereas formerly the weapon was the instrument of man, it now appears that man is the instrument of the weapons system: for a weapons system demands a rigid technical division of labour that admits of little variation in the social organization of the men operating it.' Yet there is always a tension between the need for rigid command and flexible response to unpredictable threats.

For that reason, the logic of advanced weapons systems requires that the human component is either upgraded or marginalized. As ordinary soldiers might prove vulnerable and unreliable, a 'super-soldier' is created to satisfy the system's needs. The military now enlists 'techniques that might help troops handle stress, work cohesively, learn skills faster, and fight more effectively', such as biofeedback, split-brain learning, stress management, sleep learning, and even ESP (Miller, 1988). As Chris Gray demonstrates in this book, training programmes attempt to integrate mechanical qualities of endurance with human qualities of intelligent 'quick-response', to shape a new model soldier who behaves as if he were a cybernetic organism.

While one strategy is to overcome human fragility, the other is to eliminate the weak link from the system. As the system's demands are seen to exceed human capability, there has been a drive to introduce automated, 'intelligent' and autonomous weapons systems. Designed to respond to threats in real time, these systems use remote-control cybernetic technologies to transcend human limitations. Yet proponents and even some anti-militarists have overestimated the reliability of these systems (as argued by Tom Athanasiou in this book); the human component can never be fully dispensable.

The weapons system's dual strategy – alternatively disciplining and withdrawing the human component – is becoming paradigmatic for the entire society, even for our sense of identity. Moreover, the idea of the self as machine has recurred as a pervasive phantasy – realized in harsh reality through the historical development of capitalist technologies. Prime examples have been the Taylorist and Fordist organization of work, in turn derived from military projects (Smith, 1985).

A decisive stage in mechanizing the human was reached in the early twentieth century through the efforts of 'Scientific Management'. Its founder, F. W. Taylor, developed a form of behavioural engineering that treated the body as a machine. To do this, argues Bernard Doray (1988), it was 'necessary to objectify the human subject, to reduce its complexity and to regard it not as something which speaks to another subjectivity, but as a concrete and desubjectivized manifestation of laws revealed by natural abstractions'. The consequence is an alienating condition, 'Taylorist man', characterized by a 'divorce between that part of his body which has been instrumentalized and calibrated and the remainder of his living personality'. With Fordism, that mind/body split was further structured by the assembly line, a continuous-flow production system.

In the late twentieth century we are seeing control extended to 'the remainder' of the living personality. Behavioural engineering is raised to a new level; mind, along with body, is objectified and instrumentalized. 'In post-industrial capitalism', writes Bill Nichols (1988), 'the human is defined in relation to cybernetic systems – computers, bio-genetically engineered organisms, eco-systems, expert systems, robots, androids, cyborgs'.

Moreover, through the science of cybernetics, the principle of organic life itself is defined on a continuum with that of computational machines. The mechanization of self is intensified through an ontology which assigns a common basis to biology and cybernetics. As the mind is conceived as a computer program, as something estranged, modelled on mechnical virtues, so does 'the remainder' of human subjectivity become further amenable to discipline.

VIGILANT OPERATOR

What kind of discipline? Attempts simply to deskill operators with yet more extreme automation have run up against the limits of supposedly perfect technology, which always turns out to require more human intervention than its designers had anticipated. Moreover 'the remainder' of subjectivity has a tendency to resist the menial or routine role assigned to the body.

An alternative strategy has attempted to plan for 'intelligent' human intervention by 'reskilling' the operator in terms set by the cybernetic system. This reconstitutes the worker's judgement, perhaps even inventiveness, as a creative force, now integrated symbiotically with the system's needs. It means reinvolving the operator's intellect in executing or even designing tasks. Now 'You *are* paid to think', defined as a suitably flexible, rapid response to the acknowledged unpredictability of the system, for optimal achievement of its goals.

This strategy has been led by the military, as with the 'cyborg soldier', though the model has been extended more widely. The military can be seen as paradigmatic for the 'flexible integration' with which futurologists euphemistically celebrate this 'post-Fordist' advance in capitalist work-organization. If we consider the intensified demands that the system makes upon the intellect and stamina of the worker, now called a technician or 'staffer', we may be justified in calling this a cyborg model of self-discipline. The demeaning effects can be seen in workers' experience of the 'Japanese model' at Nissan-UK (Holloway, 1987) and of the 'team concept' at General Motors, where the work-force accept responsibility for Taylorizing their own jobs (Parker and Slaughter, 1988).

Military developments in cognitive self-discipline are also embedded in the 'computer literacy' that is being promoted as a means for making the learner more employable, or even an effective citizen. As demonstrated by Douglas Noble (1988), US psychologists-turned-educators have appropriated progressive education within an amalgam of instructional technology and cognitive science, both derived from military psychotechnology. Defining the soldier as the 'human component' of a 'man–machine system', this cybernetic model has become the basis for educational reform emphasizing cognition: problem-solving, thinking skills and the micro-computer.

'Just look at the child sitting in front of his computer at school,' writes Jean Baudrillard (1988). 'Do you think he has been made more interactive, opened up to the world? Child and machine have merely been joined together in an integrated circuit.' Or, rather, the child's play may have become more interactive, but only in relation to a simulated reality. Thus arises the paradox of a regulated play.

The self-discipline mediated by computer microworlds has also served as a model for education and training more generally, or for education *as* training, and not always by using computers. A newly emerging approach is dedicated to producing an adaptable, flexible, integrated, self-controlling work-force for the embryonic regime of so-called 'post-Fordism'. This aims not simply to subordinate the worker but to integrate a 'responsible' worker into the production system.

Accordingly, note Robins and Webster (1989), elements of progressive education have been transformed into an 'instrumental progressivism'. In particular the concept of 'computer literacy', in the name of empowering the learner, has served to colonize the mind with a narrowly defined cognitive rationality that devalues intuitive, aesthetic and emotional qualities. The profiling of individuals' personal characteristics emphasizes self-disciplined work habits for flexible performance in diverse contexts, irrespective of any real interest in the content. At a conceptual level, at least, these approaches derive from a military-based model of the mind as an efficient machine fulfilling a system's predefined purpose.

Further similarities can be seen in the quasi-military tone used (by the US-based Foxboro Corporation) to market 'intelligent automation systems'. The language of its glossy publicity can be paraphrased as follows: As an industry leader, the firm provides not just hardware, but integrated systems solutions which can measure and control the entire production process. These systems will enhance productivity through 'proactive reorganization', an aggressive attempt to restructure production as a dynamic process. This features paperless order handling, 'just-in-time' methods and the single station controller (operator); thus robotics and vigilant operators form an efficient team. The firm offers gratifying careers to its employees, who form a cadre of specialists representing various disciplines. For its clients the firm provides training in process measurement and control concepts. Here students learn how to install, service, trouble-shoot and repair the system, to minimize down time. They learn to perform routine operations and respond correctly to alarm situations. The trainers share the firm's commitment to total solutions. A distributed global data base provides validated real-time information needed to make better decisions. In this way, each client firm can answer the question, 'Does the end justify the cost?'

Advertised in terms which almost parody crass amorality, the 'intelligent automation system' bears similarities with various training strategies described above. Each, in its own way, seeks to mobilize the operator's full mental involvement, now reconnected with manual tasks and/or physical endurance, together serving the system's programmed purposes and real-time demands. Is this to be the final, total solution to the problem of human unreliability? Judging from actual experience, the declared aim of total control would seem nearly impossible to realize; it warrants analysis as something more complex, even more ominous, than the rationality it claims to impose.

THE CYBORG SELF

At a psychic level, the search for total control enacts a paranoid attack on the self, a war against the self. One pioneer of artificial intelligence research, Marvin Minsky (1979), has even expressed the fear that 'the first self-improving AI machines [will] become "psychotic" in many ways'. This hypothetical mental disorder, attributed to the computer, can be seen partly as a projection of a human one, as in Minsky's much-quoted distaste for the 'bloody mess of organic matter'. Beyond the pains and pleasures of the flesh, his phrase metaphorically evokes the unpredictability of human desires, against which cybernetics (especially artificial intelligence) helps us construct a psychic defence. Paranoid rationality, expressed in the image of the machine-like self, combines an omnipotent phantasy of self-control with fear and aggression directed against emotional and bodily limitations of mere mortals. (Here we use the form of spelling that implies unconscious levels of phantasy, even though the phenomenon often becomes conscious.)

Certainly our culture promotes cybernetic images of progress with phantasies of omnipotence. Futurologists foresee global communications networks giving us unlimited access to 'information'. Such liberatory expectations underpin particularly the whole gamut of technologies referred to as home informatics. Here all human needs can be fulfilled, once they are reduced to things, to consumable goods and services. The projected scenario of the electronic household realizes the phantasy of the technological prosthesis through a man–machine nexus. Indeed, it is envisaged that all life functions – work, consumption, communication, learning, entertainment – can and will be electronically subject to push-button control.

As phantasy, this control can represent a flight from the world. In the seclusion and privacy of the home, the new technologies provide a restrictive, system-dependent form of mastery. A control no longer possible in the outside world finds expression within a private domain, in the protected environment of a microworld.

As a sublimated, compensatory control, it is also illusory. Sherry Turkle (1984) describes how infotech can 'support the desire, the needs and in extreme cases the obsession for "perfect mastery"'; they 'provide a chance to be in complete control, but they can trap people into an infatuation with control, with building one's private world'. While Turkle also describes other modes of relating to infotech, the 'perfect mastery' mode would seem central to the institutional settings analysed in this book. Beyond people's pleasurable experience of such control, we need to understand its role as a regressive compensation for people's everyday impotence and dependence.

The cybernetic state – in either the political or psychological sense – appeals to the subordination of individual reason, desire and emotion, in favour of a rationality dedicated to system maintenance. People experience this regime in complex, contradictory ways. On the one hand, people gain a sense of power and mastery in accommodating its demands. On the other, people disengage from the system with feelings of anxiety, inadequacy or vulnerability. In the context of the wider technological system, push-button omnipotence is always vitiated.

How are contradictory feelings of omnipotence and powerlessness, of mastery and dependence, effectively reconciled? Through a kind of regressive solution, the cyborg self, these conflictual elements are held in tension. By regressing to a phantasy of infantile omnipotence, we deny our dependency upon nature, upon our own nature, upon the bloody mess of organic matter.

In that sense the cyborg self can be seen as a variant of what Christopher Lasch (1985) calls the narcissistic or minimal self. Narcissism is characterized by a refusal of the distinction between the self and the surrounding world, between the self and not-self. According to Lasch, technology 'reactivates infantile appetites and the infantile need for illusions by impressing itself on people's lives as a never-ending series of miracles that obviate the need for human effort'. Infotech can be associated with narcissistic illusions of omnipotence, phantasies of controlling the external world. These evoke a longing either to remake the world in one's own image or to merge into its environment in blissful union.

Cybernetic systems appeal to that phantasy by creating a world of simulacra amenable to total control. As Bill Nichols (1988) suggests, 'cybernetic simulation renders experience, and the real itself, problematic'. It 'draws us into a realm, a design for living, that fosters a fetishized relationship with the simulation as a new reality all its own, based on the capacity to control, within the domain of the simulation, what had once eluded control beyond it'. In short, it entrances us with a 'fetishistic addiction to a process of logical simulation'. Nichols contrasts its meaning in work and leisure: 'Like face-to-face encounter, cybernetic systems offer (and demand) almost immediate response. This is a major part of their hazard in the workplace and their fascination outside it . . . This is the bane of the "automated work-place" and the joy of the video game.'

Yet management, too, whether military or industrial, can appropriate the thrill of the video game, the omnipotence phantasy of its closed world, to engage the soldier or operator in the required discipline. In the man–machine nexus, the human component interacts with a mechanized reality, a mediated and simulated reality. This indeed facilitates greater control, achieved at the cost of eroding the distinction between phantasy and reality. Through cybernetic mediation, phantasies can flourish uninhibited by a sense of the intractability of the external world.

This kind of mastery involves the technologization of self, the delegation of self to the machine. Integrating human and technological components, the man–machine nexus blurs the self and non-self. This regressive symbiosis is then expressed as a phantasy – extending the self through technological power, as well as incorporating and merging with the technological Other. Whether expressed through Promethean illusions of omnipotence and self-sufficiency, or through phantasies of self-annihilation and union with the Other, the cyborg self is fundamentally regressive, infantile, defensive. In both cases, it seeks the impossible: to abolish separation from the external world.

Although such phantasies do exist independently of infotech, they are evoked and institutionalized by military-based systems of control. From the SDI strategist to the vigilant operator to the computer-aided learner, illusory control over a 'closed world' makes the systems themselves more credible and reinforces the phantasy. Psychic defence from reality becomes part of the discipline internalized through the man–machine nexus.

OUT OF CONTROL?

In the military information society the war machine is shaping our sense of self, directly and indirectly. While the military project has always subordinated human agency to its imperatives, now infotech is increasingly implicated as mediator, even as model of the human. As social organization and social identity become programmed, processed worlds, we encounter an increasingly blurred distinction between military and civil spheres, between mechanical and human, between inner and outer realms.

Is the military information society out of control? Is there a way out of that control? Finding a way out involves both a psychological and a political challenge. We will need to overcome the duality of real impotence and phantasized omnipotence on which we depend for security. We will also need to challenge the military content borne by supposedly liberatory sciences: information theory, cybernetics, artificial intelligence, systems theory, cognitive psychology. Rather than disavowing their repressive aspects, we will need to acknowlege them – their inner connection to military paradigms, and their permeation throughout out lives.

Is it possible to subvert the dominant cybernetics from within? Some critics suggest the appropriation of elements for liberatory aims, from ecological or feminist standpoints. Extending an argument from Gregory Bateson, Bill Nichols (1988) proposes that cybernetics can offer a method for making ourselves more environmentally responsible: 'The task is not to overthrow the prevailing cybernetic model but to transgress its predefined interdictions and limits, using the dynamic of the apperceptive powers it has itself brought into being.' Yes, hypothetically, a cybernetic model of 'the environment' might help us to transgress taboos of a destructive social order. However, it could just as well adapt individuals to that order, in the name of accommodating the needs of an ecosystem, in turn ideologized as a natural order of stability.

Another critic, Donna Haraway, has also suggested a dual potential of cybernetics:

From one perspective, a cyborg world is about the final imposition of a grid of control on the planet, about the final abstraction embodied in a Star War apocalypse waged in the nature of defence, about the final appropriation of women's bodies in a masculinist orgy of war. From another perspective, a cyborg world might be about lived social and bodily realities in which people are not afraid of their joint kinship with animals and machines, not afraid of permanently partial identities and contradictory standpoints. (1985, p. 72)

Here she is playing devil's advocate against a feminism based upon mystical communion with holy Nature. By detaching the cyborg model from its present institutional context, into the realm of phantasy, her discussion can help us to analyse its manifestation in popular culture. Yet that detachment can also lead us away from confronting the social impotence that makes the phantasy appealing.

Any cybernetic model, the cyborg one included, entails the temptation of an omnipotence phantasy about controlling the world, freezing historical forces – if necessary, destroying them in rage, thus containing our anxiety, in the name of maintaining rational control. We will need to acknowledge such irrationality embedded within our rationality. In that sense, the political problem involves far more than how to select cybernetic models and how to use them. It is not a matter of being truly rational, but of struggling to achieve maturity by recognizing all the internal and external forces at work.

Such ambiguities inherent in our technology have been acknowledged, if only implicitly, in popular culture. In the film/book *Wargames* David Lightman, the boy hero, comes to meet Stephen Falkes, the creator of the US Defence computer that now threatens to unleash a global nuclear war. Explains Falkes,

The computer was not built as a result of an urgent desire of mankind to see a little yellow ball gobbling up dots in a maze. The computer is, in a very real sense, the child of war and as Wordsworth says, the child is the father of the man ... Perhaps it is all some magnificent death wish, buried deep in the collective consciousness of us all. (Bischoff, 1983)

Even if there exists no death wish as such, surely there are primitive emotions inseparable from our society's form of reason and technology; the danger lies in pretending that they are neatly separable. Some science-fiction novels and films have explored these connections in more mature ways than do many social critics of technology, in the sense of presenting apparently contradictory aspects as integral to the whole. The *Robocop* cyborg, for example, personifies infantile rage expressed through a cybernetic rationality, even though the story line concludes with a regressive solution, both psychically and politically (Glass, 1989).

As we have attempted to demonstrate, cybernetics can mediate our most primitive emotions, our sense of the natural, the rational and the real. We will need to work through these feelings and assumptions if we are to make the most of the opportunities for seeking a different path through our cyborg worlds. In diverse realms – the work-place, the school, the training scheme, the home, the video game, as well as the military itself – our resistance to their 'closed worlds' will need to be informed by a deep comprehension of their attractions as well as their horrors. In all those realms, moreover, military-derived discipline is internalized in ways that may seem benign, creative, even playful. We will need to challenge those appearances, those definitions, along with the practices themselves.

As in any oppressive regime, discovering alternatives begins with refusal – refusing the pre-programmed purposes of the military information society, in whatever subtle guises they may appear. At the same time, that refusal means struggling with contending definitions of who we are and who we can be – what it means to be human.

ACKNOWLEDGEMENTS

We should like to thank Douglas Noble, Tony Solomonides and Sherry Turkle for their editorial comments, though the final version remains our responsiblity alone.

REFERENCES

Ball, M. (1984) 'Electronics factory of the future', *Electronic Business* 15 September:164–74.

Baudrillard, J. (1988) *America*. London: Verso.

Beer, S. (1971) 'The liberty machine', *Futures* 3:338–48.

Beniger, J. (1986) *The Control Revolution: Technological and Economic Origins of the Information Society*. Cambridge, MA: Harvard University Press.

Bischoff, D. (1983) *Wargames*. Harmondsworth: Penguin.

Center for Productivity Enhancement (1987) *Bargaining for Lynn's Factory of the Future: A Case Study*. University of Lowell, MA: Productivity Center.

Doray, B. (1988) *From Taylorism to Fordism: A Rational Madness*. London: Free Association.

Edwards, P. N. (1987) *The Army and the Microworld: Computers and the Militarized Politics of Gender Identity*. Santa Cruz, CA: Silicon Valley Research Group (Working paper 12).

Ennals, R. (1986) *Star Wars: A Question of Initiative*. Chichester: John Wiley & Sons.

Giddens, A (1985) *The Nation State and Violence*. Cambridge: Polity.

Glass, F. (1989) 'The new bad future: *Robocop* and 1980s sci-fi film', *Science as Culture* 5:7–49.

Haraway, D. (1985) 'A manifesto for cyborgs: science, technology and socialist feminism in the 1980s', *Socialist Review* 80:65–107.

Harding, S. (1986) *The Science Question in Feminism*. Milton Keynes: Open University Press.

Holloway, J. (1987) 'The red rose of Nissan', *Capital and Class* 32:142–64.

Kaldor, M. (1980), 'The significance of military technology', in A. Eide and M. Thee, eds *Problems of Contemporary Militarism*. London: Croom Helm, pp. 226–9.

Lasch, C. (1984) 'Chip of fools', *New Republic* 13 August:25–8.

_____ (1985), *The Minimal Self: Psychic Survival in Troubled Times*. London: Picador.

Levidow, L. and Solomonides, T. eds (1985) *Compulsive Technology: Computers as Culture*. London: Free Association.

Lovering, J. (1987), 'The Atlantic arms economy: towards a military regime of accumulation', *Capital and Class* 33:129–55.

Marx, K. (1976) 'Fetishism of the commodity and its secret', in *Capital*, vol. 1. Harmondsworth: Penguin.

Miller, M. S. (1988), 'New toys for Robocop soldiers', *Progressive* July:18–21.

Minsky, M. (1979), 'Computer science and the representation of knowledge', in M. L. Dertouzos and J. Moses, eds *The Computer Age: A Twenty-Year View*. Cambridge, MA: MIT Press, pp. 392–421.

Mumford, L. (1964), 'Authoritarian and democratic technics', *Technology and Culture* 5:1–8.

_____ (1967) *The Myth of the Machine*. New York: Harcourt Brace-Jovanovich.

_____ (1970) *The Pentagon of Power*. New York: Harcourt Brace-Jovanovich.

Neisser, U. (1966) 'Computers as tools and as metaphors', in C. R. Dechert, ed. *The Social Impact of Cybernetics*. Notre Dame, IN: University of Notre Dame Press, pp. 71–93.

Nichols, B. (1988) 'The work of culture in the age of cybernetic systems', *Screen* 29(1):22–46.

Noble, David (1984) *Forces of Production: A Social History of Industrial Automation*. New York: Alfred A. Knopf.

Noble, Douglas (1988) 'Education, technology and the military', in Landon E. Beyer and Michael W. Apple, eds *The Curriculum: Problems, Politics and Possibilities*. Albany, NY: SUNY.

Parker, M. and Slaughter, J. (1988) *Choosing Sides: Unions and the Team Concept*. Detroit, MI: Labor Notes.

Robins, K. and Webster, F. (1989) *The Technical Fix: Education, Computers and Industry*. London: Macmillan.

Smith, M. R. ed. (1985) *Military Enterprise and Technological Change*. Cambridge, MA: MIT Press.

Turkle, S. (1984) *The Second Self: Computers and the Human Spirit*. London: Granada.

Virilio, P. (1986) *Speed and Politics: An Essay on Dromology*. New York: Semiotext(e).

Virilio, P. and Lotringer, S. (1983) *Pure War*. New York: Semiotext(e).

Weber, M. (1948/1921) 'The meaning of discipline', in H. H. Gerth and C. Wright Mills, eds *From Max Weber: Essays in Sociology*. London: Routledge & Kegan Paul, pp. 253–64.

Wiener, N. (1948) *Cybernetics: Or Control and Communication in the Animal and the Machine*. Cambridge, MA: MIT Press.

_____ (1954) *The Human Use of Human Beings*, revised edition. Boston, MA: Houghton-Mifflin; London: Free Association (1989) with a new Introduction by Steve J. Heims.

Wolin, R. (1984/5) 'Modernism vs. postmodernism', *Telos* 62:9–29.

Notes on contributors

TOM ATHANASIOU is an ecologist, computer programmer, writer and left-communist, not necessarily in that order.

PAUL N. EDWARDS is a lecturer at Kresge College, University of California at Santa Cruz, and a researcher with the Silicon Valley Research Group. His essay in this collection forms part of his PhD dissertation, 'The closed world: computers and the politics of discourse.'

CHRIS HABLES GRAY is writing his doctoral dissertation on advanced computing and the US military at Kresge College, University of California at Santa Cruz. He has been active in various non-violent direct-action campaigns since the early 1970s.

DENNIS HAYES taught at the University of Wisconsin, Milwaukee, before moving to Silicon Valley for a stint as a news reporter for a socialist weekly. Since then he has worked as a receptionist, secretary, clerk and technical writer in the electronics industry there. He is author of *Behind the Silicon Curtain: The Seductions of Work in a Lonely Era* (South End Press/Free Association Books, 1989).

LES LEVIDOW, an editor at Free Association Books, has edited several critical collections on science, technology and medicine. He also teaches 'science and society' courses in adult education and higher education.

VINCENT MOSCO is Professor of Communication, Carleton University, Ottowa; formerly he was Professor of Sociology, Queen's University, Kingston, Ontario. His most recent books are *The Pay-Per Society: Computers and Communication in the Information Age* (Toronto: Garamond, 1989) and *The Political Econcomy of Information* (Madison: University of Wisconsin Press, 1988), edited with Janet Wasko.

DOUGLAS D. NOBLE, having worked as a teacher and computer programmer, now writes on issues of technology, education and work. He is currently completing a book on the military origins of contemporary educational methods.

KEVIN ROBINS works at the Centre for Urban and Regional Development Studies, University of Newcastle. He is co-author, with Frank Webster, of *Information Technology: A Luddite Analysis* (Ablex, 1986) and *The Technical Fix: Education, Computers and Industry* (London: Macmillan, 1989).

Index

This first edition of
Cyborg World: The Military Information Society
was finished in September 1989.

It was typeset in 10/13 Plantin Roman
on an AM Comp Set 560 II
and printed on a Timson T32 on to
80g/m² vol. 18 Publishers Antique Wove.

This book was commissioned and
edited by Les Levidow,
copy-edited by Peter Phillips,
indexed by Derek Derbyshire
designed by Wendy Millichap
and produced by Simona Sideri
and Martin Klopstock for
Free Association Books.